YOUNG STUDENTS
Learning Library®

VOLUME 16

North Dakota —
Petrified Forest

NEWFIELD
PUBLICATIONS
SHELTON, CONNECTICUT

CREDITS

Page 1924 Pat Morris; 1925 ZEFA; 1927 ZEFA; 1931 ZEFA; 1932 ZEFA; 1935 ZEFA; 1936 Collins, enguin, Methuen (left), Mansell Collection (bottom right); 1944 ZEFA; 1948 Library of Congress; 1956 Hulton; 1958 Spectrum Colour Library; 1960 ZEFA; 1962 Oklahoma Tourism/Mike Shelton; 1963 Oklahoma City Convention & Tourism Bureau; 1965 ZEFA; 1967 allsport; 1969 ZEFA; 1970 Westerman Foto (bottom); 1972 Hulton (bottom), Dominic Photography (top); 1979 ZEFA (top), Oregon State Highway Division (bottom); 1981 Oregon Economic Development Department; 1984 Victoria & Albert Museum (center), Armando Curcio Editore (bottom); 1985 BBC Picture Publicity; 1986 ZEFA; 1987 Sonia Halliday; 1989 U.P.I.; 1094 ZEFA; 1096 National Park Service; 1097 Armando Curcio Editore; 1098 Fitzwilliam Museum, Cambridge; 1099 National Gallery, London; 2000 Armando Curcio Editore; 2001 National Gallery; 2016 ZEFA; 2022 ZEFA; 2025 Armando Curcio Editore; 2025 Armando Curcio Editore; 2026 Jeremy Hartley/Panos Pictures; 2027 Imperial War Museum; 2028 National Film Board; 2032 Pennsylvania Dept. of Commerce; 2033 Rex Features 2034 PA Travel Bureau (bottom).

Printed in the U.S.A.

ISBN 0-8374-9823-6

CONTENTS

▲ A group of **PELICANS** and a flock of flamingos at the edge of a lake.

NORTH DAKOTA

In the southwest corner of North Dakota lie the Badlands. They were named by pioneers who found them bad lands to travel through. Rainfall is light there, and water is scarce. Grass grows in many places, but much of the land is bare. The scenery, however, is startling. For thousands of years the Little Missouri River and the weather have been carving the rock and clay of the area into unusual shapes. The formations include steep, flat-topped hills, called *mesas,* and *buttes*, which are like mesas but not as broad. The mesas and buttes are colored in bands of red, yellow, blue, and gray. Each year, thousands travel to the Badlands to see these spectacular natural "sculptures."

The Land and Climate

The Badlands are near the Montana border in the Great Plains region of North Dakota. This region covers the whole western part of the state. Most of the Great Plains was once grassland. Large areas are still grazing country today. North Dakota's part of the Missouri Basin is in the Great Plains region. The Garrison Dam holds back part of the Missouri River, forming Lake Sakakawea, a winding lake about 200 miles (320 km) long.

The eastern boundary of the Great Plains region is formed by two rivers. The Rivière des Lacs ("River of Lakes") is in the north. It starts near Canada. The James River is in the south.

East of the two river valleys, the land slopes downward. From there on, North Dakota is prairie land. It is part of the plains that lie west and south of the Great Lakes. The prairie region is a rolling plain with dark, fertile soil. The *black belt* has especially good farming land. This belt is the part of the river valley that North Dakota shares with Minnesota. The river is the Red River of the North.

North Dakota has very little nat-ural woodland. The Turtle Mountains are wooded and so are parts of the Red River Valley and some of the smaller valleys. But in most of the state the woods were planted by people.

North Dakota lies in the center of North America. No ocean winds can warm it in winter or cool it in summer. Winters are long and cold. Strong winds from northern Canada often bring snowstorms. Summers are short and hot with very dry air. The eastern part of the state has more rain than the western part, but rainfall is not heavy. In both east and west, farmers raise large crops of wheat.

History

Europeans came late to the center of the continent. New France, New England, and Virginia were more than 100 years old by the time white people explored North Dakota. The first Europeans in North Dakota were the French, who came about 1740. The French were looking for Native Americans who would sell furs. They met tribes of two kinds. Some were settled farmers, and others were wandering hunters. Among the farming tribes were the Mandan and the Cheyenne. They lived in villages protected by walls. Their crops were corn, squash, pumpkins, and beans. The farmers hunted just enough to get some meat.

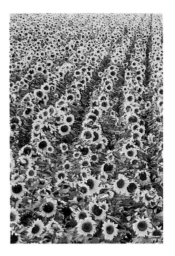

▲ The sunflower is commonly grown in North Dakota for its oil, which is used in cooking or in salad dressings. The leftover seed is not wasted; it is made into poultry feed and cattlecake.

▼ Wind has eroded the Badlands region of North Dakota, creating strange formations, including cliffs, buttes, and canyons. Sometimes winds whip up the soil making dust storms.

NORTH DAKOTA

Capital city
Bismarck
(49,256 people)

Area
70,665 square miles
(183,022 sq. km)
Rank: 17th

Population
638,800 people
Rank: 47th

Statehood
November 2, 1889
(39th state admitted)

Principal river
Missouri River

Highest point
White Butte, 3,506 feet
(1,069 m)

Largest city
Fargo (74,111 people)

Motto
"Liberty and Union,
Now and Forever, One
and Inseparable"

Song
"North Dakota Hymn"

Famous people
John Burke, Louis
L'Amour, Peggy Lee,
Lawrence Welk

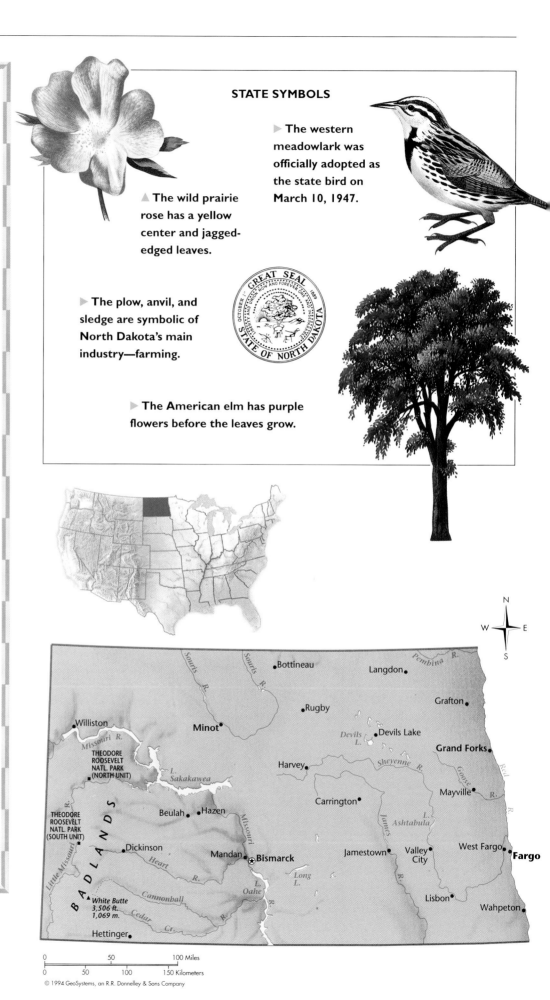

STATE SYMBOLS

▲ The wild prairie rose has a yellow center and jagged-edged leaves.

▶ The western meadowlark was officially adopted as the state bird on March 10, 1947.

▶ The plow, anvil, and sledge are symbolic of North Dakota's main industry—farming.

▶ The American elm has purple flowers before the leaves grow.

0   50   100 Miles
0   50   100   150 Kilometers
© 1994 GeoSystems, an R.R. Donnelley & Sons Company

The wandering hunters lived differently. They did not stay in one place long enough to harvest crops. Instead, they went wherever they could find game. Bison provided them with meat and with skins for *tepees* (tents) and warm robes. Deer and elk were useful, also. Two hunting tribes were the Sioux (Dakota) and the Ojibwa (Chippewa). The Sioux, especially, were feared by the farming tribes.

The southwestern part of North Dakota, claimed by France, was sold to the United States in 1803 as part of the Louisiana Purchase. Two explorers, Meriwether Lewis and William Clark, were the first to raise the Stars and Stripes in North Dakota in 1804. Northern and eastern North Dakota were held by Britain. Britain turned the land over to the United States in 1818 along with part of Minnesota.

For a while, the only white people in North Dakota were fur traders and soldiers. The soldiers lived in lonely little forts built in areas that were likely to come under attack. After 1850, white settlers came to the region in larger numbers. Some of them took land that the government had set aside for the Native Americans. White hunters slaughtered the bison that the tribes needed to survive. During and after the Civil War, Sioux warriors fought the white people. But they were too few in number to hold back the whites for long. The Sioux, led by Sitting Bull, surrendered in 1881 to U.S. troops.

North and South Dakota were part of the same territory. The settlers of both areas wanted them to be separate states. In 1889, Congress granted their wish. U.S. President Benjamin Harrison signed the papers on November 2 of that year. Which state became the 39th and which the 40th? No one can say for sure. President Harrison didn't want to put one Dakota ahead of the other. So he would not let anyone see which declaration of statehood he signed first. North Dakota is usually called the 39th state and South Dakota the 40th. But there is no way of telling which state was admitted to the Union first.

Working in North Dakota

By the time North Dakota was made a state, wheat was being raised on large farms there. Agriculture has remained the state's biggest business, and wheat is still the main crop. Only one state, Kansas, grows more wheat than North Dakota does. In North Dakota, wheat fields stretch as far as the eye can see. Tall grain elevators rise from the plain. These buildings store wheat that is waiting to be shipped.

Lack of rain in the 1920s and early 1930s brought drought and dust storms to North Dakota. Topsoil was blown away, ruining the farmland. Wheat prices dropped, and many people lost their farms. More than 70,000 people left the state during that time. In the late 1930s, wheat prices rose. Farmers worked large farms by using modern machinery and better agricultural methods.

▼ **More than 90 percent of the land in North Dakota is used for crops or pasture. Wheat, the main crop, is grown throughout the state.**

Armagh in Northern Ireland is a small town with two cathedrals and two archbishops, one Protestant and one Roman Catholic. The Roman Catholic archbishop of Armagh is Primate of all Ireland.

Today, crops earn more money for North Dakota than cattle do. Corn and oats grow in the southeastern part of the state. Food processing is the leading industry. Vast amounts of petroleum, natural gas, and lignite lie under the lands of North Dakota. Oil was discovered in 1951 in the large Williston Basin near Tioga. This basin lies under North and South Dakota, Montana, and parts of Canada. Many refineries have been built in the state to process the oil.

▶ ▶ ▶ **FIND OUT MORE** ◀ ◀ ◀
Bison; Fur; Lewis and Clark Expedition; Louisiana Purchase; Ojibwas; Prairie; Sioux; Westward Movement

NORTHERN IRELAND

Northern Ireland, also called Ulster, consists of six counties located in the northeastern corner of the island of Ireland, which lies off the west coast of Great Britain. (See the map with the article on UNITED KINGDOM.) Northern Ireland was separated politically from the rest of Ireland in 1921. In that year, the rest of Ireland (now the Republic of Ireland, or Eire) won independence from Great Britain. The residents of Northern Ireland's six counties (which were predominately Protestant) voted to remain part of Great Britain rather than become part of the predominantly Roman Catholic Republic of Ireland.

Belfast is the capital of Northern Ireland and its largest city. The Belfast shipyards are among the largest in the world. Londonderry ("Derry") is the second largest city.

The leading industries are the manufacture of textiles and clothing. Irish linen, considered the finest in the world, is produced mostly in Northern Ireland. Agriculture, especially dairy farming, is another important source of income. Flax (used in making linen), oats, animal feeds, and potatoes thrive in the moist, moderate climate.

Political problems in Northern Ireland date back to the early 1600s, when many English and Scottish Protestants settled there. The Protestants soon exceeded the Catholics in number, and a religious conflict developed. In the 1960s, protests by the Catholics against unfair treatment led to civil disorder. British troops were sent to restore order.

Today, Northern Ireland, as part of the United Kingdom, has representatives in the British House of Commons, but several of those representatives refuse to attend the House. The provisional wing of the Irish Republican Army (IRA) has vowed to achieve independence from British rule. Bombings, shootings, and other terrorist acts have led to great loss of life in Northern Ireland and other parts of the United Kingdom.

In 1985, the Republic of Ireland and Britain agreed to set up a joint commission to give the Republic an advisory role in the government of the north. But the northern Protestants opposed this plan. The conflict continues in the 1990s.

▶ ▶ ▶ **FIND OUT MORE** ◀ ◀ ◀
British Isles; English History; Ireland; United Kingdom

▼ **The Giants Causeway, a spectacular rock formation on the coast of Northern Ireland. Legend says that the giant, Finn MacCool (Fingal), built the "causeway" (road through water) to cross from Ireland to Scotland.**

NORTHERN LIGHTS

SEE AURORA

NORTH KOREA

SEE KOREA

NORTH POLE

As the Earth moves around the sun, it also spins like a top. Most tops spin on an *axis* that runs through their center. The Earth has an imaginary line running through its center, around which it spins. The northern point of this line is called the North Pole. The southern point is the South Pole. The North Pole is geographically the northern-most point on the Earth. If you look at a globe, you will see that all the *meridians* (longitude lines) meet at the pole.

About 1,000 miles (1,600 km) away from the North Pole is the *North Magnetic Pole*. This is the northern point to which your compass needle points. It is located near Prince of Wales Island in Canada's Northwest Territories. The exact position of both magnetic poles shifts slightly each year.

▶ ▶ ▶ ▶ **FIND OUT MORE** ◀ ◀ ◀ ◀
Amundsen, Roald; Arctic; Byrd, Richard E.; Compass; Exploration; Magnet; Peary, Robert

NORTH SEA

The North Sea lies between Great Britain and the northwestern part of the European continent. To the north, the sea opens straight into the Atlantic Ocean. To the southwest, the sea is linked to the Atlantic by the Strait of Dover and the English Channel. A narrow channel to the east links the North and Baltic Seas.

Ship captains who sail the North Sea know the dangers of its sudden fogs, winter gales, and strong tides and currents. Nevertheless, this sea is one of the world's busiest shipping areas. Freighters and passenger ships steam to and from busy ports such as Rotterdam, in the Netherlands; Aberdeen, in Scotland; Bremen and Hamburg, in West Germany; and Antwerp, in Belgium.

The North Sea is one of the richest fishing grounds in the world. Fishermen of several nations catch large quantities of cod on the Dogger Bank, a sandbank off the northeast coast of England.

Large amounts of oil and natural gas are under the North Sea. The North Sea is dotted with oil and gas rigs, and the oil is brought ashore by pipeline. The discovery of North Sea oil is important to the economies of Britain and Western Europe.

▶ ▶ ▶ ▶ **FIND OUT MORE** ◀ ◀ ◀ ◀
Atlantic Ocean; Baltic Sea; English Channel; Petroleum

NORTH STAR

In the Northern Hemisphere, one star is used for telling direction more than any other star, because it always stays in nearly the same place in the sky. It is the North Star, or *Polaris*, also called the *Pole Star*. Polaris is almost directly above the North Pole. The North Star is the star at the end of the handle of the constellation called the *Little Dipper.*

Other stars seem to move in the sky because of the turning of the Earth on its axis. Polaris stays in almost the same place, with the axis of the Earth pointed near it.

The first ship to reach the North Pole was the U.S. atomic submarine *Nautilus*. It traveled under the ice-covered pole on August 3, 1958. The first surface ship to reach the pole was the Soviet nuclear icebreaker *Arktika*. It broke its way through the ice to the top of the world on August 16, 1977.

◀ **The Earth's North Pole is covered by an ocean on which floats a thick layer of ice. This was proved by a submarine traveling under the ice in 1958.**

▼ **A modern North Sea trawler. For centuries, fishermen have faced the dangers of these waters.**

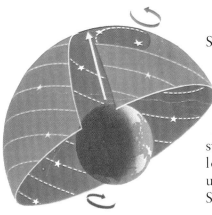

The movement of the stars across the sky is really caused by the Earth spinning on its axis. Someone far away from the Equator will see the stars move in straight lines.

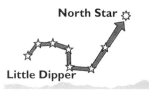

The stars can be used as a compass. If you are in the Northern Hemisphere, find the star group named the Little Dipper—the last star of the handle is the North Star.

The *Manhattan* was the first commercial ship to use the Northwest Passage.

Ship captains have used the North Star as a guide for years. Although ships have radar and radio now, Polaris still helps tell direction.

You can find the North Star if you go out on a clear night. Look for the *Little Dipper*. Find the two stars farthest from the "handle." Follow the line of these two stars upward, and you will find the North Star.

▶ ▶ ▶ ▶ **FIND OUT MORE** ◀ ◀ ◀ ◀
Constellation; Star

NORTHWEST PASSAGE

The famous voyage to the Americas by Christopher Columbus in 1492 led other explorers to search for some way to sail past the American continents and reach Asia. The Portuguese explorer Ferdinand Magellan found a route around the southern tip of South America in 1520. But explorers continued to search for hundreds of years for a "Northwest Passage" around North America.

The English explorer Sir Martin Frobisher tried several times to find the Northwest Passage during the 1570s. He explored the eastern approaches to the Canadian Arctic. Another British explorer, Henry

Hudson, reached as far as Hudson Bay in 1610. Hudson thought he had discovered the west coast of America and joyfully sailed south. When his journey was stopped at the southern end of the bay, the Arctic winter had begun. When spring came, his starving crew mutinied and set him, his 10-year-old son, and several of his loyal followers adrift in a small boat. He and his companions perished.

Other explorers followed in Hudson's wake. They explored much of the region between northeast Canada and Greenland. In 1845, Sir John Franklin, the English explorer, and his crew were lost when their boat was crushed by the Arctic ice.

In 1906, after a three-year ordeal, the Norwegian explorer Roald Amundsen completed the first trip from the Atlantic to the Pacific by the Arctic passage in a small ship. Between 1940 and 1944, a tough little ship belonging to the Canadian Mounted Police traversed the Northwest Passage in both directions.

In 1969, a huge U.S. oil tanker, the S.S. *Manhattan,* helped by the Canadian icebreaker *Macdonald,* made the passage from the Atlantic as far as the oil fields of northern Alaska. The voyage proved that specially built ships, able to combat the Arctic winters, might one day open up the Northwest Passage commercially.

▶ ▶ ▶ ▶ **FIND OUT MORE** ◀ ◀ ◀ ◀
Amundsen, Roald; Arctic Ocean; Exploration; Hudson, Henry

NORTHWEST TERRITORIES

The northern third of Canada consists of a vast wintry domain of forest, tundra, and ice. It is the largest frontier in North America. Eskimos were the first people to live here.

The land and islands north of Canada's ten provinces are divided between the Yukon Territory, next to Alaska, and the three districts of

NORTHWEST TERRITORIES

Capital and largest city
Yellowknife
(12,000 people)

Area
1,271,422 square miles
(3,292,968 sq. km)

Population
54,000 people

Created
1870

Principal river
Mackenzie River

Highest point
Mount Sir James
McBrien, 9,062 feet
(2,762 m)

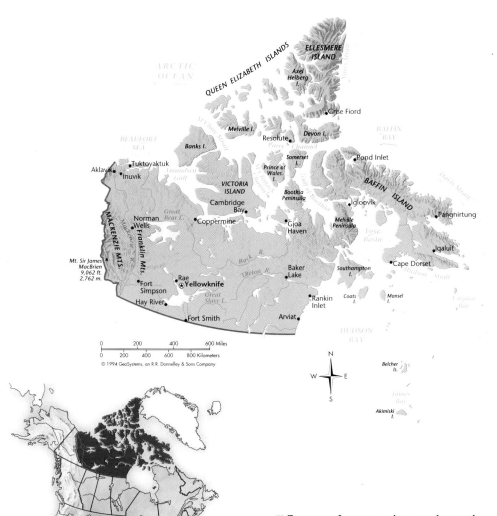

▼ **Forests of spruce, pine, poplar, and birch trees grow near the MacKenzie River in the Northwest Territories.**

▲ **One of the symbols of Canada's Northwest Territories is the flower of the mountain avens, a hardy plant found on rocky slopes and high ledges.**

Baffin Bay separates Baffin Island from Greenland. It is named for William Baffin, who explored it in 1616. Many of its harbors are north of the Arctic Circle and remain frozen most of the year.

Norway is a land of deep valleys. Where these valleys reach the sea, long saltwater lakes are present.

Mackenzie, Keewatin, and Franklin, which together form the Northwest Territories.

Half of the Northwest Territories is located north of the Arctic Circle. Much of this northern half is low-lying, but in the far north, barren, stony mountains rise to more than 7,000 feet (2,130 m). On the Canadian-mainland part are two of Canada's largest lakes, Great Bear and Great Slave, and Canada's longest river, the Mackenzie.

The territories are a land of midnight sun in summer and a three-month night in winter. In summer, the sun never rises very high above the horizon, and the temperature never becomes really warm. The northernmost islands are covered with ice and snow that never melts. The largest islands are Baffin, Victoria, and Ellesmere. Ellesmere Island is only about 500 miles (800 km) from the North Pole.

Farther south, temperatures reach about 50°F (10°C) in summer, and the growth of small bushes and moss permits caribou and reindeer to live in the region. The soil, however, always stays frozen a few inches below the surface.

Still farther south, below what is called the "tree line," the ground does not stay frozen and trees grow.

Fish and fur-bearing animals were the only known resources in the Northwest Territories for the first 300 years after its discovery by white people. The trees were not big enough to be used for lumber. But the value of this wood for making paper transformed the northern forest into an important resource.

Then oil was discovered along the Mackenzie River. Other vast oil reserves probably exist along the Arctic Ocean. Radium, gold, and uranium were discovered. There is so much copper in the ground around the tiny Arctic seaport of Coppermine that the soil is green from rusting copper particles. There is little farming, so agriculture is not important.

In 1670, England granted a fur-trading company, the Hudson's Bay Company, control over all the area drained by rivers and streams emptying into Hudson Bay and the Arctic Ocean. In 1869, this land was placed under the control of the Canadian government.

The Northwest Territories Act of 1875 gave the area its present name and created a government for it. Land was taken from the territories to form parts of the Canadian provinces. In 1920, the remaining land was divided into the three present districts, which today are governed by a commissioner and a council.

The vast area of the Northwest Territories has a smaller population than that of a small city in southern Canada or in the United States. The capital and largest city, Yellowknife, has a population of 12,000—not much larger than that of a large village. About half of the people of the Northwest Territories are of English descent, and about a quarter are Eskimos (Inuits). There are also some Native North Americans and some French Canadians. Some of the people are *Métis*—mixed French and Native North American.

▶ ▶ ▶ ▶ **FIND OUT MORE** ◀ ◀ ◀ ◀
Canada; North America;
Northwest Passage

 NORWAY

The country of Norway is part of the Scandinavian peninsula in northern Europe. Norway has a long, broken coastline. Scattered along its coast are about 150,000 islands, many of which are only bits of rock.

The coast of Norway was carved by glaciers that scraped along the rocks during the last ice age. Glaciers cut deep inlets, *fiords*, or *fjords*

into the coastline. Some fiords are more than 100 miles (160 km) long and are so wide that big ocean liners can enter them. Oslo, the capital city, lies at the head of a large fiord.

Norway is bordered on the east by Sweden, Finland, and Russia. The North Sea is on the south shore of Norway, the Norwegian Sea is on the west, and the Barents Sea is on the north.

From about mid-May to the end of July, the sun never sinks below the horizon in the "Land of the Midnight Sun," the part of Norway that is mostly north of the Arctic Circle. There is light 24 hours a day. But in winter, this northern part of Norway is dark for about the same length of time. Reindeer, polar foxes, Arctic hares, wolves, and lemmings live in northern Norway.

About one-fourth of Norway is covered with forests of spruce, pine, and birch. Much timber is made into pulp and paper. The country has little good farmland, most of which is used to grow feed for livestock. Fishing is a major business in Norway, with large numbers of cod, capelin, haddock, and herring being caught. Large amounts of oil are extracted from Norway's North Sea oil fields. Oil refining is an important industry.

Norwegians are generally a hardy people. Many are blonde and blue-eyed. In the far north of Norway live the dark-haired Lapps. Some Lapps are still nomads who follow herds of reindeer.

Norway's people are the descendants of the Vikings who raided the coasts of Europe and North America about 1,000 years ago. The Vikings settled colonies along the North Atlantic and Arctic Ocean coasts.

During the A.D. 800s, the country was united under one ruler, King Harold the Fairhaired. Later, Norway was again divided into small kingdoms. In 1397, the kingdoms of Norway, Sweden, and Denmark were united under the rule of Denmark. After centuries of rule by Denmark, Norway was controlled by Sweden from 1814 to 1905. Under Sweden, Norway had its own constitution and legislature. In August 1905, the Norwegians voted to separate from Sweden and become an independent country. In 1907, Norway became the first country in Europe to give women the right to vote.

NORWAY

Capital city
Oslo (456,000 people)

Area
125,182 square miles
(324,219 sq. km)

Population
4,245,000 people

Government
Constitutional monarchy

Natural resources
Oil and natural gas, iron ore, copper, lead, zinc, nickel, pyrites

Export products
Petroleum and petroleum products, natural gas, ships, fish, aluminum, pulp and paper, machinery, transport equipment

Unit of money
Krone

Official language
Norwegian

▶▶▶▶ **FIND OUT MORE** ◀◀◀◀
Fishing Industry; Ice Age;
Lapland; Lemming; Mythology;
North Sea; Polar Life; Scandinavia;
Scandinavian Languages; Vikings

Noses come in many shapes and sizes. A nose is called Roman if it is straight, Grecian if it is straight and continues to the forehead without any depression, aquiline if it curves out like an eagle's beak, and retroussé if it turns up at the end.

 ## NOSE

Your nose aids in breathing, and it is the organ of smell. The outer nose, or external nose, is the part you see on your face. The two openings of the nose are called *nostrils*. The dividing wall between them is called a *septum*. The lower part of the septum is made up of cartilage, which is softer than the bone in the upper part of the nose. The inner nose, or internal nose, is a hollow above the roof of the mouth. It is divided into two parts by a septum of bone. The internal nose opens at the rear into the *pharynx*, which is part of the throat.

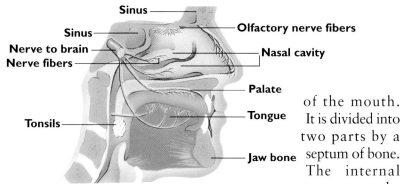

Sinus
Sinus
Nerve to brain
Nerve fibers
Olfactory nerve fibers
Nasal cavity
Palate
Tongue
Tonsils
Jaw bone

▲ When you breathe in through your nose, the air goes into the nasal cavity, which connects with the breathing tube and with the sinuses (two cavities in the skull above the nose). At the back of the nasal cavity is a surface containing *olfactory* (smell-sensitive) nerve fibers. These pass information along nerves to the brain, which interprets the smells.

The nose acts as a filter that removes almost all the dust from the air you breathe. The larger particles of dust are caught by the hairs at the lowest part of the nose. Lining the nose is a *mucous membrane*, which gives off a sticky fluid called *mucus*. The smaller particles of dust stick to the mucus. When you blow your nose, you get rid of the dust.

The mucous membrane has a very large number of tiny blood vessels, which are called *capillaries*. The blood passing through the capillaries keeps the membrane at the temperature of the rest of the body. Air passing through the nose is warmed by contact with the mucous membrane.

In the upper part of the internal nose, there is a group of cells that makes up the organ of smell. These cells are connected by nerves to the brain. Molecules enter your nose in the air you breathe. When they come in contact with the "smelling" cells, messages go through the nerves to the brain, where they are interpreted as the odor of the substance.

▶ ▶ ▶ ▶ **FIND OUT MORE** ◀ ◀ ◀ ◀
Breathing; Smell

NOUN

SEE PARTS OF SPEECH

NOVA

SEE STAR

 ## NOVA SCOTIA

Nova Scotia is a province on the east coast of Canada. Most of Nova Scotia is a peninsula jutting out into the Atlantic Ocean. Cape Breton Island, a part of the province, is located at its northern end. The peninsula is connected with the Canadian province of New Brunswick by a narrow *isthmus* (strip of land). The isthmus is bound on the north by the Northumberland Strait and on the south by the Bay of Fundy. Nova Scotia has a rugged, rocky coastline with many deep harbors. Inland are several fertile valleys and a number of rivers and lakes. The sea surrounding Nova Scotia gives it a more moderate climate than that of most of the rest of eastern Canada.

Fishing has long been a major occupation in the province. Nova Scotia cod, lobsters, and haddock are sold all over the world. Apples and other fruits are grown in the sheltered inland valleys. There is also a substantial coal industry in Nova Scotia. The mine tunnels at Sydney, on Cape Breton Island, stretch out for miles under the sea.

Large deposits of oil exist offshore in the Atlantic. Nova Scotia's capital city, Halifax, is one of Canada's major Atlantic ports.

The Viking Leif Ericson is believed

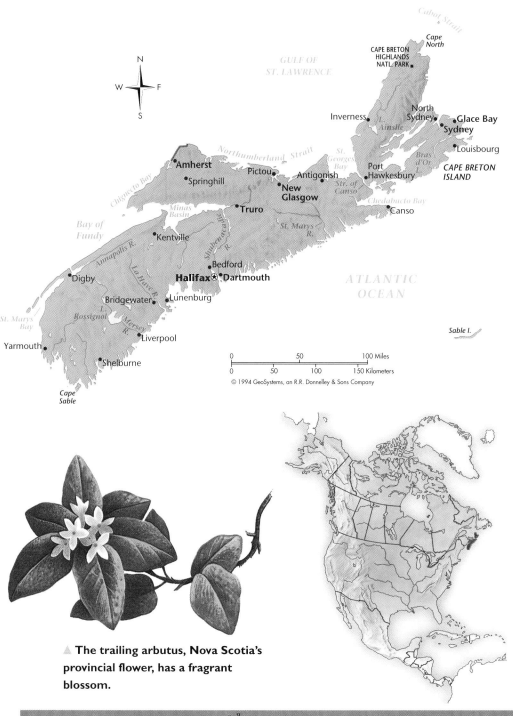

NOVA SCOTIA

Capital and largest city
Halifax
(118,000 people)

Area
20,402 square miles
(52,840 sq. km)

Population
892,000 people

Entry into Confederation
July 1, 1867

Principal river
Annapolis River

Highest point
Cape Breton Highlands
1,747 feet (532 m)

Famous people
Sir Robert Borden,
Sir John Dawson,
George Dawson, Joseph
Howe, Hugh MacLennan

▲ **The trailing arbutus, Nova Scotia's provincial flower, has a fragrant blossom.**

◀ **No part of Nova Scotia is more than 35 miles (56 km) from the sea. Fishing villages, such as Peggy's Cove, are numerous. Fishermen catch cod, haddock, herrings, scallops, and lobsters.**

to have seen the coast of Nova Scotia about A.D. 1000. The English explorer John Cabot supposedly landed on Cape Breton Island in 1497. The French established a colony in 1605 and later fought against the British for control of the area. Nova Scotia was one of the four original provinces that joined together to form the Dominion of Canada in 1867.

The name *Nova Scotia* means "New Scotland." Almost one in three Nova Scotians is of Scottish ancestry. Some Nova Scotians still speak Gaelic. Nova Scotia is famous for its Scottish festivals, when the people dress in colorful tartans and listen to the music of the bagpipes.

▶▶▶▶ **FIND OUT MORE** ◀◀◀◀
Canada; North America

NOVEL

A novel is a long story. Some novels are exciting adventure stories set in faraway places with unusual and fascinating characters. Other novels may tell of things that happen every day to ordinary people in ordinary places. Some novels are set in the future. But all novels, like most other forms of literature, are written to entertain and to give a better understanding of people and their personal experiences.

The novel developed gradually from ancient forms of storytelling, such as the *epic poem*, a long poem that told stories of brave heroes and their glorious deeds. During the 1300s, the Italian writer Giovanni Boccaccio combined a number of loosely related stories into a long work called the *Decameron*. This book inspired Geoffrey Chaucer, an English poet, to write *The Canterbury Tales*, which were similar, loosely related stories.

Picaresque novels *(picaro* means "rascal" in Spanish) were realistic stories concerning events in everyday life.

They were popular in Italy, France, and Spain. Picaresque tales were about clever, adventurous heroes who traveled from place to place, looking for—and finding—trouble. *Don Quixote* (1605–1615), by Miguel de Cervantes, was an early novel based on such tales. The English novel as it is known today began in the 18th century. During this period, Daniel Defoe and Samuel Richardson wrote the first novels in which the many adventures of the hero or heroine were really combined into one plot.

A *novelist* (a writer of novels) combines many elements in creating an entertaining, thought-provoking story. One element, the plot, is the series of events that makes up the action of the book. The plot may be very long and complicated, as is found in adventure stories and novels about a person's life. The novel *Great Expectations* (1860–1861), by Charles Dickens, has a long, involved plot covering a number of events over many important years in the life of the main character. Other novels may have simple plots dealing with only a few events over a short period of time. The novel *Franny and Zooey (1962)*, by J. D. Salinger, takes place in one day and consists primarily of three conversa-

▽ **An illustration from the novel *A Christmas Carol* by Charles Dickens. Dickens combined humor, pathos, mystery, social observation, and wicked versus kind characters in his books.**

△ **Four internationally known 20th-century novels.**
1936

tions a young man has, one with his mother and two with his sister.

The people in a novel are called the *characters*. There may be many of them in one novel, but the story usually revolves around one or two main characters. Some characters, such as Elizabeth Bennett in Jane Austen's *Pride and Prejudice* (1813), seem as real and fully developed to readers as an actual person. Other characters are purposely made not to seem like real people, because the novelist has chosen them to represent a certain idea or quality in human nature. The character named Fagin in *Oliver Twist* (1837–1839), by Charles Dickens, represents an evil kind of cleverness.

The novelist combines the elements of plot, character, *setting* (place where the action or plot occurs), and *point of view* (the character through whose eyes the author tells the story). They are combined in order to present the *theme*—the statement about life or people that the author wishes to make with the book. He or she may want to present an idea about love, youth, religion, society, or human nature. For example, *The Scarlet Letter* (1850), by Nathaniel Hawthorne, explores the problems of sin, guilt, and punishment among Puritans in New England. The novel *The Grapes of Wrath* (1939), by John Steinbeck, concerns problems faced by poor people who lost their land during the Depression in the 1930s.

Authors write many kinds of novels. *Historical* novels, such as Leo Tolstoy's *War and Peace* (1863–1869) and Charles Dickens's *A Tale of Two Cities* (1859), are fictional stories set in the past, usually in an exciting, glamorous period of history. *Suspense* novels, such as Sir Arthur Conan Doyle's *The Hound of the Baskervilles* (1902) and Wilkie Collins's *The Woman in White* (1860), are detective stories and mysteries. In these, the reader, and the characters, try to solve a sinister crime or explain a mysterious happening. *Realistic* novels are written to be as true to life as possible. They nearly always have a serious theme. Realistic novels may concentrate on social problems, personal problems, or relationships between people. Some, called *psychological* novels, concentrate on the personalities of the characters.

It would be impossible to list all the good novels that have been written, but your public library and school library contain many of them. Read one or two, and you will discover why reading a novel is an exciting way to pass the time!

▷▷▷▷ **FIND OUT MORE** ◁◁◁◁
Literature; Short Story

Mark Twain's *The Adventures of Tom Sawyer* is an example of a *humorous* novel. In one chapter, Tom describes how a teacher, absorbed in drawing a map of America, has his wig clawed from his head by a cat. The cat was lowered down from a garret, then pulled up quickly with the wig in its claws.

 ## NOVEMBER

The eleventh month of the year is November. Its name means "nine" in Latin. November was the ninth month of the first calendar of the ancient Romans. The Roman emperor Julius Caesar gave November 31 days, but the emperor Augustus later changed this to 30 days. November still has 30 days.

DATES OF SPECIAL EVENTS IN NOVEMBER

Election Day held first Tuesday after the first Monday of the month.

1   U.S. exploded world's first hydrogen bomb (1952).

2   Daniel Boone, American frontiersman, was born (1734).
President James K. Polk was born (1795).
President Warren G. Harding was born (1865).
The world's first public television broadcasting service began in London, England (1936).

4   Will Rogers, U.S. humorist, was born (1879).
The first wagon train of pioneers reached California from Missouri (1841).

5   Guy Fawkes and fellow conspirators tried to blow up the British Parliament (1605). The day is now celebrated in Great Britain as Guy Fawkes Day with fireworks and burnings of Guy Fawkes's effigy on bonfires throughout the nation.
The first transcontinental airplane flight landed at Pasadena; flown by C. P. Rogers (1911).
Sinclair Lewis became the first U.S. writer to win the Nobel Prize for Literature (1930).

7   Battle of Tippecanoe, in which General William Henry Harrison and his soldiers defeated the Shawnee tribe (1811).
The Communist Revolution began in Russia (1917).

8   X rays were discovered by the German scientist Wilhelm Roentgen (1895).

10   Martin Luther, Protestant religious leader, was born (1483).

11   The first U.S. telescope was patented (1851).
Armistice Day, commemorating the end of World War I, was celebrated until 1954. The day is now called Veterans Day.

13   Robert Louis Stevenson, British author of *Treasure Island* and other exciting stories, was born (1850).

15   The second Continental Congress approved the Articles of Confederation, uniting the 13 colonies in their struggle against British rule (1777).
The League of Nations Assembly met for the first time in Geneva, Switzerland (1920).

16   The space shuttle *Columbia* completed its first operational flight (1982).

17   Congress met in Washington, D.C. for the first time (1800).
Suez Canal was opened (1869).

18   United States and Panama signed a treaty to allow the building of the Panama Canal (1903).

19   President James A. Garfield was born (1831).
Abraham Lincoln delivered the Gettysburg Address (1863).
The *Mayflower* reached the Massachusetts coastline (1620).

22   President John F. Kennedy was assassinated in Dallas, Texas (1963).

23   President Franklin Pierce was born (1804).

24   President Zachary Taylor was born (1784).

26   First national Thanksgiving Day proclaimed by Abraham Lincoln (1864).

29   First flight over the South Pole by Richard E. Byrd and his crew (1929).
Samuel Clemens (Mark Twain), U.S. author, was born (1835).
Winston Churchill, British statesman, was born (1874).

November is bleak and gray in much of the Northern Hemisphere, as the rich, bright season of fall comes to an end. Most of the leaves have fallen from the trees, and many animals have begun to hibernate. Farmers have harvested their crops, and the fields are bare. The weather grows colder during this month. In some areas, the first snows begin to fall.

November signals the approach of winter in the Northern Hemisphere, but in the Southern Hemisphere it marks the beginning of spring.

The birthstone for November is the tawny-colored topaz. November's flower is the chrysanthemum. In the United States, Thanksgiving is celebrated in November. Thanksgiving began in 1621, when the Pilgrims, with the Native Americans, gave thanks for their first harvest in a strange new world. Election Day in the United States is also held in November.

◀ **November's flower is the chrysanthemum. November's "lucky" stone, or birthstone, is the lustrous and transparent topaz.**

▶ ▶ ▶ ▶ **FIND OUT MORE** ◀ ◀ ◀ ◀
Autumn; Calendar; Season; Thanksgiving

NUCLEAR ENERGY

Atoms are the "building blocks" of which everything in the world is made. It is almost impossible to imagine how small these tiny particles are. It is even more difficult to imagine that each atom is made up of smaller particles—*protons*, *neutrons*, *electrons*, and others. At the center of an atom is the *nucleus*, which is made up of protons and neutrons. Then there is a great empty space. Then come the electrons, which travel in *orbits* (paths) around the nucleus. We can imagine the atom to be like a tiny solar system, with the planets (electrons) orbiting the sun (nucleus). (This is not what the atom is really like, but it is as near as we can picture it.)

The tiny nucleus at the atom's center contains the most powerful force ever discovered. This force—the *strong nuclear force*—provides nuclear energy (sometimes called atomic energy).

What Makes the Energy

Chemical elements differ because their atoms have different numbers of protons. The nucleus of an atom of *hydrogen*, the lightest element, is the simplest. It contains one proton. The most complicated—and the heaviest—element that occurs in nature is *uranium*. Its atom has 92 protons and 143 neutrons in its nucleus. Scientists add these numbers 92 + 143 and call this atom "uranium 235," or U-235 for short.

A tremendous force locked inside every atom keeps all the protons and neutrons pressed tightly together. In a complicated atom, such as that of U-235, a neutron sometimes shoots away from the nucleus. No one knows what causes this, but it does happen. Because the U-235 atom slowly loses pieces of itself, scientists say it is *unstable*, or *radioactive*.

Every time a neutron flies away from the nucleus, the atom loses energy—this is nuclear energy.

One neutron, however, does not produce enough energy to be useful. But the neutron may crash into another U-235 atom and knock loose another neutron. The second atom also loses some energy. The problem is to keep the collisions going—to start a *chain reaction*. When the piece of U-235 is big enough, a great many neutrons fly about at once. They crash into other atoms and knock more neutrons loose, and many atoms

Uranium atom

Neutron

give up their energy at once. The result is a tremendous explosion—an atomic bomb. You can get an idea of its power if you realize that one pound (0.454 kg) of U-235 has as much energy as 3 million pounds (1,360,000 kg) of coal!

Putting Nuclear Energy to Work

An atomic bomb is a terrible weapon—one that can kill many people and destroy large cities. But the explosive chain reaction can be controlled in a nuclear power station.

A nuclear power station does not use pure U-235. When uranium is dug from the ground, most of it consists of the type U-238, which has three extra neutrons in its nucleus. This natural uranium does not explode, because the fast-moving

▼ **Nuclear fission releases large amounts of energy when a uranium atom is split by a slow-moving neutron. Each split uranium atom releases three more neutrons, which go on to split yet more uranium, and so on.**

▼ **In a nuclear power station, energy in the form of heat, from the controlled nuclear reaction, is used to make steam. The steam drives turbines, which generate electricity in a way similar to other power stations.**

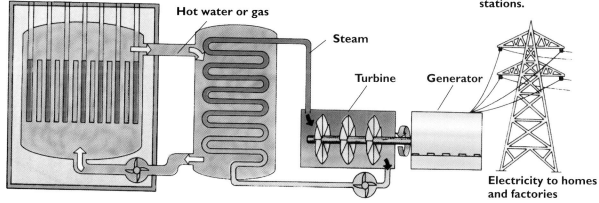

Hot water or gas

Steam

Turbine   Generator

Electricity to homes and factories

THERMAL NUCLEAR REACTOR

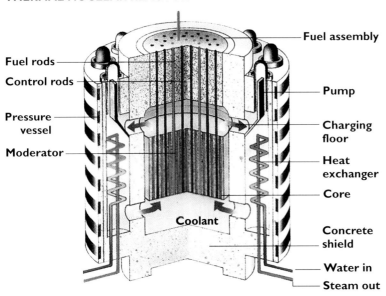

Fuel rods
Control rods
Pressure vessel
Moderator

Fuel assembly
Pump
Charging floor
Heat exchanger
Core
Concrete shield
Water in
Steam out

Coolant

In their efforts to master fusion power, scientists at Princeton University produced a temperature of 360 million degrees Fahrenheit (200 million degrees Celsius). This temperature is ten times hotter than that at the center of the sun, but it was kept at this level for only a third of a second.

▲ The core, the heart of a thermal nuclear reactor, is enclosed in a pressure vessel. Heat from the fission of uranium fuel converts water into steam for driving turbine generators to produce electricity.

neutrons escaping from the U-235 are absorbed by the U-238. To make a chain reaction happen in natural uranium, extra U-235 atoms must be added and the escaping neutrons must be slowed down. If they are moving slowly enough, they are not absorbed by the U-238. This slowing down is done by adding a substance such as carbon—called a *moderator*—to the uranium. Some of the neutrons then lose energy bouncing off the carbon atoms.

The first nuclear reactor, built by Enrico Fermi and a group of other scientists in 1942, was called a pile. To control it, the scientists used cadmium rods, which work something

◄ The "mushroom" cloud shows the spot of an atomic explosion. Nuclear bombs can cause widespread destruction, but this nuclear force can be harnessed by nuclear power stations to produce energy.

like the accelerator pedal of an automobile. When the rods are pushed into the reactor, they soak up most of the free neutrons and slow down or stop the chain reaction. When the rods are pulled out, the reaction speeds up. In some modern reactors, other substances, such as boron, are used for the rods.

Even a controlled nuclear reaction is so hot that nuclear reactors would melt if they were not cooled. The cooling system consists of water-filled pipes that run through the reactor. As the cold water in the pipes passes through the reactor, the water *absorbs* (takes up) heat and turns to steam. The steam is carried through the pipes to a large *turbine*—a special kind of fan. The steam blows out of the pipes and turns the fan, which is connected to an electric generator. In this way, nuclear energy is used to produce electricity.

Small nuclear reactors are used to drive submarines and ships. By 1993, there were more than 500 nuclear power plants in use in the world, but some people have become afraid of the use of nuclear energy following two major disasters—at Three Mile Island near Harrisburg, Pennsylvania, in 1979, and at Chernobyl, Ukraine, in 1986. However, scientists are working to make nuclear power safer.

Existing nuclear reactors gain energy from *fission*, the splitting of atoms with heavy nuclei, such as uranium. Many scientists are now working to try to gain energy from *fusion*, the joining of atoms with light nuclei, like hydrogen. Fusion power, if it can be harnessed, should be a lot safer than fission power, because it does not produce radioactive by-products.

About 1 billion metric tons of coal would have to be used annually by coal-powered stations to provide the world with sufficient electricity for all its needs. Just 135 metric tons of deuterium, one of the hydrogenlike fuels used in nuclear fusion, would give the same amount of energy.

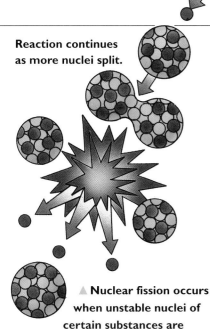

Reaction continues as more nuclei split.

▲ **Nuclear fission occurs when unstable nuclei of certain substances are bombarded with atomic particles or rays. As the nucleus splits, it releases energy and more atomic particles, which split more nuclei. A chain reaction is set up.**

▶ ▶ ▶ ▶ **FIND OUT MORE** ◀ ◀ ◀ ◀
Atom; Electric Power; Element; Energy; Explosives; Fallout; Fermi, Enrico; Hydrogen

NUCLEIC ACID

SEE BIOCHEMISTRY, CELL, GENETICS

NUMBER

It is as important to be able to use numbers as it is to read and write. Numbers are used everywhere—on calendars, clocks, telephones, price tags, and labels. Numbers are used for keeping the scores of games and for keeping track of money. Houses and streets are numbered. Scientists and engineers make constant use of numbers. All businesses must use numbers for keeping records of their products, their workers, and their money.

The words *number* and *numeral* are different in meaning. A numeral is a written mark or sign that stands for a number. The numeral that looks like this—2—stands for two. The numeral that looks like this—8—stands for eight. The numeral ½ stands for one-half.

The word *number* is often used to mean numeral, but number is actually the amount that the numeral stands for. You can write down a number using different kinds of numerals. For example, let's say you have 17 pencils. You could write this down as seventeen, 17, or /////////////////.

If you were an ancient Roman, you would have written it as XVII. No matter which *numerals* you use, the *number* (the amount) stays the same.

Numerals and Counting

All ancient civilizations had ways of counting. They had to keep track of their animals and crops, and they had to keep track of how much they bought and sold things for. The earliest way of counting was to use *counters*. Pebbles, sticks, shells, or other small objects were used as counters. Farmers with flocks of sheep kept bags of pebble counters— one pebble

WHERE TO DISCOVER MORE

Hershey, Robert L. *How to Think with Numbers.* Massachusetts; Janson Publishers. 1987.
Lewis, Brenda R. *Coins & Currency.* New York; Random House Books for Young Readers. 1993.

▽ **Most ancient number systems did not have a zero. The zero was invented by Hindu mathematicians in about A.D. 600.**

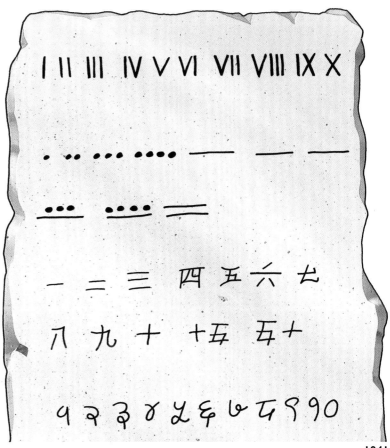

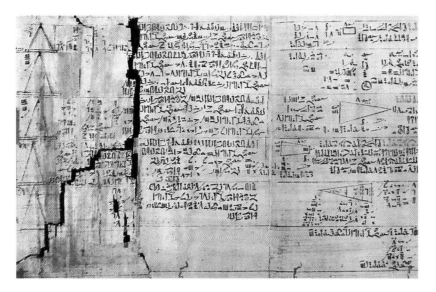

▲ Part of a long roll of *papyrus* (a sort of paper) found in Thebes, Egypt. It is full of mathematical problems, which are similar to the ones students calculate today. For example: "A cylindrical granary is of diameter 9 and height 6. How much grain goes into it?"

▼ Writing had not been invented during the rule of the Inca Empire. All records were kept on *quipus*—thick cords of different colors that had knots tied in them to convey information.

for each sheep. When they counted their flocks, they would move the pebbles from one bag to another. For each sheep they saw, they would put one pebble into the empty bag. If they had a pebble left over, they knew that a sheep was missing. If they had no pebbles left, and there was still another sheep to be counted, then they knew there was an extra sheep from somewhere else. The ancient Incas used to tie knots in a rope, called a *quipu*. Each knot stood for an animal or an amount of grain.

Fingers were also used as counters. Since a person has ten fingers, many people based their numbering on 10. When they had to count higher than ten, they used "one-more-than-ten," "two-more-than-ten" until they reached 20 ("two-tens"). Fingers are fine for telling the number of days in a week, but how could you tell someone with your fingers that there are 365 days in a year? People had to find a way to show larger numbers.

The first kind of writing was picture writing. "Three cows" would be written as a picture showing three cows. "Five days" was a picture of five suns. Pictures worked for smaller numbers, but it would be very hard to show in picture writing that there are 100 billion stars in the Milky Way! To solve this problem, people began making short lines to stand for numbers one through nine, and then

using other marks for 10, 100, 1,000, and larger numbers. The ancient Greeks used alphabet letters to stand for numbers. The Romans also used numerals that looked like alphabet letters—I=1, V=5, X=10, L=50, C=100, D=500, and M=1,000. The numbers 1, 2, 3 were written I, II, III in Roman numerals. Number 4 was written IV (the I on the *left* of V meant "one *less* than five"). Number 6 was VI (the I on the *right* meant "one *more* than five").

Roman numerals were used throughout the Roman Empire and in most of Europe during the Middle Ages, but there was one serious problem with them. It is very difficult to do arithmetic problems using Roman numerals. People used an *abacus* (an ancient device that uses beads for calculating) to add, subtract, multiply, and divide. Numerals were used only to write the answer.

About A.D. 800, Europeans discovered that the Arabs had a better way of writing numbers. Europeans called these numerals "Arabic numbers," although the Arabs actually learned them from the Hindu traders of India. Arabic numerals are the ones we use today. It took a long time for the Arabic numerals to become popular and replace Roman numerals.

Arabic numerals were better than Roman numerals because any number could be written by using only ten numerals (0, 1, 2, 3, 4, 5, 6, 7, 8, 9). Also, it was easy to do arithmetic problems with Arabic numerals. The trick in using Arabic numerals is their *position* in a number.

The position at the far right of a number stands for *ones*. The next positions to the left stand for *tens, hundreds, thousands, ten-thousands, hundred-thousands, millions,* and so on. In the number 76, the 6 stands for "six ones" and the 7 stands for "seven tens." In 743, the 3 is "three ones," the 4 is "four tens," and the 7 is "seven hundreds."

Counting Systems

The counting system (also called numeration system) used in most countries today is the *decimal system*. The word "decimal" comes from the Latin word *decem,* meaning "ten." This means the decimal system is based on ten and uses only ten numerals (0, 1, 2, 3, 4, 5, 6, 7, 8, 9). You can check this yourself by studying the decimal system in the chart that shows kinds of counting systems. Each square is a number position. The first position is "ones." The next position to the left is "tens" (1 × 10). The next position is "hundreds" (10 × 10), and the next is "thousands" (100 × 10). Each position is *ten times* higher than the one before. As you can see on the chart, 76 is 7 tens and 6 ones.

The *binary system* is based on two and uses only two numerals (0 and 1). The position of each numeral shows that it is *two times* higher than the one before. The chart shows that in the binary system, 76 is written as 1001100 (1 sixty-four, 0 thirty-twos, 0 sixteens, 1 eight, 1 four, 0 twos, 0 ones).

The *quinary system* is based on five and uses only five numerals (0, 1, 2, 3, 4). The position of each numeral shows that it is *five times* higher than the one before. In the quinary system, 76 is written as 301 (3 twenty-fives, 0 fives, 1 one).

The *duodecimal system,* based on 12, uses the numerals 0–9 and *a* and *b* (with the letters *a* and *b* standing for the two-figure numerals 10 and 11). The position of each numeral shows that it is *twelve times* higher than the one before; thus, 76 is written as 64 (6 twelves, 4 ones).

▲ **The illustration shows that numbers increase rapidly if you continue to double them. The series is: 1, 2, 4, 8, 16, 32, 64, 128, and so on. This is called a** *geometric progression.*

Kinds of Numbers

The simplest kind of number is the *counting number* also called a *whole number* or *integer.* They are the numbers we use to count things.

The fraction number is used when we want to count *part* of something, such as *half* an hour or *two-thirds* of the world. A fraction is written with two numerals—½ is one-half, ⅔ is two-thirds. The bottom number tells how many parts an object has been divided into. The top number tells how many parts you have. Fractions can also be written as *decimal numbers.*

Negative numbers are used in algebra and other kinds of mathematics. They are always written with a minus sign in front of them (-5, -26, -35). Negative numbers are used to stand for numbers that are lower than zero. You have probably heard of temperatures such as "16 degrees below zero" or "22 degrees below zero." These temperatures are written as -16° and -22°.

Even numbers (2, 4, 6, 8, and so on) are those numbers that can be evenly divided by two. *Odd numbers* (1, 3, 5, 7, and so on) can also be

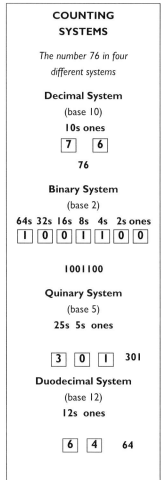

COUNTING SYSTEMS

The number 76 in four different systems

Decimal System
(base 10)
10s   ones
| 7 | 6 |
76

Binary System
(base 2)
64s 32s 16s 8s 4s 2s ones
| 1 | 0 | 0 | 1 | 1 | 0 | 0 |
1001100

Quinary System
(base 5)
25s   5s   ones
| 3 | 0 | 1 | 301

Duodecimal System
(base 12)
12s   ones
| 6 | 4 | 64

LEARN BY DOING

Here is a way to roughly count a huge number of things, such as the number of blades of grass in a field. Find out the area of the field (for example, 100 feet × 100 feet = 10,000 square feet). Block off a small area (1 foot × 1 foot = 1 square foot) and count the blades of grass in that area (for example, 525). Then determine how many times larger the field is than the area you blocked off (10,000 square feet ÷ 1 square foot = 10,000 times larger). Multiply the number of blades of grass (525) by this number (10,000) to get an estimated total. In our example, 525 × 10,000 = 5,250,000 blades of grass in the field!

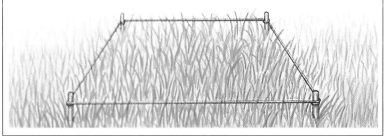

divided by two, but not evenly. *Prime numbers* (1, 2, 3, 5, 7, 11, 13, 17, and so on) are those numbers that can only be divided evenly by themselves and by the number one.

▲ Sometimes we need to round off a figure up or down. If tomatoes were 35 cents for three and you only wanted one, you could not pay 11.7 cents. You would have to round up to 12 cents.

WHERE TO DISCOVER MORE

Cosner, Sharon. *War Nurses.* New York: Walker & Co., 1988.

Heron, Jackie. *Exploring Careers in Nursing.* New York: Rosen Group, 1990.

▶ ▶ ▶ ▶ **FIND OUT MORE** ◀ ◀ ◀ ◀

Instruments That Make Use of Numbers see Abacus; Barometer; Calculator; Compass; Computer

Numbers in Everyday Life see Calendar; Clocks and Watches; Latitude and Longitude; Map; Measurement; Money; Scale; Temperature Scale; Thermometer; Time; Weight

Occupations That Make Use of Numbers see Accounting and Bookkeeping; Banks and Banking; Economics; Statistics; Surveying

School Subjects That Make Use of Numbers see Algebra; Arithmetic; Chemistry; Geometry; Mathematics; Mechanical Drawing; Music; Physics; Science

Working with Numbers see Angle; Binary System; Chance and Probability; Decimal Number; Graph; Interest; Percentage; Set; Symmetry

▽ NURSING

The profession of providing care to the sick, injured, and helpless under the direction of doctors is called nursing. Nurses also teach disease prevention and health care. In the United States, you must be licensed to work as a nurse. There are two kinds of licenses. One allows you to work as a *registered nurse* (RN). The other permits you to work as a *licensed practical nurse* (LPN) or a *licensed vocational nurse* (LVN).

In order to be licensed as a registered nurse, you must pass a course of training in an approved school and then pass a state board examination. Most nursing students are trained in a three-year course at a nursing school run by a hospital. Another way to become a registered nurse is to take a four-year college course, which leads to the degree of Bachelor of Science in Nursing. Training includes classroom and laboratory work. Student nurses also work in hospitals.

Most professional nurses are *hospital* nurses, who are full-time employees in hospitals or related institutions. Most hospital nurses do "general duty" work, following doctors' instructions about the care that each hospital patient must have. They keep charts of each patient's treatment, condition, and progress. They give any medicine prescribed by the doctor. They check to see that medical equipment is working.

A hospital nurse may have special training in addition to the basic nursing courses. This training prepares the nurse to perform special jobs or care for certain kinds of patients. *Pediatric* nurses are specially trained to care for infants and young children. *Psychiatric* nurses receive special training to care for

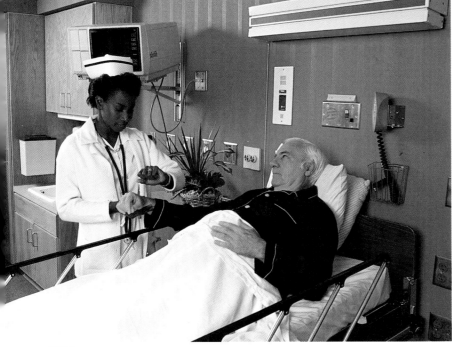

◀ For many elderly people, going into a hospital is a traumatic event. Here a nurse is taking a patient's pulse rate and making sure that he is comfortable.

patients with mental and emotional disorders. *Surgical* nurses are trained to help surgeons in operating rooms and to care for patients who have had surgery. A *private-duty* nurse is employed by sick persons or their families to give nursing care at home or extra care in a hospital.

Practical and vocational nurses take a shorter and much simpler course of training than that taken by registered nurses. They also work in hospitals under the supervision of registered nurses. Practical and vocational nurses may perform such jobs as taking patients' temperatures and pulses, giving baths, and making beds. (If necessary, registered nurses also perform these tasks.)

An occupation that has become important in recent years is that of *nurses' aide*. A nurses' aide does not have to have any special training and does not have to be licensed. He or she just needs the ability to work with people and a strong desire to help others. Aides working in hospitals help not only nurses, but also doctors and patients. Nurses' aides may make beds, serve patients' meals, read to or play with children in the hospital, or even help a patient to write a letter.

Nurses may be employed in many places other than hospitals. *Office* nurses work in doctors' private offices. They make appointments for patients to see the doctor, receive patients, and take care of the patients' records. They may also assist the doctor in examining a patient or give special tests under the doctor's supervision. *Public-health* nurses work for national, state, or local governments. *Industrial* nurses are hired by companies to care for employees.

Once, almost all nurses were women, but now there are many male nurses in the profession also.

▶ ▶ ▶ ▶ **FIND OUT MORE** ◀ ◀ ◀ ◀
Barton, Clara; Career; Cavell, Edith Louisa; Hospital; Nightingale, Florence

NUT

A nut is the fruit of a plant. Each nut has a shell, containing the *kernel*, or seed—the part that you eat.

Peanuts are the most popular nuts in the United States. Peanuts are not true nuts but are related to the pea family. They grow under the ground, and each shell (which is really a pod) usually contains two nuts. Peanuts are eaten roasted, salted, or dried. They are used in making cookies and, of course, peanut butter. Peanuts are crushed to get peanut oil, which is often used in cooking.

Pecans are one of the hickory family of trees. Raising pecans is important in Southern states, such as Georgia and Louisiana.

Pecan trees are fast-growing. The nuts are nourishing.

Chestnuts are scarce in the United States. There have not been chestnut trees in the United States since 1911, when a plant disease killed them all. (There are many *horse chestnut* trees in the United States, but horse chestnuts are not good to eat.) All of the edible chestnuts sold in the United States are imported from Europe. The prickly outer covering of a chestnut is called a *burr*. Inside is the brown chestnut shell, and inside the shell is the meat of the chestnut. Chestnuts should be cooked before they are eaten.

The *black walnut* is a native American nut. The *English walnut* is native to Europe, but is also grown in the United States. Black walnuts grow wild in the United States, but English walnuts do not. Both types of walnuts have very hard shells.

When the American Civil War broke out there were no trained nurses. Most of the nursing for both armies was done by untrained volunteers.

Walnut

Sweet chestnut

Brazil nut

Peanut

Filbert (hazelnut)

Horse chestnut

Nuts come in all shapes and sizes. But they all have at least one hard outer casing. This has to be removed before the nut kernel can be eaten.

▲ Coconuts are grown in many tropical lands. They provide food and oil, and their fibers are used for coconut matting.

Filberts (or *hazelnuts*), *beechnuts*, *hickory nuts*, and *almonds* are also grown in the United States, but many nuts you buy in the store come from faraway lands. *Brazil nuts* come from the valley of the Amazon River in South America. Mozambique is the world's largest producer of *cashews. Pistachio nuts* come mainly from the Middle East. *Macadamia nuts* are from Australia but are also raised in Hawaii.

▶ ▶ ▶ **FIND OUT MORE** ◀ ◀ ◀
Carver, George Washington; Fruit; Nutrition; Palm; Plant Products; Seeds and Fruit

NUTRITION

Some health experts call the human body a machine, but machines do not change once they are built. Human beings never stop changing. Every moment, some part of you changes. Old cells die, and new ones take their place. New cells can only be made because of the food you eat.

The United States produces thousands of kinds of food. Some fruits, vegetables, and meats are sold fresh, but much of our food is processed. *Processed food* is changed in some way at a factory. Cake mixes, potato chips, canned and frozen foods, puddings, ice cream, hot dogs, bread, and soft drinks are examples of processed foods. Processed foods give people a greater variety of things

to eat, and they usually do not take much time to prepare, but processing removes many of the *nutrients* (vitamins and minerals) from foods. People may enjoy the taste of processed foods, but most of these foods do not give people enough of the body-building nutrients they need. Without proper nutrients, cells throughout the body must struggle very hard to do their work. Your body may constantly feel tired. You become impatient, depressed, or "crabby" and unable to pay attention to anything. These are some of the first signs of *malnutrition*.

Malnutrition is a weakening of the body caused by eating too little food or eating food that lacks enough of the nutrients that keep your body strong and healthy. A team of doctors studied two groups of people in India. One group lived on food rich in nutrients. These people developed strong bones and powerful muscles. They were intelligent, fast workers. The other group ate food without enough nutrients. The people in this group developed weak bones, did not grow as tall, and were not as active or strong. Their children were poor at schoolwork. These people were suffering from malnutrition.

Important Nutrients

A very important nutrient is *protein*. Not all proteins are equally valuable. They all have *amino acids* (substances found in all living cells), but some proteins have more than others. Meat has 18 kinds of amino acids. Dried peas and beans and nuts have just a few, but if you eat the right mixture of these foods, your body will get all the amino acids it needs.

A person could survive by eating only protein, but he or she would not feel well and would have no energy. Most energy is provided by *carbohydrates* (starches and sugars). Bread, potatoes, rice, pasta, and cereals, plus cookies and cakes contain carbohy-

---

QUIZ

1. What are nutrients?
2. Is cholesterol good or bad for you?
3. What are the most important minerals for good health?
4. What foods are high in vitamins?
5. What foods are called carbohydrates?

(Answers on page 2048)

LEARN BY DOING

To find out whether you are eating a balanced diet, keep a record of everything you eat for a whole week. Then see if you have eaten enough beans or meat—for fat soluble vitamins and protein—and sufficient green vegetables and fruit for vitamin C and fiber. To be healthy, you should have very few sugary or fatty foods on your list.

drates. They "burn" quickly and give you pep. If too many foods with extra sugar (candy, cookies, and cakes) and fats (cookies, potato chips and fried foods) are eaten, the body stores them as fats. Foods with too much fat or sugar can be harmful.

Early in the 1900s, scientists discovered vitamins. Now we know that vitamins are important in various ways to good health.

The human body also needs *vitamins* and *minerals* for strength and healthy tissues. The most important minerals are *calcium, phosphorus, iron,* and *iodine.* Besides these, *trace minerals* (minerals found in very small amounts), such as manganese, copper, zinc, and cobalt, are needed. A well-balanced diet provides enough vitamins and minerals of each kind.

unbleached contain the most nutrients. Most white breads contain very few nutrients. The nutrients in wheat lie just under the hull of the kernel. These nutrients are lost when wheat is milled into flour. Bleaching removes even more nutrients. Many manufacturers add some vitamins and call the product "enriched," but they have wasted the natural vitamins. Vitamins added later are not enough. Breads and cereals are also rich in fiber, which helps your body to digest foods more easily.

4. *Protein.* Everyone needs two servings of protein every day. The best proteins are in meat, fish, and eggs. Other, less costly, proteins are in nuts, peas, and dried beans.

Fats

Proteins

Carbohydrates

Vitamins and minerals

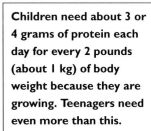

▲ A healthy diet is a balanced diet, containing proteins, carbohydrates, fats, vitamins, and minerals in the correct proportions. Too much, or too little, of each kind is unhealthy.

Diet

Protein, carbohydrates, fats, vitamins, and minerals should be eaten every day. To help people plan, buy, and prepare nutritious meals, experts have a Daily Food Plan.

1. *Milk and milk products.* Children need a quart (950 ml) of milk every day. Either natural cheese or ice cream may substitute for part of the milk. Milk contains *calcium,* which is vital for your bones to grow. One to three servings of butter or margarine supply enough vitamin A.

2. *Fruits and vegetables.* Several fruits and vegetables should be eaten each day. Fresh fruits and vegetables are the best. Frozen ones are next best.

3. *Breads and cereals.* These should be eaten along with rice and pasta at least six times a day. The foods made of whole grains and left

Wheat germ (the rich center of the wheat grain) can be added to many foods for both vitamins and flavor.

Cooking can destroy some nutrients. Vegetables have the most nutrients when eaten raw (although some, like potatoes, should *never* be eaten raw). If you cook vegetables, cook them only for a short time.

▶ ▶ ▶ ▶ **FIND OUT MORE** ◀ ◀ ◀ ◀
Diet see Dairy Products; Fish; Food; Fruit; Meat; Nut; Vegetables; Vegetarian; Water **Human Body** see Blood; Bone; Brain; Circulatory System; Digestion; Gland; Growth; Human Body; Muscle; Nervous System; Respiration; Skeleton **Nutrients** see Carbohydrate; Fats and Oils; Protein; Vitamins and Minerals

Children need about 3 or 4 grams of protein each day for every 2 pounds (about 1 kg) of body weight because they are growing. Teenagers need even more than this.

Cholesterol is a type of fat found in eggs, meat, and shellfish. Too much of it can increase the risk of a heart attack.

OAKLEY, ANNIE (1860–1926)

Annie Oakley was only 6 years old when she began helping to support her family by selling rabbits, pheasants, and quail she had shot with her father's rifle. She was born Phoebe Anne Oakley Mozee in a log cabin in Darke County, Ohio. She became a crack shot with rifles, pistols, and shotguns. At age 15, Annie entered a shooting contest and defeated the well-known marksman and vaudeville star, Frank Butler. Five years later she married Butler, who became her partner in stunt shooting and then her show-business manager.

In 1885, Annie became a star in Buffalo Bill's Wild West Show and gave shooting exhibitions throughout the United States. She performed many times before the kings and queens of Europe. Annie thrilled audiences at Queen Victoria's Diamond Jubilee in 1887 in London.

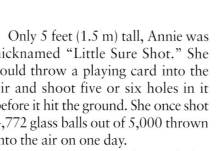

▶ **A photograph made in 1899 of the sharpshooter Annie Oakley.**

Only 5 feet (1.5 m) tall, Annie was nicknamed "Little Sure Shot." She could throw a playing card into the air and shoot five or six holes in it before it hit the ground. She once shot 4,772 glass balls out of 5,000 thrown into the air on one day.

Irving Berlin's musical comedy *Annie Get Your Gun* is based on her life.

▶▶▶▶ **FIND OUT MORE** ◀◀◀◀
Buffalo Bill; Rodeo

OASIS

SEE DESERT

OBESITY

SEE HEALTH

OBSERVATORY

An observatory is a place for studying the stars, planets, and other bodies in space. Weather stations are sometimes called observatories, but *observatory* usually means a place for *observing* (watching) the skies. Most observatories are built on high hills in the countryside, where the air is clear.

The first observatory was built in China in 2600 B.C. This observatory, like most early observatories, was used for measuring and calculating time. Early *astronomers* (scientists who study the bodies in space) kept careful records of when certain stars and planets were at certain places in the sky. They particularly studied the moon and watched how it changed shape. By doing this, they were able to come up with a calendar.

Early observatories did not have telescopes. But early astronomers, just by watching the sky and keeping records of what they saw, were able to map the visible part of the universe and discover some important astronomical laws.

The first astronomer to use a telescope was Galileo Galilei, in

A.D. 1610. From then on, almost every observatory had a telescope. Galileo's telescope was a *refracting* telescope—light passes through two or more glass lenses that collect the light and magnify the object observed.

Most of the large telescopes built after 1900 have been *reflecting* telescopes. In a reflecting telescope, the light is reflected (bounced) off a huge curved mirror and then into a lens. The world's largest reflecting telescope is at Zelenchukskaya, Russia. Its mirror is 236 inches (6 m) across and weighs 78 tons (71 metric tons), but it has failed to provide sharp images. Reflecting telescopes can be much larger than refracting telescopes, because the mirror can have a solid support on one side. The large lens of a refracting telescope can be supported only around its edges, so it sags because of its own weight.

Telescopes need large lenses or mirrors because large ones collect more light than small ones. Most telescopes today are used to study distant bodies in space. Little of the light given off by these bodies reaches the Earth, so the usefulness of a telescope depends more on how much light it can collect than on how much it can magnify an object.

The nearest star is so far away from Earth that the star's light, moving at 186,000 miles (300,000 km) a second, takes about four years to get here. Other stars are much farther away.

Today, most observatories are used for *astrophysics,* the science of the physical makeup of stars, star clusters, and *galaxies* (groups of billions of stars). Scientists find out what a body is made of by studying the electromagnetic radiation (light, radio waves, X rays, and so on) it gives off.

Stars can be studied with an optical telescope and a *spectroscope.* The telescope picks up light from a star, and the spectroscope splits the light into different colors (wavelengths). By studying the different wavelengths of light given off by a star, scientists can tell what the star is made of.

In 1990, the Hubble Space Telescope was launched in the cargo bay of the space shuttle *Discovery.* Unfortunately, one of its two mirrors was flawed, and the telescope was unable to return clear images. In 1993, astronauts were sent into space to repair the telescope.

SOME IMPORTANT OBSERVATORIES

Name	Location	Opened	Interesting Feature
Jodrell Bank Observatory	Jodrell Bank, England	1949	Has the world's first radio telescope capable of pointing in any direction
Kit Peak National Observatory	Tucson, Arizona	1962	Has the world's largest solar telescope
Mauna Kea Observatory	Mauna Kea, Hawaii	1991	The world's largest segmented mirror (400 inch)
Mount Palomar Observatory	Mount Palomar, California	1948	Has the largest reflecting telescope in the United States (200 in)
National Radio Astronomy Observatory	Socorro, New Mexico	1981	Has the world's largest radio telescope
Special Astrophysical Observatory	Zelenchukskaya, Russia	1974	Has the world's largest reflecting telescope
Yerkes Observatory	Williams Bay, Wisconsin	1897	Has the world's largest refracting telescope

▶ ▶ ▶ ▶ **FIND OUT MORE** ◀ ◀ ◀ ◀
Astronomy; Lens; Radiation; Radio Astronomy; Star; Telescope

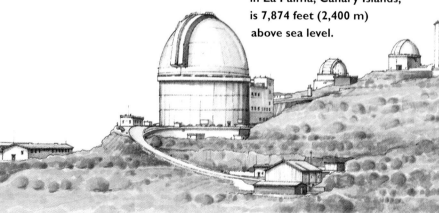

▽ **Modern observatories are built on tall hillsides and mountains, far away from city lights, which could blur the view. This observatory in La Palma, Canary Islands, is 7,874 feet (2,400 m) above sea level.**

OCEAN

For centuries the oceans were vast, mysterious places. Explorers such as Christopher Columbus sailed across the oceans in fear and ignorance. Gradually people mapped the oceans and learned what their boundaries are and what winds blow across them. But our knowledge of what lies underneath the ocean surface is very recent. A great deal of it has been learned in the last 40 years. We now know that the oceans are a far more fantastic part of the Earth than the early explorers could ever have guessed. Very recently, we have realized that the oceans are really all just parts of one big ocean, the "world ocean."

The world ocean is a large body of salt water that covers 71 percent of the Earth's surface. The Earth is the only planet in the solar system with such a large quantity of water. The continents divide the ocean into the Atlantic, the Pacific, the Indian, the Antarctic, and the Arctic oceans. Smaller bodies of water, such as the Mediterranean Sea, the Gulf of Mexico, and Hudson Bay, are all part of the ocean, but they are largely closed in by land. Seas that are completely surrounded by land, such as the Caspian Sea (between Russia, Kazakhstan, and Iran), are not part of the world ocean.

Ocean Water

Seawater is said to have a high *salinity* (saltiness) because at least 80 elements are dissolved in it. The large amounts of chlorine and sodium, which combine to form sodium chloride (common salt), make the ocean water taste very salty.

Water pressure in the ocean increases by 14.7 pounds per square inch every 33 feet (1.03 kg per sq. cm every 10 m). As people go deeper down in the ocean, their equipment needs to be stronger. Scuba divers can go down only about 100 feet (30 m). Wearing pressurized suits, divers have been able to descend to 600 feet (180 m) below the surface. In 1960, the *Trieste*, a U.S. Navy *bathyscaphe* (a deep-sea research vessel similar to a submarine), made the deepest dive on record—35,800 feet (10,900 m). This was at the Marianas Trench in the Pacific Ocean. The *Trieste* withstood a pressure of 16,000 pounds per square inch (1, 125 kg per sq. cm)!

> As you go down beneath the surface of the ocean, colors begin to disappear as different wavelengths of light get filtered out. First the reds disappear, then the yellows and greens. A hundred feet (30 m) down, blue is the only color left. Below a depth of 3,000 feet (1,000 m), there is complete darkness. The only light in these depths comes from fish that make their own light.

▶ The "oceans" of the world are really only a single ocean, as can be seen from this map. Under the ocean's surface, large-scale *currents* cross thousands of miles. Some bring warm waters; others bring cold. The currents affect the weather of the countries they reach.

1. Davis Strait
2. Labrador Sea
3. Greenland Sea
4. Norwegian Sea
5. Barents Sea
6. Laptev Sea
7. Bering Sea
8. Philippine Sea

Ocean Movements

Waves are the most easily seen kind of ocean movement because they happen at the surface. Waves are caused by wind blowing over the water, making it move in a circle (downward and upward). When waves from out in the ocean travel from deep water to shallow water, the ocean bottom interferes with the downward motion of the wave, so the wave rises higher above the surface. When it gets too high, the top of the wave falls forward, forming a breaker. A very dangerous kind of wave, called a *tsunami*, is caused by undersea earthquakes or erupting volcanoes that start a huge wave rolling at speeds up to 500 miles an hour (800 km/h). Boats at sea do not notice this wave because it is only about 3 feet (1 m) high, but by the time it reaches land it may, with little warning, have built up to 100 feet (30 m) high. When it hits land, it causes great damage. Tsunamis are sometimes called *tidal waves*, but they are not caused by tides.

Less easily observed movements of water are *currents*. Currents are streams of water that flow through the ocean along well-mapped routes. There are two kinds of currents: *surface currents*, which extend from the surface down to about 700 to 1,000 feet (200 – 300 m), and *deep-sea currents*, which flow much farther below sea level.

Currents that flow toward the poles from the equator are *warm currents*. They come from hot, tropical regions where the sun beats down and heats up the surface waters. The Gulf Stream is an example of a warm current.

Currents that flow from the poles toward the equator are *cold currents*. Their waters come from icy regions in the north and south. Cold water sinks because it is denser and heavier than warm water, so cold currents flow beneath the warm currents.

Tides are the regular rise and fall of sea level. At high tide the water reaches farther up the coast than at low tide. Tides occur because the gravity of the moon and the sun pull on the Earth's waters. Most parts of the world have high and low tides twice a day. Enclosed seas, such as the Mediterranean, hardly have tides at all.

The Ocean Floor

People used to think that the ocean floor was flat, but this is not true. Along most coastlines is a *continental shelf*. This is a wide, flat area extending in places 40 miles (65 km) out to sea and sloping gently downward to 360 to 600 feet (110–180 m). The ocean floor then plunges steeply downward. This steep descent is called the *continental slope*. At the bottom of the slope is the *abyss*, the deep ocean floor.

The ocean bottom is very rugged in places. Mountain ranges, volcanoes, canyons, and great *abyssal plains*, the flattest places on Earth, can all be found under the ocean. One mountain range, the Mid-Atlantic Ridge, stretches from Iceland to Antarctica. Ranges like this are called *mid-ocean ridges*. Mountains that rise above sea level are called *seamounts*. Some islands are the tops of seamounts. Underwater volcanoes spew red-hot lava into the sea. The lava quickly cools when it comes into contact with the cold water, forming dark, glassy *pillow lavas*.

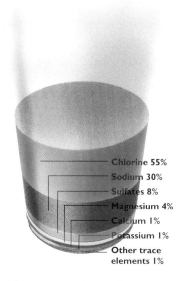

Chlorine 55%
Sodium 30%
Sulfates 8%
Magnesium 4%
Calcium 1%
Potassium 1%
Other trace elements 1%

▲ **The sea contains sodium chloride (common salt), which makes it taste salty, as well as other minerals. The Dead Sea is the saltiest of all the world's oceans.**

▼ **The highest ocean wave ever recorded was seen during a Pacific Ocean hurricane in 1933. It measured 112 feet (34 m) high. Ocean waves are caused by the pull of the sun and the moon, the wind, and under-the-sea volcanic action.**

The deeper you dive in the ocean, the more the weight of the water presses down on you. In the deepest part of the Pacific Ocean, nearly 7 miles (11 km) down, the pressure is more than 7 tons on every square inch (a metric ton on every square cm). Yet people traveling in special vessels have been able to go this deep and live.

▼ A cross-section through one of the world's oceans shows that the sea bed is not flat and level but more like a continental landscape. The sea bed is cut by deep valleys and forced up by underwater mountains and volcanoes. It is on the continental shelf areas that fish are caught and oil exploration takes place.

Ocean trenches are narrow, steep clefts that plunge to depths far below the ocean floor. Trenches are usually found along the edges of continents.

Mid-ocean ridges and ocean trenches mark the divisions between the giant rigid plates that form the Earth's crust. Mid-ocean ridges are found at *constructive margins*. Here, molten rock rises from great depths into a gap between the plates, adding to the sea floor as the plates move apart. Ocean trenches are found at *destructive margins*, where one plate is sliding under another.

Submarine canyons are narrower than trenches and not as deep. Canyons are found near the mouths of rivers that pour into the ocean. Canyons were probably formed by river water that *eroded* (wore away) the ocean floor when the sea level was lower.

The ocean floor is covered by layers of *sediment* (soil particles and other matter) that has sunk to the bottom. Sediments building up over millions of years, covering the rock beneath it, and in time becoming solidified itself. In bringing up samples of sediment, scientists have discovered the fossils of very ancient plant and animal life.

Oceanic Life

As on land, all life in the ocean depends on plants. The plants in the sea are often very small, and some are almost like particles of dust. They live near the surface, where they can use the energy from sunlight to make

their own food from the minerals in the seawater. Deep in the ocean it is completely dark.

The plants float about wherever the currents in the ocean take them. Floating with them are billions of little animals. Some are almost as small as the plants. Others are the young of larger animals, such as fish. All these tiny plants and animals are known as *plankton*, which means "drifters." The smallest animals feed on the plants of the plankton, and larger animals eat the small animals. Strangely enough, the biggest animal in the world, the great blue whale, feeds on *krill*, tiny shrimplike creatures that are part of the plankton.

Some of the most fantastic ocean life has been discovered not on the surface but 1½ miles (2.4 km) under the Pacific Ocean in the Galápagos Rift. A number of bacteria and animals live there, far from the light of the sun. They get their energy from *hydrothermal vents*, fountains of hot water and gases spouting from the deep ocean floor. The creatures found there include huge blood-red worms and large clams.

Ocean Resources

People are just beginning to discover the vast natural resources of the ocean. Fish and other sea animals are the most used resources. They are plentiful, and, if people use great care in how they fish, they will not decrease their numbers. Most whales, however, are in danger of extinction because people have killed so many of

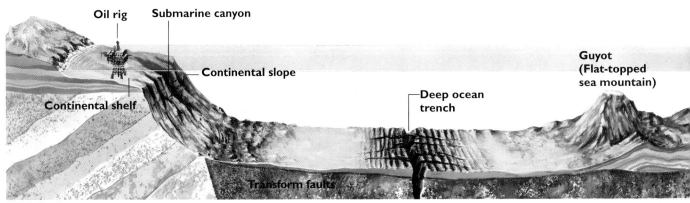

Oil rig
Submarine canyon
Continental slope
Continental shelf
Deep ocean trench
Guyot (Flat-topped sea mountain)
Transform faults

them. The world's supply of lobsters and shrimps may also be decreasing.

Aquaculture means "seafarming," raising marine plants and animals in the same way a farmer raises crops and animals on land. People have been raising oysters, clams, and seaweed for a long time. Now scientists are experimenting with ways to raise and harvest a large variety of seafood.

The ocean contains deposits of useful minerals. Many lie in sand and gravel near coasts. They include gold, tin, titanium, and magnetite (an ore of iron). Shallow deposits are already being mined by dredgers, and there are plans to work in deeper water. These deposits have come from the land, washed down by rivers, but in the deep ocean there are other minerals that have apparently come up from deeper in the Earth's crust.

Lying on part of the ocean floor, especially in the northern Pacific, are lumps called *manganese nodules*. These nodules are rich in minerals, particularly manganese, nickel, cobalt, and copper. However, so far, few of these have been mined.

Under the continental shelf are rich deposits of oil and natural gas. These deposits are being exploited off the coasts of the United States, Australia, Indonesia, Malaysia, and Nigeria, and in the North Sea.

▶ The oceans are filled with a rich variety of fish and plants that survive even in the dark, cold depths.

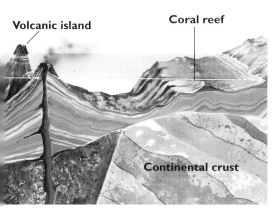

Volcanic island

Coral reef

Continental crust

FACTS ABOUT THE OCEANS' AREA

The total area covered by the Earth's oceans is about 140,000,000 square miles (362,000,000 sq. km). This is just over 70 percent of the Earth's surface area. The largest ocean is the Pacific, with an area of about 63,800,000 square miles (165,000,000 sq. km). The smallest is the Arctic Ocean, with an area of about 5,440,000 square miles (14,100,000 sq. km).

VOLUME The total volume of the Earth's oceans is about 310,000,000 cubic miles (1,292,000,000 cu. km). The total weight of the water is about 1,450 thousand million million tons (1.32 million million million metric tons).

DEPTH The average depth of the oceans is about 11,700 feet (3,566 m). The Pacific is the deepest ocean, with an average depth of about 14,000 feet (4,267 m). The deepest part of the ocean is the Marianas Trench in the Pacific; it is about 36,000 feet (10,970 m) deep.

▶ **Mining boats dredge up manganese nodules from the seabed with a suction scoop. Manganese is mainly used in making steel.**

The flattest plains on Earth lie beneath the oceans at depths of 2 to 4 miles (3 to 6 km). These plains are so flat that any lump more than 3 feet (1 m) high is a mountain.

QUIZ

1. How much of the Earth's surface does the world ocean cover?
2. Would you say that the Great Lakes (in the northern U.S.) are part of the world ocean?
3. What is a *tsunami*?
4. Is the Gulf Stream a warm or cold current?
5. Name two of the useful minerals found in the ocean.

(Answers on page 2048.)

▼ **Sonar is used by ships to measure the water depth. Sound waves reflect back from the sea bed, as seen on the screen.**

Exploring the Ocean

Interest in the bottom of the ocean began when people started laying telegraph cables across the ocean floor in the 1850s. One of the people helping to lay cables was a U.S. naval officer, Matthew Fontaine Maury. Maury collected information on winds, currents, and water temperatures to help navigators at sea. He studied the ocean bottom using *sounding lines*. These were ropes that were weighted with cannonballs and that had hollow tubes at the ends. The tubes were driven into the sea bottom by the weight of the cannonballs, and samples of the sediments were trapped in the tubes. Maury was then able to study the microscopic sea life embedded in the ocean bottom, as well as make discoveries about the bottom's formation.

Scientific exploration of the ocean developed even more in 1872 when the British warship H.M.S. *Challenger* began a 3½-year voyage around the world. Techniques of undersea exploration were developed even further during World War II, when people spent time and effort trying to detect submarines.

In 1968, the United States joined with five other countries—France, Great Britain, Japan, the former Soviet Union, and West Germany— in the Deep Sea Drilling Project. This was carried out by the drilling ship *Glomar Challenger*. The ship has

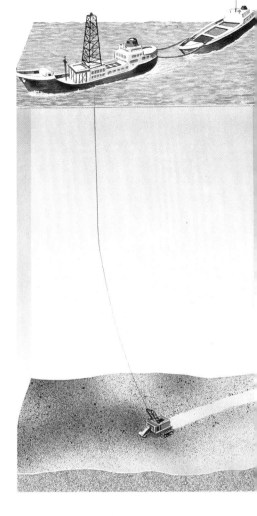

been roaming the oceans ever since, drilling holes deep into the seabed to find out what the Earth's crust is like under the oceans.

People Under the Sea

Divers have been exploring the sea for hundreds of years. More than 5,000 years ago people used to dive for pearls and sponges in the Mediterranean Sea, holding their breath when they dived. Diving suits came into use in the 1800s. Divers wearing these suits are supplied with air pumped from the surface. Diving suits are very heavy and cumbersome, but people still use them for some kinds of underwater work.

Skin diving, in which the diver carries his or her own air supply, was made possible by a Frenchman, Jacques-Yves Cousteau. He invented a portable air supply, the *aqualung*, in the 1940s. With aqualungs, divers

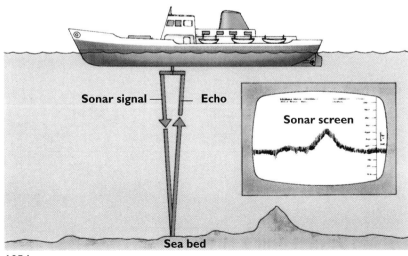

Sonar signal — ┃ ┃ — Echo

Sonar screen

Sea bed

have been able to explore and photograph under water in shallow seas.

Exploration of the deeper parts of the ocean is carried out on special diving vessels. In 1934, two U.S. scientists, William Beebe and Otis Barton, were lowered 3,028 feet (925 m) down into the Atlantic in a *bathysphere*. The bathysphere was a round windowed chamber with lights that could be shone out into the blackness of deep ocean waters. But the bathysphere was dangerous because if the cable lowering it had snapped, the vessel would have plunged straight to the ocean bottom.

A far safer vessel was the *bathyscaphe*, invented by a Belgian named Auguste Piccard. The bathyscaphe was made up of a large floating tank and a small observation sphere. Piccard's bathyscaphe was the first vessel in which scientists could study the ocean at great depths for long periods of time.

A later diving vessel is the U.S. research submarine *Alvin*, which is built especially strong to withstand great pressure. It has been tested to a depth of 22,000 feet (6,700 m). It carries a crew of three. Scientists aboard it discovered the strange worms in the Galápagos Rift.

Scientists have been trying to find ways in which people can live in homes built under the sea. In 1962, Cousteau led an experiment called *Conshelf I*, in which two *aquanauts* (undersea explorers) lived for a week in a steel chamber on the sea floor. It was anchored in the Mediterranean 40 feet (12 m) below the surface. *Conshelf II* was an experiment in 1963 in which five persons lived 36 feet (11 m) below sea level for a whole month. Two years later, Cousteau built *Conshelf III*, a large underwater house in which six aquanauts lived for three weeks at a depth of 330 feet (100 m). Similar experiments were carried out in 1964, 1965, and 1968 by the U.S. Navy with *Sealab I, Sealab II,* and *Sealab III*

in the Pacific Ocean.

In 1990, The World Ocean Circulation Experiment (WOCE) came into being. Scientists from more than 40 nations are conducting a 10-year program studying oceans. Satellites, ships, floating platforms, and thousands of scientific instruments are being used.

▶▶▶▶ FIND OUT MORE ◀◀◀◀
Exploration and Use of the Ocean
see Boats and Boating; Byrd, Richard E.; Cousteau, Jacques-Yves; Diving; Drilling Rig; Fishing Industry; Maury, Matthew; Natural Resources; Navigation; Petroleum; Sailing; Scuba Diving; Ships and Shipping; Submarine; Swimming
Geography and Geology
of the Earth see Antarctica; Arctic; Continental Drift; Earth History; Equator; Geography; Geology; Map; Mineral; Plate Tectonics
Ocean Life see Algae; Bioluminescence; Clams and Oysters; Deep-sea Life; Dolphins and Porpoises; Echinoderm; Electric Fish; Fish; Fossil; Gulls and Terns; Hydra; Jellyfish; Lichen; Marine Life; Mollusk; Octopus and Squid; Protozoan; Seabirds; Seahorse; Seals and Sealions; Sharks and Rays; Shell; Sponge; Tropical Fish; Walrus; Whales and Whaling
Ocean Surface and Depths see Atlantic Ocean; Climate; Glacier; Gulf Stream; Iceberg; Indian Ocean; Pacific Ocean; Salt; Sand; Seacoast; Tide; Wave; Wind

WHERE TO DISCOVER MORE
Gibbs, B. *Ocean Facts*. London: Usborne Publishing, 1991.
Neal, Philip. *The Oceans*. Vermont: Trafalgar, 1993.

▼ **Submersibles are much smaller than submarines, but they can dive to far greater depths. They have room for crew members, and are used for laying, inspecting, and repairing underwater pipelines and telephone cables. Submersibles are also used to service oil rigs, map the ocean floor, and survey shipwrecks. A robot helper can be sent to small and dangerous places.**

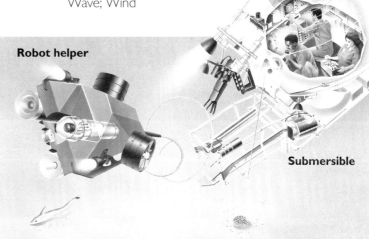

Robot helper

Submersible

DATES OF SPECIAL EVENTS IN OCTOBER
1   The first U.S. jet plane was flown (1942).
2   Mahatma Gandhi, Indian political leader, was born (1869).   Thurgood Marshall sworn in as first black **U.S. Supreme Court** justice (1967).
3   Ethiopia was invaded by Italy (1935).   The reunification of Germany (1990).
4   President Rutherford B. Hayes was born (1822).   *Sputnik I,* the first space satellite, was launched by the former Soviet Union (1957).
5   President Chester A. Arthur was born (1830).   President Harry Truman made the first televised address from the White House (1947).   The Great Chicago Fire began (1871).
6   The first showing of a part-talking movie, *The Jazz Singer,* starring Al Jolson, in New York (1927).
10   The U.S. Naval Academy was opened at Annapolis, Maryland (1845).   Spiro Agnew resigned as Vice President of the United States (1973).
11   Eleanor Roosevelt, the wife of President Franklin D. Roosevelt and a tireless worker for rights of minorities, was born (1884).
12   Christopher Columbus reached the island of San Salvador in the Bahamas (1492).
14   William the Conqueror invaded England from France (1066) and became king of England.   President Dwight D. Eisenhower was born (1890).   John Brown led a daring raid on the U.S. arsenal at Harpers Ferry, West Virginia (1859).   Eugene O'Neill, U.S. dramatist, was born (1888).
17   John Burgoyne, British general, surrendered at Saratoga to American Revolutionary forces (1777).
19   The British surrendered to the American Revolutionary War forces under General George Washington at Yorktown, Virginia (1781).
20   Christopher Wren, great British architect, was born (1632).   John Dewey, U.S. philosopher and education pioneer, was born (1859).
21   Ferdinand Magellan entered the present-day Strait of Magellan at the tip of South America (1520).   Battle of Trafalgar was won by the British (1805).
22   Sam Houston was inaugurated as the first president of the Republic of Texas (1836).   The Metropolitan Opera, one of the world's greatest operatic centers, opened in New York City (1883).
23   The Hungarian Revolution began (1956).
24   United Nations Day. Church bells ring and special prayers of peace and brotherhood are said all over the world.
25   The English won the Battle of Agincourt, a decisive victory over the French, during the Hundred Years' War (1415).   Pablo Picasso, the great modern artist, was born (1881).
26   The Erie Canal was opened to traffic (1825).
27   The Federalist Papers first published in *New York Independent Journal* (1787).   President Theodore Roosevelt was born (1858).
28   Harvard College in Cambridge, Massachusetts, was founded (1636).
29   The great stock market crash in the United States (1929).
30   President John Adams was born (1735).
31   Martin Luther nailed his 95 theses to a church door in Wittenberg Germany (1517).   Halloween. Children dress up in fancy costumes and play "trick or treat" on the neighbors.

O'CONNOR, SANDRA DAY (1930–)

Sandra Day O'Connor was the first female justice to sit on the bench of the U.S. Supreme Court. She was born in El Paso, Texas, on March 26, 1930, but spent her childhood on the Day family ranch near Duncan, Arizona. She studied law at Stanford University, where she met her husband, John Jay O'Connor III.

As a young lawyer, she practiced in Arizona, and from 1965 to 1969,

▶ Sandra Day O'Connor, the first woman to become a U.S. Supreme Court Judge.

she served as assistant attorney general for the state. In 1969, she was elected to the Arizona Senate as a Republican and became majority leader, the first woman ever to hold such a position. She became a judge in 1974.

In 1981, President Ronald Reagan chose Sandra O'Connor as his first appointee to the U.S. Supreme Court. Known as a conservative, Justice O'Connor has won respect for her independent judgments, particularly in regard to constitutional questions about religion. She is a strong supporter of police and prosecutors.

▶▶▶▶ **FIND OUT MORE** ◀◀◀◀
Supreme Court

OCTOBER

October is the tenth month on our calendar. It was the eighth month on the ancient Roman calendar. *Octo* means "eight" in Latin. It once had only 30

◀ The calendula flower and the opal stone are symbols for the month of October.

days, but in 45 B.C. Julius Caesar added another day. October's flower is the calendula, often called the "pot marigold." October has two birthstones. One is the tourmaline, a gem of many colors. The other is the opal, which glows with firelike brilliance.

October is crisp and cool in most of the northern parts of the world. Its days are golden with sunshine and bright with red and yellow autumn leaves. Large orange pumpkins lie in the fields, ready to be picked. Children carve them into scary jack-o'-lantern faces for Halloween, October 31. Columbus Day is celebrated in October, too. Christopher Columbus, sailing across the ocean, landed in the Americas on October 12, 1492.

Sometimes in the early mornings in October, there is frost on the grass and on the windowpanes. A few late flowers still brighten the gardens. Cider and crunchy red apples are sold at roadside stands. In the southern part of the world, beyond the equator, gentle springtime is bursting into bloom in October.

▶ ▶ ▶ ▶ **FIND OUT MORE** ◀ ◀ ◀ ◀
Autumn; Calendar; Halloween; Month

OCTOPUS AND SQUID

Both octopuses and squids are highly developed *mollusks.* They live in the sea and have soft bodies.

The octopus has a large, football-shaped head and enormous eyes that are very similar to those of higher animals. It has excellent vision and a good nervous system. Its strong, hard beaklike jaws are used to crush and tear apart its prey—usually crabs. Eight *tentacles,* or arms, extend from around the head of the octopus. The tentacles help the octopus to creep along the rocks and coral deposits on the ocean bottom. Each arm has two rows of suckers underneath, which act like suction cups. With these suction cups, the octopus can grip its prey and other objects.

The octopus has cells in its skin filled with color pigments. When the octopus is frightened or excited, the cells change shape. This changes the distribution of color pigments and the color of the skin. The octopus at times appears to be blushing!

Contrary to popular belief, most octopuses are small creatures, less than 1 foot (30 cm) across from the tip of one arm to the tip of the opposite arm. Several kinds of octopuses may be up to 28 feet (8.5 m) across, but such giants are rare. Octopuses

The octopus is the most intelligent of the animals without backbones. It can be trained to find its way through a maze and to solve simple problems, such as removing the stopper from a sealed jar containing food.

▼ The octopus is not as dangerous as many people think. In fact, it is often eaten by various big fish that attack its arms. One of its defenses is to change its color to match its surroundings in order to *camouflage* (hide) itself.

are preyed on by eels, fish, seals, other marine animals, and even people.

The squid has ten tentacles; a long, pointed body; and two triangular fins. It uses the fins to move through the water. A squid may be from 2 inches (5 cm) to 30 feet (9 m) in length. Giant squids are the largest of all animals without backbones. Squids feed on fish, which they grasp with two of their longest tentacles, called "grasping arms."

▲ The squid is one of the fastest animals in the sea. It has excellent eyesight, which makes it a good hunter. Its tentacles are covered with suckers. These hold the prey firmly while the squid bites it.

▼ The statue of Christopher Columbus which stands in Ohio's state capital. The statue was given to the state by the citizens of Genoa, Italy—the explorer's birthplace.

Both octopuses and squids usually creep along slowly. If danger comes, they move quickly by shooting streams of water out of a *siphon* on the body—just as a jet plane is propelled forward by the streams of hot gas from its engines. When moving in this way, the squid shoots backward! Squids and octopuses can also shoot an inky fluid into the water. The ink not only confuses the enemy by hiding the octopus or squid, but also dulls the enemy's sense of smell.

Many tales have been told about fierce attacks by octopuses and squids on human beings. Most of these stories are exaggerated. Despite these age-old tales, fishermen continue to catch and sell the sea creatures, which make tasty meals.

▷▷▷▷ **FIND OUT MORE** ◁◁◁◁
Marine Life; Mollusk

OGLETHORPE, JAMES

SEE GEORGIA

OHIO

Ohio's admission into the Union was complicated by a very unusual mistake. Ohio was admitted as a state in 1803. But by some strange error, Congress did not *ratify* (approve) the state's admission. This error was not discovered until 1953!

Ohio is unusual in another way. It has given this country more Presidents than any other state except Virginia. Ulysses S. Grant, Rutherford B. Hayes, James A. Garfield, Benjamin Harrison, William McKinley, William H. Taft, and Warren G. Harding were born in Ohio. For this reason, the state is called the "modern mother of Presidents."

The Land and Climate
Ohio is a north-central state. Michigan and Lake Erie are north of it. The winding Ohio River forms the southern and southeastern borders. Pennsylvania is on the other side of Ohio's eastern boundary. Across the straight western boundary is Indiana. The Scioto River divides Ohio into two parts. The state capital, Columbus, is on this river.

A gently rolling plain lies west of the Scioto. It is part of the plains that are west and south of the Great Lakes. In Ohio, most of these plains are called Till Plains. But the northern tip is called the Great Lakes Plain. Campbell Hill, northwest of Columbus, is the highest point in the state.

East of the Scioto, the land rises. This area is called the Allegheny Plateau. Most of the plateau is hilly, but a strip of flat plain lies close to Lake Erie. A small part of the hilly, fertile bluegrass region is in south-central Ohio.

Winters in Ohio are cold, and summers are warm and humid.

OHIO

STATE SYMBOLS

The sun over the mountains illustrates that Ohio is the first state west of the Allegheny Mountains.

The scarlet carnation came from southern Europe.

The Buckeye tree is named for its shiny brown seeds that look like the eyes of white-tailed buck deer.

The cardinal's song is so pretty that at one time the birds were sold as pets. Laws have now been passed to protect cardinals.

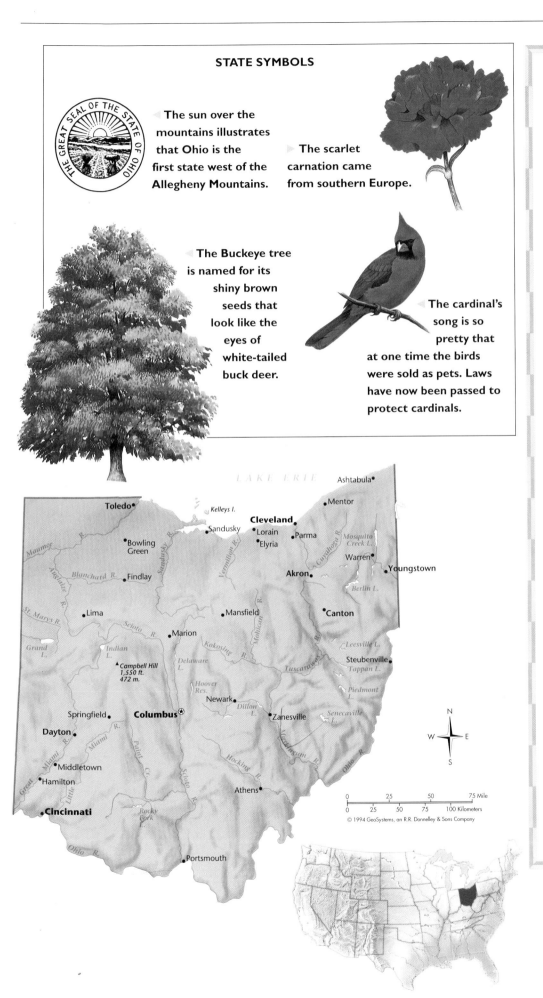

Capital and largest city
Columbus
(632,910 people)

Area
41,222 square miles
(106,764 sq. km)
Rank: 35th

Population
10,847,115 people
Rank: 6th

Statehood
March 1, 1803
(17th state admitted)

Principal rivers
Great Miami River
Scioto River
Ohio River

Highest point
Campbell Hill
1,550 feet (472 m)

Motto
"With God, All Things are Possible."

Song
"Beautiful Ohio"

Famous people
Neil Armstrong, Thomas Alva Edison, John Glenn, Zane Grey, Jesse Owens, Tecumseh, James Thurber, Orville Wright

© 1994 GeoSystems, an R.R. Donnelley & Sons Company

One of Ohio's nicknames is the "Buckeye State." It received this name because many buckeye, or horse chestnut, trees grow there.

▲ The great Serpent Mound in Ohio was built by the Hopewell tribe and is 1,641 feet (500 m) long. It is one of several animal-shaped mounds which survive today.

▶ Cincinnati seen at night, from across the Ohio River. Cincinnati lies close to the Kentucky border.

History

Native Americans called Mound Builders were some of the earliest inhabitants of the region. The Mound Builders had disappeared long before European explorers arrived in the 1600s. But some of the mounds they built remain undamaged.

In the early 1700s, French fur traders found a number of tribes living in Ohio's wooded river valleys. The Iroquois were in the northeast and center. The Delawares had moved into the southeast. In western Ohio lived the Ottawas, the Shawnees, and the Miamis.

France claimed a large area that included Ohio because of French explorations there. But Britain claimed the same region. British fur traders from Pennsylvania and Virginia had built trading posts in the region. Ohio was one of the prizes that France and Britain fought for in the French and Indian War. Some tribes helped the British, and some helped the French. When the British won, they took practically all the French-claimed land east of the Mississippi River.

But the region south of the Great Lakes was not British for long. The United States gained it as a result of winning the Revolutionary War. Settlers began moving into this area, then called the Northwest Territory, in 1788. Some former soldiers came down the Ohio River by boat. Where the Muskingum River joins the Ohio, they started a town that they named

Marietta, after Marie Antoinette. She was queen of France at the time the French helped the United States win the Revolutionary War. Cincinnati was founded the next year, in 1789. It also was built on the Ohio River. When the settlers moved into Ohio, forest covered nearly all of the land. They cleared whatever land they needed for farming.

Settlers took away more and more Native American land for their towns and farms. The tribes united to fight the white people and save their land. In 1794, General Anthony Wayne marched a small army to northwestern Ohio. The two sides met in a place where a windstorm had felled many trees. Wayne and his soldiers won the Battle of Fallen Timbers. With this defeat, the Native American tribes lost Ohio.

Many more settlers then moved in. In 1800, Congress divided the Northwest Territory into two parts. Ohio was made a state in 1803.

Waterways have meant a great deal to Ohio's development. The first steamboat west of the mountains reached the state in 1811. Steamboats made the rivers more useful than ever. And soon canals, such as New York's famous Erie Canal, linked Ohio with the East. Ohioans could then ship goods by water all the way to the Atlantic Coast.

Ohio was settled mostly by people from the northeast of the country. Most were strongly against slavery. Some Ohioans helped slaves escape

from the South. Troops from Ohio played a big part in winning the Civil War.

Working in Ohio

The location of the state has much to do with its success in manufacturing. It is situated in the middle of the most densely populated part of the United States. Ohio factories, therefore, have millions of customers close at hand. A network of airlines, railroads, and highways carries Ohio's products to customers. The state has access to two major water routes—the Ohio River and Lake Erie. Ohio's location makes it a convenient meeting place for the two things that manufacturing must have—raw materials and fuel. The principal raw material is iron ore, which comes from mines in Minnesota and Wisconsin. Heavy freight like this can be moved most cheaply by water. Iron ore comes most of the way by ship on the Great Lakes. The principal fuel is coal. Some is mined in Ohio, but much comes from West Virginia and Pennsylvania. The manufacturing centers of Ohio grew up close to the coal fields.

Ohio ranks third in the country for money earned in manufacturing. It has thousands of manufacturing plants. Much equipment for transportation (cars, buses, and trucks) is made in Cleveland, Dayton, and Toledo. Akron is known for its rubber manufacturing; Cincinnati, for its jet engines; and Canton, for its roller bearings. Steel, glass, chemicals, and office machines are also made in Ohio.

Mining is a significant source of income for the state. Coal, gravel, sand, and salt are mined, and petroleum and natural gas are drilled in Ohio.

The minerals and manufacturing industries that enrich Ohio also pose a threat. Lake Erie had become very polluted by the 1970s, but Federal cleanup measures have improved conditions there.

Fertile soil and a good climate help Ohio's agriculture. Corn is the state's biggest crop. Wheat, tomatoes, and soybeans are other money-making crops. Much of the corn is fed to the hogs and cattle raised in Ohio. Dairy farms all over the state provide many products. Tourism is another important industry in the state.

▶▶▶▶ **FIND OUT MORE** ◀◀◀◀
French and Indian War; Fur; Great Lakes; Indian Wars

OIL

SEE FATS AND OILS, PETROLEUM

OIL SHALE

SEE PETROLEUM

OJIBWAS

The Ojibwa, or Ojibway, tribe was once one of the largest Native American tribes in North America. These people lived in the Great Lakes regions of what are now the states of Minnesota, Wisconsin, and Michigan, and the Canadian provinces of Ontario and Manitoba. The Ojibwas speak the Algonkian, or Algonquian, language. Their name *Ojibwa* means "to roast until puckered up" in Algonkian. This name refers to the puckered seams they sewed on their moccasins. Early European settlers found it hard to pronounce "Ojibwa" and called the tribe the "Chippewa."

> **Seven United States Presidents were born in Ohio: Ulysses S. Grant, Rutherford B. Hayes, James A. Garfield, Benjamin Harrison, William McKinley, William Howard Taft, and Warren G. Harding. Garfield, Hayes, McKinley, and Harding are buried there also, along with Presidents William Henry Harrison and Grover Cleveland.**

▲ The Ojibwas bent branches to make a *supple (flexible),* but strong, dome-shaped frame for their wigwams. This they covered with birch bark or animal skins.

The Ojibwas hunted and fished in the forests, marshes, and lakes. They gathered wild fruit. In the fall, the women would paddle to the shallow places of the Minnesota lakes, where wild rice grew. They would lean the rice stalks over their canoes and beat them until the rice grains fell into the canoes.

Ojibwa families lived in dome-shaped *wigwams*. These houses had wooden frames and were covered with long strips of birch bark. The Ojibwas also used birch bark as writing paper. They drew small pictures on the birch bark to represent different events and, in this way, kept a record of tribal affairs. The Ojibwa tribe helped the French fight the British in the French and Indian War, but they sided with the British in the Revolutionary War and in the War of 1812. They signed a peace treaty with the United States government in 1815 and later sold most of their territory to the government. More than 55,000 Ojibwa Native Americans now live on reservations in Michigan, Minnesota, Wisconsin, North Dakota, and Ontario, Canada.

▶▶▶▶ **FIND OUT MORE** ◀◀◀◀
Algonkian; French and Indian War; Native Americans; Sioux; War of 1812

OKLAHOMA

A race for free land! Western Oklahoma was opened up for settlement in an exciting way. Thousands of homesteaders came on foot, on horseback, and in covered wagons to dash for the free land. They were to start when a shot was fired. Some people began ahead of time and claimed their land sooner than they should have. These cheaters gave Oklahoma its nickname, the "Sooner State." Oklahoma is also sometimes called the "Boomer State."

The first *land run*, or *land rush*, in Oklahoma was held on April 22, 1889, when government land was opened to any settler who wanted it. Small farms were staked out, and tent villages sprang up. Other land rushes were held in later years. The land had been territory set aside by the government for Native Americans.

The Land and Climate
Oklahoma lies west of Arkansas, south of Kansas, and north of Texas. It looks like a hand with a finger pointing west. The finger, a strip only 34 miles (55 km) across, reaches as far as Colorado and New Mexico. This strip is called the *panhandle*.

Western Oklahoma is in the Great Plains. The plains are almost level but slope toward the southeast. East of the Wichita Mountains, another plain begins. It is a branch of the plains that curve around the Great Lakes. Here, also, the land slopes toward the southeast. Two highlands rise on the state's eastern border and extend into Arkansas. The northern highland is the Ozark Plateau. The southern one is the Ouachita Mountains. The Arkansas River flows between them.

Oklahoma summers are long and sometimes very hot. The air is dry and winds sweep over the plains. Winters are cold but usually short. Great differences in *precipitation* (rain-and snowfall) are found in the

> Oklahoma City is one of the largest cities in area in the United States. It covers about 650 square miles (1,680 sq. km).

▼ The great Oklahoma land rushes gave settlers a chance to race for land that they could get for free. Some people cheated and began the race early.

state. Oklahoma lies across the line where the dry western part of the United States meets the moist eastern part. The Great Plains section of Oklahoma has less than 28 inches (71 cm) of precipitation in an average year. The panhandle is extremely dry. More rain falls in the eastern part.

History

Many tribes used the land that is now Oklahoma as a hunting ground for buffalo. Wichita, Caddo, Quapaw, Plains Apache, and Osage were some of the tribes that hunted there. Spanish explorers were the first Europeans in Oklahoma. Later, French fur traders came. All of Oklahoma except the panhandle was part of the Louisiana Territory claimed by France. The United States bought the territory in 1803.

In the early 1830s, the U.S. Government removed southeastern Native Americans from their land and sent them west. By doing this, white settlers were able to claim the tribal lands for themselves. During the next ten years, these tribes were forced to march to Oklahoma. More than 3,000 people died from cold, hunger, disease, and exhaustion along the route Native Americans called the "Trail of Tears."

The "Five Civilized Tribes" were the first Native Americans sent west. They were the Creek, Choctaw, Chicasaw, Cherokee, and Seminole tribes. They were called "civilized" because many had been to mission schools and had become teachers, lawyers, and owners of farms and businesses.

They had founded towns and set up governments. A Cherokee named Sequoya had invented an alphabet for his people, who then printed a newspaper with columns both in their language and in English.

Some Native Americans had adopted the white people's custom of farming with slave labor. They brought black slaves to Oklahoma.

William F. Cody (1846–1917) was famous as "Buffalo Bill." As a buffalo hunter, it is said he killed more than 4,000 animals, which led to his nickname. Later, he became an entertainer in his *Buffalo Bill's Wild West Show*, displaying his legendary shooting skills.

When the Civil War broke out, many Native Americans took the Confederate side. After the war, the government took about half of the land of these Native Americans and settled other Native Americans on some of it. The government also bought land from the tribes. During the 1860s and 1870s, cattle ranchers, coal miners, and railroad workers moved onto tribal lands, which were later opened to settlers in 1889 through the land rushes.

Oklahoma was divided into two territories, *Indian Territory* and *Oklahoma Territory*. The territories soon asked to be made states. The Native Americans wanted to name their state "Sequoya." But in 1907, both territories were admitted to the Union as one state, Oklahoma.

The state capitol in Oklahoma is surrounded by wells. One of them had to be drilled at an angle so that oil could be extracted from under the capitol building.

OKLAHOMA

Capital and largest city
Oklahoma City
(444,719 people)

Area
69,919 square miles
(181,089 sq. km)
Rank: 18th

Population
3,145,585 people
Rank: 28th

Statehood
November 16, 1907
(46th state admitted)

Principal rivers
Arkansas River
Canadian River
Red River

Highest point
Black Mesa 4,973 feet
(1,516 m)

Motto
Labor Omnia Vincit
("Labor Conquers All Things")

Song
"Oklahoma!"

Famous people
Woody Guthrie, Will Rogers, Maria Tallchief, Jim Thorpe, David L. Payne, Lynn Riggs, Frederick Remington, Mary Decker Slaney

STATE SYMBOLS

◄ Oklahoma, the first territory or state to adopt an official flower, chose the evergreen mistletoe plant.

▲ The scissor-tailed flycatcher was adopted in 1951, replacing the bobwhite.

▲ On the star are the symbols of the Five Civilized Tribes, who were the first people to settle in the territory of Oklahoma.

◄ The redbud tree is a glorious sight when the reddish pink flowers bloom in early spring.

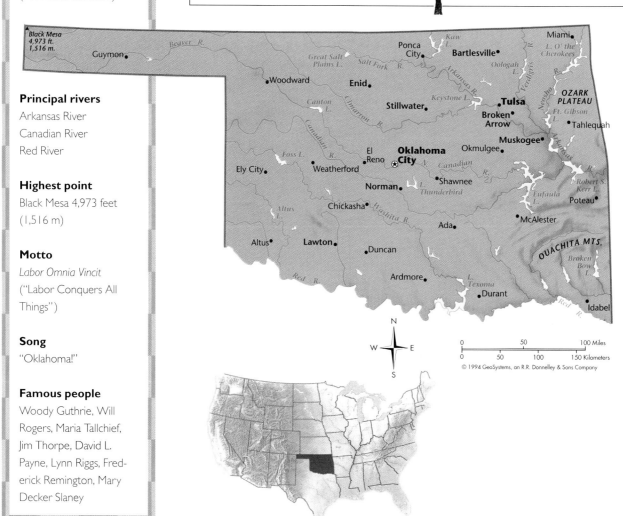

© 1994 GeoSystems, an R.R. Donnelley & Sons Company

Working in Oklahoma

At first, nearly all Oklahomans earned a living in agriculture. Some raised cattle, but most grew crops. Cotton and corn were the main crops raised for sale. But wheat grows better than either of these crops in places where there is little rain. In the 1930s, wheat became the main crop. Much of Oklahoma's land turned into a "dust bowl" in the 1930s, when there were long, dry spells. The topsoil turned to dry powder and wind blew it away. Thousands of Oklahoma families were forced to leave their farms. Many went to California in search of work. Some people became migrant workers, moving from place to place with the crops. This was the time of the Great Depression in the country, when jobs were scarce.

Livestock now brings in more money than all the crops put together. More than 5 million head of cattle graze in Oklahoma today. The livestock industry earns Oklahoma nearly $3 billion every year.

The other big businesses in Oklahoma are manufacturing and the drilling of oil and natural gas. Either oil or natural gas is found in most of Oklahoma's counties. Often the two are found together. The state capitol in Oklahoma City is even built on a working oil well! Many oil companies have their headquarters in Tulsa, which is known as the "Oil Capital of the World."

The rivers of Oklahoma were the routes of early explorers and fur traders. The Arkansas River Navigation System, completed in 1971, made it possible for boats and barges from the Mississippi River to reach Oklahoma ports on the Arkansas River. To keep the water deep enough for boats all year, 17 dams were built across the Arkansas River. *Locks* allow boats to pass the dams. Catoosa, Oklahoma, is now a port, handling freight for nearby Tulsa.

Visitors to Oklahoma can see a history of the West at the National Cowboy Hall of Fame and Western Heritage Center in Oklahoma City. The center is sponsored by 17 western states. Indian City, U.S.A., near Anadarko, displays villages typical of Plains tribes. Frontier City, U.S.A., near Oklahoma City, is a copy of a frontier town of the late 1800s. Oklahoma has other museums and craft centers showing pioneer and Native American life. The Will Rogers Memorial in Claremore honors the cowboy-humorist Will Rogers, who was born in Oklahoma.

▶▶▶▶ **FIND OUT MORE** ◀◀◀◀

Cherokees; Choctaws; Creeks; Rogers, Will; Seminoles; Sequoya; Westward Movement

 ## OLIVE

The olive has a distinguished history. More than 2,000 years ago, in the original Olympic Games in Greece, the winner of an event would receive an olive branch as a "gold medal." The ancient Romans pickled olives in brine and considered them a great delicacy.

Olive trees are evergreens that thrive in the Mediterranean climate

Pawhuska, in the state of Oklahoma, was the first place in America to form a Boy Scout Troop. The troop was formed in 1909.

◀ The Red River region provides fertile land for growing cotton, which is still an important part of Oklahoma's economy.

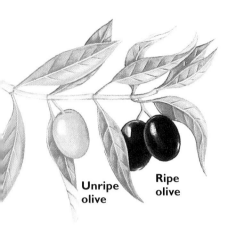

Unripe olive

Ripe olive

▲ The oil we get from pressing ripe olives is used in many ways. It's used for cooking and in salad dressings, medicine, and many different beauty products.

▲ The Olympic Games logo. Five rings are linked together to represent the sporting friendship of all peoples and to symbolize the five competing continents.

of Greece and Italy. They also grow in other warm dry places such as California and Arizona. The trees grow up to 25 feet (7.6 m) and live for hundreds of years. Their delicate fruit, which we call olives, must be picked by hand. Green olives, which are unripe, can be pickled or stuffed. Ripe black olives can be eaten as they are.

Olives can also be processed to form olive oil, which is considered one of the tastiest and healthiest of all cooking oils. Olives are pressed until they release their oil. Most olive oil is filtered to remove impurities. Unfiltered olive oil, which many people prefer, is called virgin oil.

▶▶▶▶ **FIND OUT MORE** ◀◀◀◀
Fats and Oils; Greece

OLYMPIC GAMES

In the year 776 B.C., a religious festival was held by the ancient Greeks to honor their chief god, Zeus. Such festivals had probably been held since about 1370 B.C. The site of the festival of 776 B.C. was in the southwestern part of Greece, in a place called Olympia. The Greeks decided to hold the Olympian games at the *sanctuary* (holy place) of Zeus. The games were held every four years until A.D. 393, when the Roman emperor Theodosius ordered them to be discontinued because they had become corrupt.

The Olympian games were almost forgotten until 1894, when interest in them was revived by a Frenchman, Baron Pierre de Coubertin. He succeeded in establishing the International Olympic Committee, which enlisted the aid of sports organizations and individuals from various countries. The committee organized the first modern Olympic Games, held in Athens, Greece, in April 1896. The Olympics have been held every four years in different cities around the world, except during World Wars I and II (1916, 1940, and 1944). Starting in 1994, the Winter Olympics and Summer Olympics have been held alternately every two years.

Professional and amateur athletes of all nations can participate in the Olympics. The various events are intended as contests among athletes, rather than among nations.

It is a great honor for a country to be selected to host the Olympics. The host cities for Summer Olympic Games have been Athens (1896), Paris (1900), St. Louis (1904), London (1908), Stockholm (1912), Antwerp (1920), Paris (1924), Amsterdam (1928), Los Angeles (1932), Berlin (1936), London (1948), Helsinki (1952), Melbourne (1956), Rome (1960), Tokyo (1964), Mexico City (1968), Munich (1972), Montreal (1976), Moscow (1980), Los Angeles (1984), Seoul (1988), Barcelona (1992), Atlanta (1996).

Winter sports became a part of the Olympic Games in 1924. The Winter Olympics can be held only in a nation with mountains and much snow. For example, the 1980 Winter Olympics were held in Lake Placid, New York, and in 1984, in Sarajevo, Bosnia. Calgary, Canada, hosted them in 1988, Albertville, France, in 1992, and Lillehammer, Norway, in 1994.

In the Olympics, as in most international sports competitions, distances are measured by meters, instead of by feet or yards. (However, the marathon, a long foot race, is 26 miles, 385 yards—about 42 km.) Well-trained athletes from all over the world compete for individual and team honors. The winner of each event receives a gold medal. A silver medal is awarded for second place and a bronze medal for third place.

In the Winter Olympics, most medal winners have come from nations with long, cold winters. The Netherlands, Norway, and the former Soviet Union usually have the best speed skaters. Winning bobsled and toboggan teams have come from the snowy mountainous regions of Austria, Germany, Italy, and Switzerland. Athletes from Austria, France, Germany, Italy, Switzerland, and the Scandinavian countries generally excel in the skiing contests. The former Soviet Union captured many medals in figure skating.

try's Olympic team. The United States Olympic Committee (U.S.O.C.) supervises the selection of the U.S. Olympic team. The U.S.O.C. also organizes a nationwide campaign for contributions to pay for the travel and living expenses of the U.S. team. In some nations, the expenses of the Olympic team are paid for by the government.

Since the first modern Olympic Games, performances by athletes have

▼ **A complex of new and updated sports facilities made up the Olympic ring in a landscaped park on the slopes of Monjuïc Hill, Barcelona, Spain—the site of the 1992 Summer Olympic Games and also the site of the 1929 Games.**

Most track-and-field and swimming medalists have come from the former Soviet Union, Germany, and the United States. Many champion gymnasts have been from Romania. American athletes have won the most medals of any country. One of the greatest U.S. Olympic athletes was Jesse Owens, who won four gold medals in one day in 1936.

Today, the Olympic Games are highly organized. Many countries have national Olympic Committees that hold tryouts among qualified athletes for membership on the coun-

greatly improved. This is partly due to better training methods and to sophisticated, new equipment. But sometimes, sportsmen use drugs to help build up muscle in their bodies. This is illegal, and athletes are given random checks to see if they have used drugs. During the 1988 Olympics, a routine check revealed that the Canadian sprinter Ben Johnson had used drugs. He was stripped of his gold medal.

The Olympics are often affected by politics. In 1936, Hitler used the Berlin Olympics to promote Nazism. The Moscow Olympics of 1980 were

Only nine nations took part in the first modern Olympics, held at Athens in 1896. Now, more than a hundred nations compete, and there are more than 13,000 competitors.

OLYMPIC FACTS

The 1900 Games were so badly organized that it wasn't until 1965 that one cyclist discovered he had won a silver medal at them!

In 1904, the first man to finish the marathon race was disqualified when it was discovered that he had traveled nearly half of the course by car.

When the 1976 Olympics opened in Montreal, several of the sports complexes were still not fully built.

The Olympic Oath taken by all the athletes is: "In the name of all competitors I promise that we will take part in the Olympic games, respecting and abiding by the rules which govern them, in the true spirit of sportsmanship for the glory of sport and the honor of our teams."

Tennis and the 10,000-meter race for women were added as Olympic sports in the 1988 Seoul Games.

WHERE TO DISCOVER MORE

Coffey, Wayne. *Olympic Gold.*
Colorado: Blackbirch
Press, 1992.
Duder, Tessa. *Journey to
Olympia, the Story of the
Ancient Olympics.*
New York: Scholastic, Inc.,
1992.

▲ **Eugene O'Neill, U.S. playwright, who won the coveted Pulitzer prize four times.**

There is a large stone sculpture of Alexander Graham Bell at Brantford, Ontario. The inventor of the telephone lived there for a few months between leaving Scotland and moving to Boston.

not attended by more than 60 nations who opposed the former Soviet Union's invasion of Afghanistan. South Africa was once banned from the Olympics for its apartheid policies. After abandoning these policies in 1991, South Africa was welcomed to the 1992 Olympics.

▶▶▶▶**FIND OUT MORE**◀◀◀◀
Marathon Race; Owens, Jesse; Sports; Track and Field

OMAN

SEE ARABIA

O'NEILL, EUGENE (1888–1953)

Eugene Gladstone O'Neill was the first U.S. playwright to be awarded a Nobel prize for Literature. Four of his plays won Pulitzer prizes.

O'Neill was born in New York City. His father was a famous actor, and O'Neill worked as an actor, too. He also worked as a sailor and a newspaper reporter. He once briefly searched for gold in the country of Honduras in Central America.

While O'Neill was recovering from tuberculosis in 1912, he began writing for the theater. O'Neill's early plays were performed by the Provincetown Players in Provincetown, Massachusetts, and in Greenwich Village, part of New York City.

Several of O'Neill's plays concern family problems and are based on his own tragic family life. *A Long Day's Journey into Night*, published after O'Neill's death, is a tragic play about the unhappy life his parents had and its effects on their children. *Ah! Wilderness* is set in O'Neill's childhood world, but this play is not tragic. Other outstanding plays include *Desire Under the Elms*, about a conflict between father and son, and *The Iceman Cometh*, about

the *illusions* (false beliefs) of people.

▶▶▶▶**FIND OUT MORE**◀◀◀◀
Drama; Literature

ONION

SEE BULB

ONTARIO

Ontario is the second largest province in Canada (the province of Quebec is larger). Ontario is about the size of Texas and California combined. More than a third of Canada's people live in Ontario.

Geography
The name *Ontario* probably came from two Huron words meaning "beautiful lake." More than half of northern Ontario is a low, rolling, rocky plateau covered with forests, lakes, and rivers. The land in the north is too rocky and the soil is too thin for farming, but it is a treasure trove of natural resources. Most of Canada's nickel, uranium, and platinum is mined in this area, as is a major share of its gold, copper, and iron ore. Wood products from the extensive forests are a major export. On the north, Ontario has a saltwater coastline along Hudson Bay.

The southern part of Ontario has borders on four of the five Great Lakes. Canada's richest farmlands lie in southern Ontario. Tobacco and vegetables are major crops in the southwest. The Niagara peninsula is famous for fruits and wines.

History
The first white person to visit parts of what is now Ontario was Henry Hudson. In 1611, Hudson claimed the Hudson Bay area for Britain. French explorers Samuel de Champlain and Etienne Brulé arrived in 1613 and 1615.

▲ **A view of Toronto, Ontario, showing the sky dome—the Toronto Blue Jays baseball team's stadium.**

ONTARIO

Capital and largest city
Toronto
(3,700,000 people)

Area
344,090 square miles
(891,090 sq. km)

Population
9,747,000 people

Entry into Confederation
July 1, 1867

Principal rivers
Albany River
St. Lawrence River

Highest point
Timiskaming District
2,275 feet (693 m)

Famous people
Mazo de la Roche, John Diefenbaker, John Kennedy Balboaith, W. L. Mackenzie King, Margaret Atwood, Agnes Campbell MacPhail, Lester Pearson

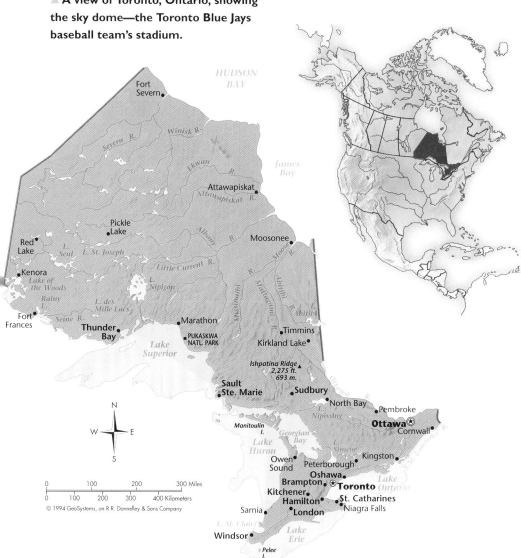

▲ **The white trillium, Ontario's floral symbol, blooms during April and May. This wild flower is found in woodlands.**

> **Ontario is a province of rivers and lakes. It has about 250,000 lakes, covering nearly one-sixth of the province.**

▶ **Sightseers have to wear raincoats with hoods to protect themselves from the massive spray of Ontario's spectacular Niagara Falls.**

Although opera only developed about 400 years ago, more than 42,000 operas and operettas have been composed, and more are being created all the time.

The French built several forts and fur-trading posts, but they made no attempts to colonize the region. Strong competition developed between the British and the French over the valuable fur trade. In 1763, at the end of the Seven Years' War between France and Great Britain, the Treaty of Paris established the region as British territory.

During and after the Revolutionary War, large numbers of colonists in the United States who wished to remain British subjects settled in Ontario. By 1791, the colony had its own government. During the War of 1812, U.S. troops invaded Ontario and burned its capital to the ground. British forces retaliated by setting fire to Washington, D.C.

Ontario was one of the four provinces that joined together in 1867 to form the new nation of Canada.

People

Three of every four residents of Ontario live in cities or towns. Toronto, the capital of the province, has a population of about 700,000 people—although nearly 4 million people live in metropolitan Toronto. The city of Hamilton, 30 miles (48 km) from the capital, is also growing rapidly.

Other major cities include Ottawa, Canada's capital, and Windsor, which, like its neighbor Detroit, is a major automobile-manufacturing center. Sudbury is famous for its nickel mines. An annual Shakespeare festival is held in the city of Stratford.

About nine out of ten people in Ontario speak English as their first language, and about six out of ten people are of British descent. Germans, Italians, Dutch, Poles, and Ukrainians also form important groups in Ontario. Many Native North Americans live in the province, mostly on 170 reservations.

Ontario's businesses and industries are growing rapidly. Half of

Canada's manufacturing is done in the province, whose major industries produce steel, automobiles, machinery, and food products. The St. Lawrence Seaway is used continually by ships carrying Ontario's products to markets in the United States, Europe, and other countries.

Southern Ontario is heavily populated. Someday, there may be one solid city from Detroit to Montreal! The northern part of Ontario will probably offer a frontier for exploration and development for many years to come.

▶▶▶▶ **FIND OUT MORE** ◀◀◀◀
Canada; Fathers of Confederation; Toronto

 OPERA

Imagine you are in a darkened theater. On stage are actors. Behind the actors you can see the scenery. Down in front of the stage, in what is called the *pit*, are an orchestra and a conductor. As the orchestra plays, the actors on stage do not speak their lines—they sing them!

This is *opera*—a combination of drama and music. Operatic dramas

△ **Pamina, the heroine of Mozart's opera *The Magic Flute*. She falls in love with an Egyptian Prince, Tamino. 1970**

are usually serious, but there are several comic operas and funny scenes in tragic operas. The music is usually complicated and difficult to sing well. Only the most skillful singers can handle it. The cast is usually made up of a few main characters (the soloists) and a chorus (a group of singers who act as a crowd of people involved in the action of the plot). Some operas have scenes in which dancing is performed by a small ballet group.

Operas usually begin with an *overture*—an introduction played by the orchestra alone. Once the curtain goes up, the soloists and chorus sing throughout most of the drama. *Arias* (songs sung by soloists) are the important points in an opera. In an aria, a character sings about his or her feelings and thoughts, or about what he or she is going to do.

Between arias, the soloists may sing back and forth to each other in a kind of musical discussion called *recitative*. Besides singing arias, soloists often join together to sing *duets, trios, quartets, quintets,* or *sextets* at various points in the opera. The chorus usually has several songs to sing, either alone or with the soloists. The music follows the action and mood of the plot.

Operas are usually performed in special buildings called *opera houses.* A *choreographer* creates the dances, and the *chorus master* rehearses the singers. The *conductor* leads the

entire opera performance from his or her place in the pit. The soloists, chorus members, and dancers all follow the directions of the conductor.

The ancient Greeks blended drama and music, but opera as we know it today developed in Italy in the late 1500s. At first, the music was used mainly for background. But by the end of the century, the drama and the music were equally important.

In the late 1600s, opera became extravagant, with magnificent scenery and huge casts of people. Arias were written into the plots, and the dramas demanded more acting. Women were trained to sing the female roles. Previously, the women's parts had been sung by men or boys. Some composers began writing full-length comic operas. Before 1750,

comic operas were short, funny little scenes performed for audiences as entertainment between the acts of a serious opera.

During the 1800s, *grand opera* developed. Grand operas are gigantic productions, full of powerful singing. The vocal parts are extremely difficult to sing and are a real test of a vocal musician's skill. They also require a wonderful voice. Giuseppe Verdi was one of the great composers of grand opera.

Richard Wagner, who was composing at about the same time as Verdi, had his own ideas about opera. He thought the music, the words, and the acting should all work together as a music-drama. Wagner wrote his own *libretto* (the story and words of

The world's largest opera house is the Metropolitan Opera House, at Lincoln Center, in New York City. It can seat 3,800 people.

▲ A spectacular performance of *Aida* in Verona, Italy. People go to the opera not only to hear the music but also to watch the drama and see the stage scenery and costumes.

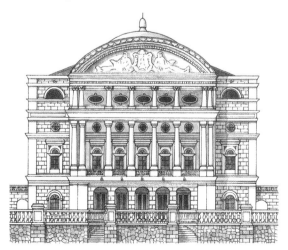

◄ When opera became popular in the 1800s, many elegant opera houses were built. This is the famous opera house in Manaus, in the Brazilian Jungle.

an opera), unlike most composers who used words from plays or hired poets to create the lines. Wagner also used a short melody (called a *leitmotiv*) to stand for each important character, idea, or object in the drama. When a particular character came on stage or was mentioned in the lines, that character's *leitmotiv* could usually be heard in the music.

▲ Luciano Pavarotti has done much over the last few years to make opera popular. Here he is singing in Donizetti's *L'Elisir d'Amore*.

Since the 1850s, many operas have been based on true-to-life stories or experiences. And operas are being staged in many different ways. The Italian-born U.S. composer Gian Carlo Menotti has written operas especially for radio and television. Menotti's opera *Amahl and the Night Visitors* is usually broadcast at Christmastime.

Famous popular operas include Mozart's *The Magic Flute, The Marriage of Figaro* and *Don Giovanni* (1780s); Rossini's *The Barber of Seville* (1816); Verdi's *Aida, La Traviata, Otello,* and *Rigoletto* (1850s–1870s); Puccini's *Madame Butterfly* (1904); and Bizet's *Carmen* (1875) to list just a few. Famous recording opera stars include Enrico Caruso, Maria Callas, Dame Joan Sutherland, Dame Kiri Te Kanawa, Placido Domingo, Luciano Pavarotti, and José Carreras.

Operetta

Operettas are sometimes called "light operas." They are like operas but are lighthearted. They also include some speaking dialogue. The settings are often make believe, with colorful scenery and elegant costumes. The plot of an operetta is always based on romance, in which the good characters win and the evil characters are punished. Operetta music is full of happy tunes, and the dancing is light and cheerful.

Franz von Suppé was probably the first composer to create real operettas. He made romance the main part of the plot, with the waltz an important part of the music. After von Suppé, most operettas had a big waltz scene that was an important part of the plot.

Some of the most successful European operettas were written by Franz Lehàr, Johann Strauss Jr., and the team of Gilbert and Sullivan. In the United States, operettas included both comedy and romance. Victor Herbert was the first great U.S. operetta composer. His works, such as *Babes in Toyland* and *Naughty Marietta*, have been performed all over the world.

▶▶▶▶ **FIND OUT MORE** ◀◀◀◀
Ballet; Drama; Gilbert and Sullivan; Handel, George Frederick; Mozart, Wolfgang Amadeus; Music; Musical Comedy; Opera; Singing; Strauss, Johann; Stravinsky, Igor; Verdi, Giuseppe; Wagner, Richard

 ## OPINION POLL

People's opinions can influence governments, industries, and other organizations. Research firms are hired to conduct opinion polls (ask questions and analyze answers) on a great many subjects. A political party might want to know what the voters of a certain state think about the party's candidate. A manufacturer might want to know if people prefer its product in a green or a red box.

It would take too long to ask the opinions of everyone, everywhere, so

▲ George Gallup, founder of the famous Gallup political polls.

QUESTION:
Do you like to wear hats?

Boys		
YES	15	(75 percent)
NO	0	(0 percent)
UNDECIDED	5	(25 percent)
Total polled	**20**	**(100 percent)**

Girls		
YES	5	(25 percent)
NO	10	(50 percent)
UNDECIDED	5	(25 percent)
Total polled	**20**	**(100 percent)**

Total		
YES	20	(50 percent)
NO	10	(25 percent)
UNDECIDED	10	(25 percent)
Total polled	**40**	**(100 percent)**

According to this poll, 75 percent of the boys like to wear hats. But only 50 percent of the *entire* sample like to. What does this mean?

LEARN BY DOING

You can take your own opinion poll. Decide on some questions that people might be interested in. Pick a sample group, such as everyone in your class. You do not have to record people's names, only whether they are boys, girls, brown-haired, blond-haired, and so on. When you have received all the answers, make a chart like the one on this page to analyze the results.

Public-opinion research began in the 1920s. Elmo Roper, Louis Harris, and George H. Gallup are three well-known U.S. *pollsters* (poll takers). The Gallup Poll is famed for its political predictions.

▶ ▶ ▶ ▶ **FIND OUT MORE** ◀ ◀ ◀ ◀
Statistics

OPOSSUM

More than 80 *species* (kinds) of opossums live in North and South America, from the Canadian woods to the Andes Mountains. Opossums are *marsupial* mammals. Other marsupials, such as the kangaroo, live in Australia. Some opossums live only on land, while others live on both land and water. Some will eat nearly anything, others eat only insects, and still others eat only marine animals. Most opossums sleep during the day and hunt for food at night.

Opossums are not completely developed when they are born. Four to 14 babies may be born at one time. Each baby is no bigger than a thumbnail! The newborn opossum crawls into a pouch on the mother's abdomen and stays there until it is fully developed. After about three months, the babies come out and ride around on the mother's back. Eventually, they are big enough to go off by themselves.

The largest opossum is the common species of the eastern United States. It is about 30 inches (76 cm) long, including its long, hairless tail. The opossum is covered with long, gray hair with an undercoat of soft,

▲ **A mother opossum and her babies. Newborn babies live in their mother's pouch. Later she carries them on her back.**

a carefully selected group of people, called a *sample,* is chosen to represent a larger group. The sample may be only 5 percent of the larger group, but it must represent the makeup of the larger group. For example, if 30 percent of the larger group are teenagers, 30 percent of the sample must be teenagers.

The people in the sample are then questioned. The questions may be asked by a trained interviewer (who must be careful not to influence the answers), or they might be printed on a *questionnaire.* It is very important that the questions be worded in a fair way. They must also be worded so that they can be answered with "yes," "no," or "undecided." It is easier to add up simple answers.

The answers received from the sample are analyzed in order to determine the opinions of that group. The sample may be broken down into smaller groups—for example, teenagers, housewives, Democrats, teachers, or high school graduates. The results are used as an indication of the opinions of the larger group.

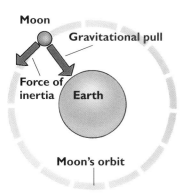

Moon
Gravitational pull
Force of
inertia
Earth
Moon's orbit

▲ This illustration shows
how the shape of an orbit
depends on the difference
between the force of
gravitation and the force
of inertia.

▶ Artificial satellites
launched at a high enough
speed go into orbit around
the Earth. If their speed is
increased even further, they
move into a higher orbit or
escape and drift into space.

woolly fur. The opossum sometimes hangs upside-down by wrapping its tail around the branch of a tree. When frightened, the opossum lies completely still and appears to be dead. This habit is the source of the expression "playing 'possum," describing someone who is pretending to be dead or injured.

▶ ▶ ▶ ▶ **FIND OUT MORE** ◀ ◀ ◀ ◀
Mammal; Marsupial

OPTICAL FIBER

SEE FIBER OPTICS

OPTICAL INSTRUMENTS

SEE LENS, MICROSCOPE, TELESCOPE

ORATORIO

SEE CHORAL MUSIC

ORBIT

The moon moves in an orbit around the Earth, and the Earth moves in an orbit around the sun. The moon is a satellite of the Earth. The Earth is a satellite of the sun. An orbit is the path of an object in space around its center of attraction. How is the Earth the center of attraction for the moon?

The Earth attracts the moon by the force of *gravitation* or *gravitational pull*. This is the same force that makes an object fall toward the ground or floor if you drop it. The object is attracted to the Earth in the same way the moon is attracted to the Earth. In fact, every object attracts every other object by gravitation. Gravitational force between two objects depends on their *masses* (quantities of matter they are made of) and on how close together they are.

The moon doesn't fall into the Earth because the Earth's gravitational pull is not the only force acting on it. The moon has *inertia*. This inertia is the tendency of an object to keep on moving at the same speed in a straight line unless some other force acts on it. If inertia were the only force acting on the moon, the moon would shoot off into space in a straight line. But gravitation pulls it toward the Earth with just enough force to balance the outward push of inertia. And the moon keeps moving around the Earth in an orbit that is almost a perfect circle.

The inward pull of gravity is a *centripetal force*—a force that pulls an object toward a center of rotation. The outward push of inertia (away from an axis or center of rotation) is called *centrifugal* force. There isn't really any centrifugal force applied from the outside, but just the straight-ahead force of inertia and the inward pull of gravity. These are perfectly balanced in a stable orbit.

An orbit is not a circle, although it can be very nearly a circle. The shape of an orbit depends on the difference between the force of gravitation and the force of inertia. *Artificial* (man-made) satellites are put into orbit at a precise height above the Earth and with a precise speed, to ensure that gravity and inertia exactly balance each other.

If gravitation is stronger than inertia, the satellite will be pulled closer to the Earth and sooner or later will crash into it. If the force of inertia is too strong, the satellite will curve past the Earth in what is called an

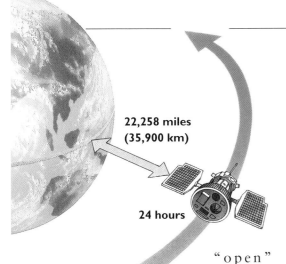

22,258 miles (35,900 km)

24 hours

"open" curve. This means it will curve around the Earth once, then escape into space. If gravity and inertia are balanced, the satellite will keep on orbiting the Earth—that is, it will travel in a "closed" curve.

In an *ellipse,* or closed curve, which is like a flattened circle, the satellite flies back out into space until its inertia becomes weaker than the force of gravitation. Then it curves around and begins falling back toward the Earth. As it gets closer, the satellite goes faster, and this increases its inertia again. Its inertia becomes stronger than gravitation, and it curves around the Earth and back out into space for another trip through the same orbit. The satellite is at its *perigee* when it is closest to the Earth and at its *apogee* when it is farthest away. The orbit of an artificial satellite can be changed by slowing down or speeding up the satellite with small rockets.

An open curve may be either a *parabola* or a *hyperbola.* Most comets, for example, have parabolic

Hyperbola

Parabola

Ellipse

Apogee

Perigee

orbits, but a few come around the sun regularly. Halley's comet is one of these. Its orbit is an ellipse, but so flattened that it resembles a parabola near the sun. In a parabolic orbit, a satellite has just enough inertia to escape the Earth's gravitational pull completely, but its distance from Earth gets greater more and more slowly. In a hyperbola, the satellite has enough inertia to escape, and it also has some extra inertia.

Spacecraft that are sent from the Earth to Mars must leave the Earth's gravitation in a hyperbolic orbit. If they have only a parabolic orbit, they will have enough inertia to escape the Earth's gravitation, but it will take them a much longer time to reach even the nearest planet.

Geostationary satellites orbit the Earth once every 24 hours, the same time it takes the Earth to spin on its axis, so that the satellites remain in the same spot above the Earth's surface.

Scientists use machines called *centrifuges.* These spin very quickly and are used to separate liquids of different densities. As it spins, a centrifuge throws the dense liquids toward the sides with more force than it does the less dense liquids. The liquids are thus separated.

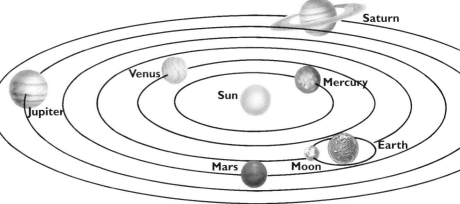

Saturn

Venus

Mercury

Sun

Jupiter

Earth

Mars

Moon

The basic movements of objects in orbit were discovered by Johannes Kepler, a German astronomer, around 1600. He accepted Copernicus' ideas that the sun is the center of the solar system. Kepler studied the observations made by his teacher, Tycho Brahe, of the orbit of Mars around the sun. From this study, he developed three laws concerning the motion of planets in orbits. These laws are true also for the movement of satellites and other spacecraft. Strangely enough, Kepler did not know about gravitation.

A view of the universe put forward by Nicolaus Copernicus (1473–1543). The Church refused to believe that the sun and not the Earth was at the center of the universe. Copernicus's theory went against the words of the Bible, so his ideas were banned.

▶▶▶▶ **FIND OUT MORE** ◀◀◀◀
Comets; Copernicus, Nicolaus; Gravity and Gravitation; Kepler, Johannes; Motion; Satellite; Solar System

The illustration shows open, *hyperbolic* and *parabolic,* orbit curves and closed, or *elliptical,* ones.

Actor and comedian Danny Kaye directed 1,342 majorettes leading some 4,524 players in the largest marching band ever recorded. This was at the Dodgers Stadium, Los Angeles, in 1985.

ORANGE

SEE CITRUS FRUIT

ORCHESTRAS AND BANDS

Many schools and community groups have orchestras or bands. If you play an instrument or plan to learn music, you would probably enjoy playing in one of these groups. Young people's bands often perform at concerts and in parades. Junior high and high school orchestras and bands also play for football games, musical

Orchestras

The word *orchestra* comes from an ancient Greek word meaning "dancing place." In ancient Greek theaters, the dancing place was the area between the audience and the stage. Today, that area is known as the pit. Orchestras that accompany stage performances (operas, musicals, and operettas) are located in the pit and are called *pit orchestras*. Other kinds of orchestras include *jazz* or *rock orchestras* that specialize in playing jazz or rock music. *Chamber orchestras* are small groups of string and woodwind players.

▶ A common way of arranging the instruments of the orchestra on stage. Stringed instruments are nearest the conductor. Percussion and brass are the farthest, being the loudest.

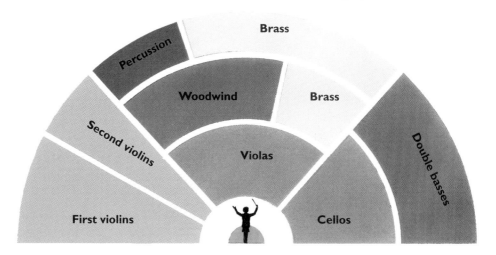

▼ The most important single member of the orchestra is the conductor. He or she controls the tempo and mixture of sounds played by the orchestra.

plays, dances, and other events. The earlier you start playing with an orchestra or band, the more musically skilled you will become.

The *symphony orchestra* is the largest and most varied instrumental group, having anywhere from 60 to 120 musicians. About half of a symphony orchestra is made up of strings—*violins, violas, cellos, double basses*, and *harps*. The violins are the most prominent instruments. They are divided into *first violins* (which carry the main melodies) and *second violins* (which play secondary or accompanying melodies). The *woodwind* section contains flutes, oboes, clarinets, bassoons, and often other instruments—for example, a piccolo, an English horn, or a contrabassoon (the lowest-pitched instrument in the orchestra). The *brass* instruments include trumpets, French horns, trombones, and tubas. Among the various *percussion* instruments are the timpani (kettledrums),

snare drums, bass drums, cymbals, gongs, bells, chimes, xylophones, triangles, and tambourines. Pianos, organs, and harpsichords are also used in symphony orchestras.

The *conductor* leads the orchestra. He or she must direct the musicians' *rehearsals* (practice sessions) and make sure the music is played correctly. The conductor guides the musicians so that the entire orchestra plays as if it were one great instrument. The conductor sets the *tempo* (speed) at which the music is played and determines the *interpretation* (or style) in which the music will be played.

Most conductors use a *baton* (a short, white stick) when directing. Others use only their hands. With facial expressions as well as hand and body movements, the conductor gives signals to the musicians. Each signal has a meaning that the musicians transfer to their playing.

Orchestras were first organized in Italy during the 1600s to accompany operas. Through the years, many improvements were made in the various instruments. Their pitch and tone quality became more exact, and their flexibility and tonal range became greater. Composers began writing music for symphony orchestras, such as symphonies, tone poems, concertos, and overtures.

Bands

Marching or *military bands* and *concert bands* are the two basic kinds of bands. *Jazz, rock,* and *dance bands* are smaller bands that specialize in playing certain types of music. Bands have always been important in circus performances. *Rhythm bands* of simple instruments (wood blocks, triangles, tambourines, and so on) are widely used in schools to teach music.

Concert and marching bands have the same brass, woodwind, and percussion instruments as an orchestra, with the addition of baritone cornets and saxophones. In marching bands, the sousaphone replaces the tuba

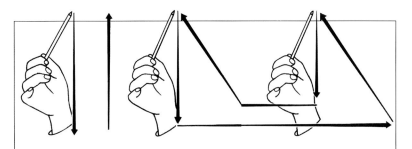

Following the direction of the arrows you can see how a conductor indicates 2, 3, and 4 counts, or *beats,* in a bar. The short stick the conductor uses is called a baton. It helps the members in the orchestra to see the conductor's movements more clearly. By watching it closely, they can all keep the correct beat or time, beginning and ending their pieces in harmony. They also watch the conductor's expression and body movements for other commands, which help them to interpret how a piece of music is to be played—such as in a jolly or sad mood.

because it is easier to carry, and the glockenspiel replaces the xylophone for the same reason.

Members of marching bands dress in colorful uniforms. The leader is called a *drum major.* He or she walks at the head of the band carrying a long staff that extends far above the head. The drum major directs the music and the marching by moving the staff in various ways. Marching bands are most often seen at parades, football games, and military events. Well-trained bands often march in complicated patterns that form letters or pictures to show their skill at drill.

Some bands contain only certain instruments. *Brass bands* have only brass instruments. *Drum and bugle bands* and *bagpipe bands* are others of this type. *Steel bands* are popular in the West Indies; all the instruments in these bands are made from steel oil drums or barrels.

Concert bands perform seated on a stage. The conductor directs with a baton. Concert bands often play orchestral music that has been arranged so that stringed instruments are not needed. Perhaps the best-known

The West Indians are famous for their steel drums made from oil drums. The sounds they produce vary from a powerful ringing to a happy vibrating beat. The music is colorful and joyous.

WHERE TO DISCOVER MORE

Blackwood, Alan. *The Orchestra: An Introduction to the World of Classical Music.* New York: Millbrook Press, 1993.

Hill, Stephanie. *Special Delivery Symphony.* New York: Astor Books, 1993.

▲ **Each flower on the early purple orchid has a three-lobed lip that acts as an insect-landing place.**

composer of band music was John Philip Sousa. His many exciting marches, such as *The Stars and Stripes Forever,* are still popular with audiences. Modern composers are now writing more music especially for bands.

Popular music or rock bands are quite different from traditional bands. Most of them use electric guitars (one of which is usually a bass guitar, to play the lowest notes), a set of drums, and various other electronic instruments.

▶▶▶▶ **FIND OUT MORE** ◀◀◀◀
Bagpipe; Brass Instruments; Circus; Harp; Jazz; Music; Musical Comedy; Musical Instruments; Piano; Popular Music; Sousa, John Philip; Stringed Instruments; Woodwind Instruments; Xylophone

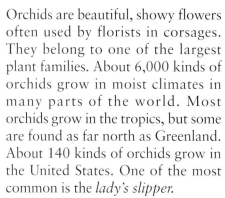 **ORCHID**

Orchids are beautiful, showy flowers often used by florists in corsages. They belong to one of the largest plant families. About 6,000 kinds of orchids grow in moist climates in many parts of the world. Most orchids grow in the tropics, but some are found as far north as Greenland. About 140 kinds of orchids grow in the United States. One of the most common is the *lady's slipper.*

Orchids grow on the ground in temperate regions. Tropical orchids may grow high up in trees. Tree orchids attach themselves to the tree and send their roots into the air to take in food and water. Orchid seeds are tiny. One plant may produce 3 million seeds.

Plant breeders have developed about 9,000 different kinds of orchids, in addition to the natural varieties. Breeders grow tropical orchids in greenhouses and sell them to florists.

▶▶▶▶ **FIND OUT MORE** ◀◀◀◀
Greenhouse; Plant; Plant Breeding

 OREGON

The pioneers who made the long, dangerous journey to Oregon in the 1800s had to cross hot, dry deserts and dusty prairies. Water was scarce. These people were pleasantly surprised, then, by the mild, rainy climate of Oregon's western valleys. The pioneers began to joke that they would need webbed feet to get through the rainy winter season. Because of this, Oregonians are often called "Webfoots."

The Land and Climate
Oregon lies near the northwest corner of the United States. The state of Washington is north of Oregon, and California and Nevada lie south of it. The waves of the Pacific Ocean break along the coast of the state. Across its eastern border is Idaho. Oregon's shoreline is bordered by mountains. The Coast Ranges, the lowest part of the state's mountain ranges, covers three-fourths of the coastline. Cows graze here in pastures among the forested hills. The Klamath Mountains are below the Coast Ranges, in the southwestern corner of the state. The state's richest mineral deposits are found in the Klamath Mountains.

East of the Coast Ranges is a beautiful valley. The Willamette River flows north through it to the Columbia River. Early settlers liked this valley better than any other part of Oregon. Today, the state's largest cities are here. Most of Oregon's factories are located in and around the cities. Between the cities are dairy farms, orchards, and green fields of crops.

The high Cascade Range lies on the eastern side of the Willamette Valley. This rugged mountain range has some of the tallest peaks in North America. Much of the land east of the Cascades is desert or almost so. The northern half is a highland. Part of it is a dry plateau that is the wheat-growing region of Oregon. The grain has to be grown by *dry farming*. A crop is planted only every two years. Between plantings, the soil collects water. The moisture of two years is needed to produce a single crop. The Blue Mountains cover the rest of the northern half of the state. They are mostly covered with forest.

The southern half of eastern Oregon is part of the Great Basin. It has short mountain ranges with flat valleys between them. The land is so dry that most rivers end by soaking into the ground or evaporating. Lakes are very shallow, and they shrink in size in summertime.

The differences between western and eastern Oregon are due largely to differences in precipitation. West winds bring moisture from the Pacific Ocean. As the winds rise to cross the Coast Ranges and the Cascades, the air becomes chilled. It drops most of its moisture in the form of rain or snow. Winter snows are very heavy in the Cascade Range. The climate of western Oregon is mild as well as wet. Ocean winds cool the land in summer and warm it in winter.

It is easy to see why eastern Oregon is different. The Cascades wall it off from the ocean. Winds from the water cannot cool it very much in summer or warm it in winter. It is hotter in summer and colder in winter than western Oregon is. It is much drier, too. By the time the winds have crossed the Cascades, they have lost most of their moisture. Most of the rain that does fall in the east comes down on its mountains.

History

The first Europeans to see Oregon saw it from the water. Sailor-explorers from Spain and Britain began coming in the 1500s. From the decks of their ships, they saw only the beautiful wooded coast. They learned nothing about the Native Americans who lived in Oregon.

The native peoples of western Ore-

gon were the Tillamook, Kalapuia, and Chinook tribes. They caught salmon in the rivers and gathered shellfish on the beaches. Elk and deer provided them with meat and skins. These tribes hollowed out tree trunks to make canoes. They chopped logs into thick boards and built houses from the boards.

East of the Cascades, the tribes did not live nearly as well. Their food was scarce. For this reason, they were *nomads* (wanderers) and had to go where food could be found. Some fished for salmon in the rivers. Others gathered roots and seeds to eat.

Captain Robert Gray of Boston sailed the *Lady Washington* into an

The volcanic mass of Mount Hood towers above the surrounding scenery of the Cascade Range. It is the highest point in Oregon.

Portland, an important West Coast port, is overlooked by the snow-capped Mount Hood. Portland boasts the largest woodland park in any U.S. city, 6,000 acres (2,400 hectares) in total.

OREGON

OREGON

Capital
Salem
(107,786 people)

Area
96,981 square miles
(251,180 sq. km)
Rank: 10th

Population
2,842,321 people
Rank: 29th

Statehood
February 14, 1859
(33rd state admitted)

Principal river
Columbia River

Highest point
Mount Hood
11,235 feet (3,424 m)

Largest city
Portland
(437,319 people)

Motto
"The Union"

Song
"Oregon, My Oregon"

Famous people
Mark Hatfield, Chief
Joseph, Joaquin Miller,
Linus Pauling,
Paul Simon

STATE SYMBOLS

▼ The Douglas fir is not a real fir tree, but it is closely related to the hemlock trees.

▶ The Oregon grape produces sour berries, frequently eaten by bears.

▲ The thirty-three stars show Oregon to be the 33rd state.

▶ The western meadowlark was officially adopted on July 18, 1927, as the state bird.

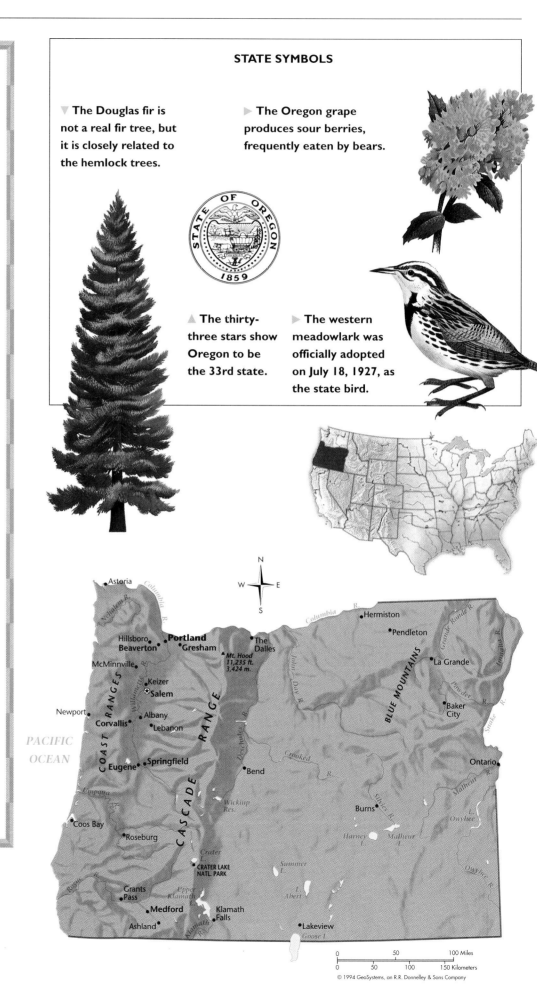

© 1994 GeoSystems, an R.R. Donnelley & Sons Company

Oregon bay in 1787. This was the first time U.S. citizens landed in Oregon. Five years later, Gray sailed another ship, the *Columbia,* to Oregon. He sailed up a great river and named the river after his vessel. In 1805, Meriwether Lewis and William Clark traveled to the mouth of the Columbia River from the east.

A U.S. citizen named John Jacob Astor built the first fur-trading post in Oregon at Astoria in 1811. A period of trade began. The Native Americans exchanged furs with the white people for guns, kettles, nails, and cloth. In the 1830s, settlers began coming to the area in covered wagons. At that time, both Britain and the United States claimed the Oregon region. In 1846, the two nations signed a treaty dividing British and U.S territory in North America at the point where Washington's northern boundary is today.

When Oregon became a territory in 1848, it included what is now the state of Washington. Later, Washington became a separate territory. Oregon became a state in 1859. More and more settlers arrived. The white settlements alarmed the Native Americans, and war broke out. The two sides fought each other as late as the 1870s. The tribes were finally forced to move to reservations.

By this time, railroads had been built across the continent. It was now easy for easterners to reach Oregon. Soon all the land in the Willamette Valley had been taken. Farmers went into the dry lands east of the Cascades to grow wheat. Lumberjacks pushed into the mountains to fell timber.

Recent decades have seen waves of people arriving from California. They prefer the unspoiled countryside and more relaxed way of life in Oregon.

Working in Oregon

Lumbering is now Oregon's most important industry. The state's leading manufactures are lumber, paper,

and other wood products. Agriculture comes second. Livestock and crops are about equal in value. Hay and wheat are the two largest crops. Fruits and vegetables are grown and processed in large quantities in the Willamette Valley. Oregon's natural beauty attracts many visitors, making tourism the state's third most important industry. Crater Lake, a brilliant-blue lake formed in the crater of an extinct volcano in the Cascade Range, is a favorite attraction. So is Mount Hood, a snow-covered peak in the Cascades, where people can ski all year round.

▲ **Crater lake formed when the top of Mount Mazma collapsed into the mountain, forming a basin. This gradually filled with water. Wizard Island, in the middle, appeared when lava erupted from volcanic action.**

▶▶▶▶ **FIND OUT MORE** ◀◀◀◀
Chinooks; Fur; Lewis and Clark Expedition; Oregon Trail; Westward Movement

OREGON TRAIL

Long lines of covered wagons rumbled along the Oregon Trail in the 1800s, carrying pioneers from the Mississippi Valley to the Pacific Coast. The trail extended about 2,000 miles (3,200 km) from Independence, Missouri, to the Columbia River in Oregon. (See the map with the article on WESTWARD MOVEMENT.) It followed the Platte and

WHERE TO DISCOVER MORE

Marsh, Carole. *Meow! Oregon Cats in History, Mystery, Legend, Lore, Humor & More.* Georgia: Gallopade Publishing Group, 1991.

Sanders, Richard S. *Government in Oregon.* Oregon: MESD Press, 1991.

The Rockies along the Oregon Trail caused the early pioneers many hardships. Guides were needed to show them the way through the most difficult passes.

Sweetwater rivers, crossing the Green River to the Bear River in Idaho. Then it crossed the Snake River and the Blue Mountains and came down to the Columbia River near the Umatilla. For a time, the Oregon Trail ended at that point, and wagons were floated on rafts to Fort Vancouver from there. But to avoid rapids in the river, the trail was later extended another 100 miles (160 km) to the Willamette Valley.

Paths made by fur trappers and Native Americans were the beginnings of the trail. The Lewis and Clark expeditions blazed a section of it in 1804. In 1811, a group of fur traders employed by John Jacob Astor followed the Lewis and Clark trail to Oregon to set up fur-trading posts. They returned by way of the Platte River, instead of the Missouri, tracing another section of the trail. An explorer named John Charles Frémont traveled westward in 1843 and added new information about the trail. That year also saw the first large wave of settlers along the trail.

The Oregon Trail was well established by 1846 and was heavily traveled by settlers seeking new lands in the West.

▶ ▶ ▶ **FIND OUT MORE** ◀ ◀ ◀
Lewis and Clark Expedition; Oregon; Westward Movement

This very beautiful 200-year-old organ has had the pipes built into an ornately carved cabinet.

 ORGAN

The organ has been called the "king of musical instruments" because of its great power and wide range of tones. The word *organ* most often refers to a *pipe organ*, although there are several other kinds. A pipe organ is made up of a *console*, hundreds of pipes, and a *wind-chest*. The *console* is where the organist sits to play. The console has several *manuals* (keyboards) played with the hands, and a set of 30 or more foot pedals. Above and around the manuals are rows of knobs and levers, called *stops*. The organist uses stops to open up the pipes.

The pipes of an organ are usually shaped like cylinders, ranging from 7 inches (18 cm) to more than 60 feet (19 m) in length. All pipes are connected to a wind-chest—a large chamber that is kept full of air. Air is pumped into the chest by *bellows* (air pumps) or by great electric fans. The air presses against the mouths of the pipes. By pressing keys or foot pedals, the organist opens the mouths of various pipes. Air rushes into the opened pipes, making the pipes sound their tones until the keys or pedals of the organ are released.

The pipes are arranged in *ranks*. Each rank is a complete set of tones of a certain quality. For example, one rank may make flutelike sounds and contain pipes for all the tones a flute can play. Another rank may make cellolike sounds and contain pipes for all the tones a cello can play. Some ranks of pipes can make tones that are lower than on any other musical instrument. When an organist wants to use a particular rank of pipes, he or she pulls out one of the stops on the console. This removes the covers on the mouths of the pipes and makes them ready to be played by pressing the keys and foot pedals.

The electric organ was invented by Laurens Hammond in 1935. The tones of an electric organ are made electronically: A small vibration in an electronic component is *amplified* (made louder) to produce the sound.

▶ ▶ ▶ ▶ **FIND OUT MORE** ◀ ◀ ◀
Cathedral; Electronic Music;
Harmonica; Music;
Musical Instruments; Music Box

ORGANIC COMPOUND

SEE CHEMISTRY

ORGANIZATION OF AMERICAN STATES

In 1826, the liberator of Latin America, Simón Bolívar, dreamed of an organization of North and South American nations. More than 120 years later, in 1948, such an organization was created. It is called the Organization of American States (OAS). Its purpose is to promote the unity and welfare of the American nations and to defend their independence. The members are listed in the box opposite. Cuba was excluded from OAS activities in 1962, because it was thought to be "exporting revolution," but it still retains its membership.

The Inter-American Conference meets every five years. A council handles problems between these sessions. In an emergency, the foreign ministers of the countries decide what to do. In 1965, the OAS met and decided to send a peace commission to the Dominican Republic to help end fighting there. Since that event, however, the OAS has become relatively obscure and unimportant.

▶ ▶ ▶ ▶ **FIND OUT MORE** ◀ ◀ ◀
Bolívar, Simón

ORGAN TRANSPLANT

SEE MEDICINE, SURGERY

ORIENTAL ART

The art objects pictured with this article are examples of the art of China, Japan, Turkey, and Persia. The art of these and other Oriental countries has a rich and beautiful history. A few museums and galleries in the United States—such as the Freer Gallery of Art in Washington, D.C.—are devoted to the art of the Orient. Shown here are a few glimpses of a great history of art on the world's largest continent.

To a great extent, Oriental art is inspired by religion. It is seldom made to be useful. More frequently it is made for beauty—to spark thoughts of love, peace, and the finer things of life in people who view it.

Among the oldest surviving pieces of Oriental art are those from the Shang dynasty. The Shang people lived on the central plains of China, beginning about 1500 B.C. They discovered how to make an alloy called *bronze* (a blend of copper and tin). They began making beautiful objects using it. They made ceremonial vessels, possibly for use in religious rites. Since the Shang period in China, there have been many great periods of Chinese art.

Sculptors in many Oriental countries have been inspired by Buddha, thought by many to be a great man of India. Buddha founded one of the world's religions. He is often shown sitting in what is called the lotus position, with his legs folded, *contemplating* (thinking about) life. It was after Buddha died that many sculptors began making statues of him. Some beautiful ones were made in the Gupta period, the greatest period of art in India. Sculpture in the Gupta period used rounded and refined figures.

From India, the influence of Buddha spread to the east—through central Asia to China and Japan—and to the southeast, to Thailand. As Buddhism spread to various countries,

THE MEMBER COUNTRIES OF THE ORGANIZATION OF AMERICAN STATES:

Antigua, Argentina, Bahamas, Barbados, Belize, Bolivia, Brazil, Canada, Chile, Colombia, Costa Rica, Cuba, Dominica, the Dominican Republic, Ecuador, El Salvador, Grenada, Guatemala, Guyana, Haiti, Honduras, Jamaica, Mexico, Nicaragua, Panama, Paraguay, Peru, St. Kitts-Nevis, St. Lucia, St. Vincent, Suriname, Trinidad and Tobago, the United States, Uruguay, and Venezuela.

▲ This bronze cauldron from the Shang dynasty was possibly used in religious ceremonies to honor and worship ancestors.

▶ **Wall paintings from the Gupta dynasty show vivid scenes of Indian life. This picture taken from ancient caves at Ajanta, India, shows dancers and musicians entertaining a royal household.**

▼ **One of a set of 12 prints made by the Japanese artist Kuniyoshi. It is called *View of the Post-stations of Hodogaya* and dates from about 1835.**

▲ **A Muslim prayer carpet, made in Turkey in the 1700s.**

sculptors in each country adapted the statue of Buddha to the art and costume of their land. For example, a statue of Buddha made in Thailand often shows him wearing a type of headdress that befits a leader in Thailand.

One kind of Japanese art that has had an influence on Western artists is the Japanese print. From the 1600s to the 1800s, a succession of Japanese printmakers developed printmaking from a very simple form to a highly complicated art using several colors. One great printmaker was Ando Hiroshige, who died in 1858. He was the last of the great printmakers of Japan.

By Hiroshige's time, an art that had started with simple black-and-white woodblocks 300 years earlier had become a highly developed art, involving several blocks. Each of these blocks was used to print a different color onto the sheet of paper. When all the areas of different color had been printed, the result was a picture that looked as if it had been painted in lots of colors.

But there is no use of *shadow* in a Japanese print. There are large, flat *planes* (areas) of solid colors. These two characteristics of Japanese prints were imitated by Western artists, including Edgar Degas, Mary Cassatt, and Winslow Homer. Japanese printmakers were skilled also in the use of "negative space"—that is, space on the print where the bare paper shows.

Another of the many kinds of Oriental art is the Oriental carpet. From Turkey eastward through central Asia into the southern part of the former Soviet Union and northern India, the making of beautiful carpets has long been an art. Particular designs have been traditional among certain groups of people.

One kind of carpet, the *prayer carpet*, has long been a religious art of the Muslims—of whom there are about 600 million in Asia. The prayer carpet is important to a Muslim because he or she must kneel and face Mecca to pray five times a day. Many Muslims take a prayer rug with them wherever they go. The Muslim kneels on the rug with the point of the arch facing Mecca. The design of the prayer niche, or *mihrab*, is traditional, with the keystone arch at one end and the columns on each side of the carpet. Red and blue are the colors traditionally used in such rugs. A very famous carpet-making center is Anatolia, in Turkey.

ORIGAMI

SEE PAPER SCULPTURE

ORTHODOX CHURCH

The Eastern Orthodox Church is the third largest branch of Christianity. It has about 80 million members. Most of them live in Greece; the countries of Eastern Europe as well as Cyprus; some countries of the former Soviet Union, such as Russia and Ukraine; the Middle East; and southwest Asia. Almost 4 million believers in the Orthodox Church live in the United States. *Orthodox* is Greek for "true belief." Members of the Orthodox Church believe that it was founded by Jesus Christ and his apostles.

For 1,000 years, Christianity was undivided. But then disagreements arose. Emperor Constantine moved the capital of the Roman Empire from Rome to Constantinople (now Istanbul, Turkey) in A.D. 330. The Roman Empire was divided into the Western Empire, ruled from Rome, and the Eastern Byzantine Empire, ruled from Constantinople. In 1054, Christianity split in two. The *pope* headed the western, or Roman Catholic, church. A *patriarch* in Constantinople ruled the Eastern, or Orthodox, church.

Today, the Eastern Orthodox Church has four *patriarchates*. They are large religious groups, headed by patriarchs in Istanbul (formerly Constantinople), Jerusalem (in Israel), Antioch (in southern Turkey), and Alexandria (in Egypt). There are also self-governing Orthodox churches in the United States, Russia, Ukraine, Greece, Albania, Cyprus, Finland, Bulgaria, Czech and Slovak Republics, Romania, and certain independent states in the former Yugoslavia. The patriarch of Constantinople is the spiritual leader of all the Orthodox churches. He governs only the Istanbul patriarchate, however.

Beautiful religious paintings, called *icons*, decorate the churches and are sometimes used in the services. Easter is the most important feast in the Orthodox Church. It is usually celebrated later than in other Christian churches, because the Orthodox Church uses the old Julian calendar. The feast is highlighted by a midnight candlelight resurrection service. Orthodox priests are allowed to marry. The Orthodox and Roman Catholic churches have very similar religious beliefs.

Icons are portraits of Jesus Christ, the Virgin Mary, and other saints. They play a large part in worship rituals of the Orthodox Church. Candles are lit before them, they are often kissed, and people pray in front of them.

▶ ▶ ▶ ▶ **FIND OUT MORE** ◀ ◀ ◀ ◀
Calendar; Christianity; Easter

ORWELL, GEORGE (1903–1950)

George Orwell was the pen name of an English author and social critic. His real name was Eric Arthur Blair. Orwell was born in Motihari, India. He was educated in England and then returned to India. In 1927, Orwell moved to Europe and devoted his time to writing. His first book, *Down and Out in Paris and London* (1933), is based on his experiences in those cities. *Homage to Catalonia* (1938) describes fighting in the Spanish Civil War.

Orwell was deeply interested in politics. He hated dictatorships. He was afraid that people's individual freedoms were being taken away. His

George Orwell, the British writer who created worlds where no one had any freedom to be themselves.

▲ **Ottawa's parliament building dominates the Ottawa River and surrounding city.**

two most famous books, *Animal Farm* (1945) and *Nineteen Eighty-four* (1949), are Orwell's efforts to warn the world of what might happen. *Animal Farm* is a story about animals who take over their farm and try to establish a Communist government. But the pigs become dictators, and the other animals lose their freedom. This book is based on what Orwell thought had happened to Communism in Russia.

Nineteen Eighty-four is set in a terrifying future where no privacy or freedom exists. A few dictatorships, constantly at war with each other, rule the world. Children are encouraged to spy upon their parents and to report them to the "Thought Police" if they say anything against the state's rulers. Some people think Orwell predicted a possible future accurately.

▷▷▷▷ **FIND OUT MORE** ◁◁◁◁
Dictator; Literature; Novel

OSTRICH

SEE FLIGHTLESS BIRDS

OTTAWA

Ottawa, the capital of Canada, stands on the Ottawa River in the province of Ontario. The city has more than 300,000 people. Facing Ottawa on the north bank of the river is the industrial city of Hull in the province of Quebec. Hull is part of the metropolitan area of Ottawa, whose population totals 718,000. The city of Ottawa includes the lower Rideau River, which flows into the Ottawa River over the 37 foot– (11 m–) high Rideau Falls. The Rideau River is part of the Rideau Canal, a waterway linking Ottawa with Lake Ontario.

Some Ottawans speak only English or French, but many speak both languages. Ottawa is a major commercial and financial center. Its largest industry is the lumber, wood-pulp, and paper industry.

The first settlement on the site of Ottawa was made in 1826 by British soldiers. The town that grew there was called Bytown until 1855, when it was renamed "Ottawa," after the Algonkian word *adawe*, meaning "to trade." (Algonkians were known as great traders.) Ottawa became Canada's capital in 1857. Its most striking landmark is Parliament Hill. The hill is dominated by Peace Tower, which commemorates Canada's war dead. The tower rises above the parliament buildings. A fire destroyed most of these buildings in 1916, but they were rebuilt by 1920. Other notable buildings include Rideau Hall—the official residence of Canada's governor general—and the Anglican and Roman Catholic cathedrals.

▷▷▷▷ **FIND OUT MORE** ◁◁◁◁
Canada; Ontario

OTTER

The otter belongs to the same animal family as the badger, skunk, and weasel. The head of the otter is broad and flat, with short rounded ears. Its legs are short but strong. Its feet are clawed as well as webbed. Its long, smooth body, covered with chestnut brown fur, enables it to swim through water quickly. It may stay underwater for several minutes. The otter feeds on fish, crabs, frogs, birds, and other small animals that live in or near the water.

The freshwater otter lives in an underground burrow along the bank of a river or stream. Since the entrance to the burrow is underwater, the burrow provides good protection from other animals.

▲ **Otters are well adapted to living both on land and in the water. On land they will hunt rabbits and *voles* (smal rodents).**

Otters are very playful animals. In the winter, they sometimes like to make slides in the snow, and take turns sliding down a hill on their stomachs.

A female otter has from two to five babies at one time. The baby otters are called kittens. The mother takes care of the kittens for about a year, cradling them on her chest as she swims on her back. She teaches them to hunt and swim. Also known as river otters, freshwater otters hunt fish, frogs, and crayfish.

Otters are found all over the world except in Australia. Large numbers of otters once lived in North America, but hunters killed many thousands of them for their valuable fur.

Sea otters live in the waters along the coast of California, in Prince William Sound, and in the waters off the Aleutian Islands. They feed on crabs, fish, and shellfish, such as clams and oysters. When a sea otter catches a fish, it eats the fish while floating on its back, using its chest as a table. If a sea otter finds an oyster or clam, it will lay the shellfish on its chest. Then it will break the shell with a stone held in its front paws. The sea otter cracks the shell just as you might crack nuts with a hammer or stone.

At one time, sea otters were in great danger of becoming extinct because they were hunted for their fur. The sea otter is now protected by government regulations. Only people with special licenses can hunt sea otters—and then only in limited numbers.

▶ ▶ ▶ ▶ **FIND OUT MORE** ◀ ◀ ◀ ◀
Mammal; Weasel

OTTOMAN EMPIRE

A thousand years ago, a group of Islamic tribes called the Seljuk Turks lived in western Asia. They were very warlike people, fighting among themselves and against nearby tribes. They conquered the Persian Empire and the people who lived in the lands that are now Israel, Iraq, and Syria. One branch of the Seljuk Turks was called the Ottomans.

In 1299, Osman, the leader of the Ottomans, declared war against the Turks' Christian neighbors in the Byzantine Empire. The Ottomans conquered all of the Byzantine Empire (except for the capital city of Constantinople) by the end of the 1300s. By that time, they had also conquered all of the other Seljuk tribes, as well as Macedonia and Bulgaria. Osman's great-grandson, Muhammad II, finally captured Constantinople in 1453. The Ottomans then began to move into parts of Asia and Africa.

The empire conquered by the Ottoman Turks was strongest under Suleiman the Magnificent, who ruled from 1520 to 1566. His troops conquered all of eastern Europe as

The endangered South American giant otter can be more than 6 feet (2m) in length. There are not many of these otters left, because they have been hunted for their valuable fur.

▲ Suleiman the Magnificent, greatest of all the sultans of the Ottoman Empire, besieges the city of Bucharest in what is today called Romania.

▲ The otter will use its very strong tail to hold itself upright in order to look out for any possible enemies.

far as the outskirts of Vienna, now the capital of Austria. The Turks were never able to take Vienna, however. They were driven back from the gates of Vienna twice in famous battles with the Austrians.

After these defeats, the Ottoman Empire slowly grew weaker. Nearby countries began to conquer some of the Ottoman lands. By the time of World War I, the Ottoman Empire had lost most of its European possessions. Mustafa Kemal, a general in the Turkish army, took command of the Turks in 1922 and founded the Turkish republic in 1923. He was elected Turkey's first president in 1925. He changed his name to *Atatürk* ("father of the Turks"') in 1934.

▲ An election scene in Istanbul in 1923. Mustafa Kemel was elected first president of the Republic of Turkey. The votes were collected in urns, which were carried in triumph through the streets.

▶ ▶ ▶ ▶ **FIND OUT MORE** ◀ ◀ ◀ ◀
Bulgaria; Byzantine Empire; Islam; Macedonia; Persia; Turkey

OUTLAW

From about 1845 to 1885—the height of the period known as the Old West—thousands of people moved west to claim land the government was giving away. They established towns, farms, and ranches very quickly. The only law officers were sheriffs and marshals,

▼ Jesse James was a notorious outlaw of the American West. He and his gang delighted in robbing trains and banks. Often innocent witnesses would be killed in the shoot-out.

and even they were scarce. During these years, some persons called outlaws—gunmen, or bandits—took advantage of the unsettled conditions.

Two brothers named Frank and Jesse James organized a gang of outlaws in 1866. They roamed the West for 16 years, robbing banks and trains and murdering innocent people. If there were witnesses they were usually threatened so that they were too scared to give evidence against the gang. Jesse James never was captured—he retired. He grew a beard and changed his name. He was later shot by one of his own gang members for the reward money!

One of the most notorious outlaws in the Old West had one of the shortest careers of all time. His name was William H. Bonney, but he became known as Billy the Kid. His only education was what he learned on the muddy streets in the West. He began his career of murder when a man who had befriended him was shot. Billy set out to get revenge and, it was reported, had killed three men by the time he was 17. Billy went on to add to the "notches on his gun" (kill more people). He was shot at the age of 21 by a sheriff.

Butch Cassidy and the Sundance Kid gained reputations as amiable but determined outlaws. Butch, especially, was known as a cheerful, persuasive man. Legend says that he and his partner never killed a person except in self-defense. But they did rob banks all over the West until they had to leave the country to escape capture. A famous movie about them was released in 1969.

OWENS, JESSE (1913–1980)

The greatest competitor of the 1936 Olympic Games was a black athlete, Jesse Owens. He won four gold medals in the Games. His victories were unusually dramatic because the Olympics that year were held in Nazi Germany. The Nazi dictator Adolf Hitler believed that Germans were superior to other peoples in everything, including athletics. Hitler had also declared that blacks were an inferior race. So it was doubly pleasing to the United States that Jesse Owens was the outstanding performer of these Games.

Owens was born in Decatur, Alabama, the son of poor sharecroppers. He had ten brothers and sisters. His family moved to Cleveland when he was a small boy. He became a member of the track team in high school and was elected president of the student council. He later worked his way through Ohio State University, where he was a track star.

As a member of the 1936 U.S. Olympic Team, Owens won gold medals in the 100-meter dash, the 200-meter dash, and the running broad jump. He set two Olympic records. He won his fourth gold medal as a member of the U.S. team in the 400-meter relay race.

▶ ▶ ▶ ▶ **FIND OUT MORE** ◀ ◀ ◀ ◀
Olympic Games

OWL

The owl is a bird of prey found on every continent except Antarctica. Owls have large heads; big eyes; and short, hooked beaks. Their feathers are soft and fluffy. Owls have a feathered fringe on the front of each wing. These soft feathers enable the owl to swoop silently down on its prey. The owl's strong legs are covered by feathers. Each foot has four toes, ending in long, sharp *talons*, or claws. The outer toes can be bent inward so that the owl can grasp its prey.

Most owls are night hunters. They feed on small mammals, birds, insects, and occasionally fish. Although the owl can locate its prey using only its sharp sense of hearing, its excellent eyesight is also helpful. Its large eyes, located at the front of its head, are fixed in their sockets. Undisturbed by any side vision, the owl can "zero in" on its prey with amazing accuracy. The pupil of the owl's eye can be greatly *expanded* (opened), giving it good night vision.

Owls are usually bewildered and helpless in the glare of sunlight. When surprised, an owl hisses like a cat and makes a clicking noise with its beak. Some owls have a shrieking cry, and others have a musical "hoot."

▲ Jesse Owens, the great U.S. athlete, performs in the running broad jump for which he won a gold medal in the 1936 Olympic Games.

▽ The color of owls' feathers helps *camouflage* (hide) them in their natural setting. All owls hunt at night. Their sharp hearing and silent flight helps them catch their prey.

Long-eared owl

Snowy owl

Great horned owl

The ghostlike barn owl of many folk tales has a white face. It gives an eerie shrill cry. Rodents, like mice and rats, are its chief prey.

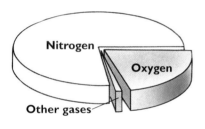

Almost four-fifths of the air we breathe is nitrogen. Oxygen, the gas we need to survive, makes up only one-fifth.

Owls build their nests in hollow trees, caves, barns, deserted buildings, and underground burrows. The *burrowing owl* of western North America often lives in the deserted burrows of prairie dogs (its favorite food) or digs its own. Owls live alone or in mated pairs. They range in size from the *elf owl*, 5½ inches (14 cm) tall, to the *great horned owl*, 25 inches (64 cm) tall with a wingspread of 5 feet (1.5 m).

Owls have heart-shaped, human-like faces, and their large, serious eyes and dignified appearance have given them the reputation of being wise birds. Ancient Greeks believed the owl was the companion of Athena, the goddess of wisdom.

Owls are nearly always harmless and useful birds. *Barn owls* are very common in the southern United States. They feed on harmful rodents. A barn owl may eat ten mice a day. This saves about 250 pounds (110 kg) of grain that would have been eaten by the ten mice in one year.

▶ ▶ ▶ ▶ **FIND OUT MORE** ◀ ◀ ◀ ◀
Bird; Birds of Prey

OX

SEE CATTLE

OXIDATION

SEE OXYGEN

LEARN BY DOING

You need oxygen and water to make iron or steel turn rusty. You can test this for yourself. Put small pieces of steel wool in tubes filled with (1) tap water, (2) boiled water, (3) just air, and (4) tap water containing salt. Where the steel wool is wet or damp and in contact with oxygen, in the air or dissolved in water, it rusts. It does not rust in boiled water because boiling water removes the air. Steel wool will rust fastest in salt water, because salt speeds up the oxidation process.

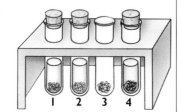

OXYGEN

Oxygen is the third most abundant of all the elements. Free (uncombined) oxygen is a gas that makes up about one-fifth of the volume of the air. Oxygen makes up 89 percent of the weight of pure water. Oxygen makes up half the weight of the Earth's crust, where it is combined with many other elements.

Oxygen is colorless, odorless, and tasteless. It dissolves slightly in water, enabling fish to get oxygen to breathe. If oxygen is cooled to 297°F below zero (-183°C), it becomes a liquid.

Oxygen is extremely important to all living things. No animal can exist without it. When you breathe air into your lungs, the oxygen in the air enters your bloodstream. The blood carries the oxygen to all the tissues of your body. The oxygen combines with digested food in the cells of the tissues. This produces energy.

Oxygen combines with many other chemical elements to make a very large number of compounds. These are called *oxides*, and the process in which they are made is *oxidation*. When oxygen and another element are combined rapidly, heat and light are given off. Rapid oxidation is called *combustion*, or burning. Things burn brighter in oxygen than they do in air.

Oxygen combines slowly with some elements. For example, iron in damp air oxidizes slowly. This produces *iron oxide*, or rust. The decaying of dead plant and animal matter is caused by slow oxidation, which is aided by molds and bacteria.

Acetylene and *hydrogen* are two gases. Each can be burned in pure oxygen to produce a very hot flame used for *welding* (melting together) metals. In hospitals, patients with lung troubles are given pure oxygen to breathe. Mountain climbers take along tanks of oxygen that they must breathe, because there is less oxygen in the air high above the ground. High-flying airplanes also carry oxygen and use it in their cabins at high altitudes. Fuel for space rockets usually contains liquid oxygen, called *LOX*.

Most often, oxygen is found in a form where two atoms are joined together. However, sometimes three oxygen atoms join together to form a rather different gas known as *ozone*. Ozone is very bad to breathe.

▶ ▶ ▶ ▶ **FIND OUT MORE** ◀ ◀ ◀ ◀

Air; Atmosphere; Bacteria; Chemistry; Hydrogen

 ## OZONE LAYER

The ozone layer is part of the Earth's atmosphere. It lies in the stratosphere, which is about 20 miles (32 km) above the Earth's surface.

The ozone protects the Earth from harmful ultraviolet rays, but scientists have discovered evidence of a "hole" in the ozone layer. Such a hole would allow ultraviolet rays to enter the atmosphere, creating a risk of cancer for humans and threatening other animals and plants.

Ozone is a form of oxygen, containing three oxygen atoms in each molecule. It is formed when ultraviolet rays hit oxygen, which normally has two molecules. The rays split these molecules and send them off on their own. Each single molecule then merges with more oxygen to form ozone. More ultraviolet rays can then break down ozone into separate oxygen molecules.

Because ozone is constantly being created, converted, and created again, scientists say that it is in equilibrium. Each reaction absorbs ultraviolet rays, ensuring that they go no further than the stratosphere.

Ozone's ability to react so quickly has also begun to threaten it. Many modern products, such as certain plastics, refrigerators, and aerosols, contain ingredients called chlorofluorocarbons (usually called CFCs). These CFCs can escape into the stratosphere and react with the ozone.

The CFC molecules contain chlorine, which robs ozone of a molecule and turns it back into oxygen without its absorbing any ultraviolet rays. A single CFC molecule can affect 100,000 ozone molecules. Evidence now shows that the ozone layer has been affected. Overall it has lost about 2 to 3 percent of its ozone. The problem is most severe over the Antarctic, where magnetic forces and cold temperatures have added to the problem. The "hole" represents nearly a 95 percent loss in places!

There are many measures to ban CFCs and other products that affect the ozone layer.

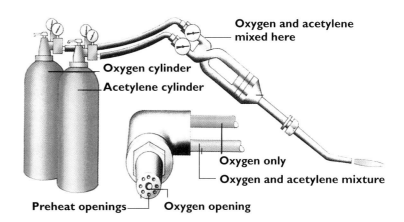

Oxygen and acetylene mixed here

Oxygen cylinder

Acetylene cylinder

Oxygen only

Oxygen and acetylene mixture

Preheat openings

Oxygen opening

△ **Oxyacetylene welding is one way of joining metal parts. Two gases are needed: oxygen and acetylene. Acetylene burns in oxygen to produce a very hot flame. It will even burn underwater.**

There can be no fire without oxygen. La Paz, the capital of Bolivia, is about 12,000 feet (3,700 m) above sea level. At this height there is so little oxygen in the air that the city's fire engines are hardly ever used.

◁ **The ozone layer, at a height of about 20 miles (32 km) above the Earth's surface, protects us from the harmful effects of ultraviolet radiation from the sun.**

Ultraviolet radiation

20 miles (32 km)

15 miles (24 km)

Ozone layer

7½ miles (12 km)

Earth

Ultraviolet radiation	Oxygen molecule	Oxygen atom (O)	Oxygen molecule (O_2)	Ozone (O_3)

**DEVELOPMENT OF
THE LETTER P**

The Semitic P
c. 1500 B.C.

The
Phoenician P
c. 1000 B.C.

The Greek P
c. 600 B.C.

The Roman P
c. A.D. 600

 PACIFIC ISLANDS

Most of the islands in the Pacific Ocean are in its southern and southwestern waters. The ocean bed in this area is deep in some places and quite shallow in others. The shallow places are formed by underwater hills or mountains. Many of these mountains are volcanoes.

Some of the Pacific islands are volcanoes that have risen high above the surface of the water. These volcanic islands are often large, with rugged mountain peaks. The Pacific island of New Guinea is the second largest island in the world. Only Greenland, in the North Atlantic Ocean, is larger. Other Pacific islands are formed from *coral*—the stony skeletons of tiny sea animals. These animals usually live on mountain peaks that lie just under the surface of the water. The coral is built up over the years until it rises above the water. Many of the coral islands are *atolls*—ring-shaped islands with a lagoon in the center. The spectacular scenery and white sandy beaches attracts many tourists to the islands.

The islands of the South Pacific are often known as *Oceania*. These islands lie in three general groups. *Melanesia* ("black islands") is the group that lies scattered north and northeast of the continent of Australia. To the north of Melanesia lies *Micronesia* ("little islands"). To the east are the islands known as *Polynesia* ("many islands"). The islands of Hawaii are included in the Polynesian group.

The waters of the North Pacific Ocean are very deep. There are fewer

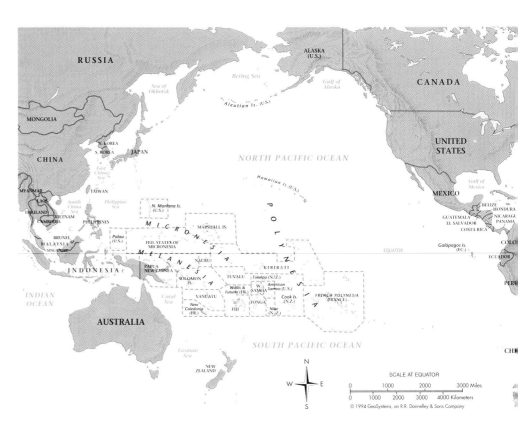

PACIFIC ISLAND NATIONS

	Area sq. miles	Area sq. km	Capital	Population
Fiji	7,056	18,274	Suva	741,000
Kiribati	281	728	Bairiki, on Tarawa	71,000
Nauru	8	21	Nauru	9,000
Solomon Islands	10,983	28,446	Honiara	329,000
Tonga	270	699	Nuku'alofa	96,000
Tuvalu	9.7	25	Fongafale	9,000
Vanuatu	5,700	14,763	Vila	159,000
Western Samoa	1,097	2,842	Apia	165,000

Fiji

Kiribati

Nauru

Solomon Islands

Tonga

Tuvalu

Vanuatu

Western Samoa

islands in this region than in the South Pacific. One group of islands in the North Pacific is the Aleutians. These islands lie off the south coast of Alaska and are part of that state.

Some Pacific islands are independent nations. They are Fiji, Kiribati, Nauru, Tonga, Tuvalu, Vanuatu, Western Samoa, and the Solomon Islands. Such island nations as Japan, Indonesia, Taiwan, and the Philippines lie near the coast of Asia. Many Pacific islands are possessions, territories, or dependencies of other nations. The Federated States of Micronesia, which include the Caroline Islands, and the Marshall Islands have a free association status with the U.S. The Mariana Islands, except Guam, have formed the Commonwealth of the Northern Marianas. New Caledonia is a French overseas territory in Melanesia.

▶▶▶▶ **FIND OUT MORE** ◀◀◀◀
Coral; Island; Melanesia; Micronesia; Pacific Ocean; Polynesia; Volcano

PACIFIC OCEAN

The Pacific Ocean is the largest and deepest body of water in the world. It stretches between North and South America on the east and Australia, the Malay Archipelago, and Asia on the west. Its northern boundary is the Bering Strait, through which it connects with the Arctic Ocean. The Pacific's southern boundary is Antarctica. Its greatest length from north to south is about 9,900 miles (15,900 km). Its greatest width is about 10,400 miles (16,700 km).

The Pacific Ocean is deepest in the long trenches that lie parallel to some of its coastlines. The greatest depth yet found, more than 36,000 feet (11,000 m), is in the Marianas Trench, off the Mariana Islands. The ocean floor also has many underwater mountains. Some, called *guyots*, have flat tops. The Pacific has several underwater *ridges*, or chains of mountains. *Continental shelves*, or plateaus, extend from the continents into the Pacific for varying distances.

Currents in the North Pacific move in a clockwise direction. Together they form one large circular current. The California Current flows southward. When it turns westward, it is called the North Equatorial Current. It moves north along Asia's coast, where it is called the Japan Current. The eastern flow back across the Pacific is called the North Pacific Current. Currents in the South Pacific move in a counterclockwise direction.

Many small islands and island groups lie in the central, southern, and western parts of the Pacific. They are divided into three groups, according to their location and the types of people who live there. *Melanesia* is the southwestern group of islands. *Micronesia* consists of the islands

PACIFIC OCEAN

▶ **A typical pagoda in Nanjing, or Nanking, China. Chinese pagodas usually have an uneven number of stories—this has nine—and have eight sides. It is believed that pagodas bring wealth and happiness to the area.**

north of Melanesia, and *Polynesia* includes the islands scattered across the central Pacific.

Asian peoples began exploring the Pacific more than 2,000 years ago. Europeans began exploring the Pacific from the western side in the early 1500s. In 1513, Vasco Nùñez de Balboa became the first European to sight the Pacific from its eastern shore. In 1520, Ferdinand Magellan named the ocean Pacific (peaceful) because it was so calm.

▶▶▶▶ **FIND OUT MORE** ◀◀◀◀
Balboa, Vasco Nùñez de; Magellan, Ferdinand; Melanesia; Micronesia; Ocean; Pacific Islands; Polynesia

▼ **A typical Pacific island shoreline with abundant palm trees fringing a sandy beach. An outlying coral reef keeps the waters shallow and calm.**

PAGODA

A pagoda is a type of building found in many Asian countries. Pagodas are usually temples or shrines belonging to the Buddhist religion.

Most pagodas are built in the shape of a tower, with several *tiers,* or stories. Each story is smaller than the one beneath it. The different stories of a pagoda represent a journey from Earth to heaven. Upward-curving roofs project outward from the building at each story. A tall *spire,* or mast, is on the top of most pagodas. Pagodas may be round, square, or many-sided.

Pagodas were first built in ancient

India. Many Indian pagodas were shrines containing holy objects. Buddhist preachers introduced the idea of the pagoda into other Asian countries. Chinese pagodas were decorated with ivory carvings and colorful tiles. Bells were often hung from the roofs. Pagodas in Japan are usually square and built of wood. The Horyuji pagoda at Nara, Japan, is decorated with beautiful wood carvings. In Burma, devout Buddhists *construct* (build) pagodas as a holy task. Most Burmese villages have at least one pagoda.

Some pagodas are found in Europe. Most were built in the 1700s, when Chinese architecture was popular in Europe. They were built for decoration, however, not for religious use.

▶▶▶▶ **FIND OUT MORE** ◀◀◀◀
Buddhism; Temple

PAINE, THOMAS (1737–1809)

Thomas Paine was a writer on politics and religion, who was involved in the Revolutionary War. He was an outspoken defender of democracy and has become a hero of all lovers of liberty.

Paine was born in Thetford, England, the son of a poor Quaker corset maker. He came to Philadelphia in 1774. He became an editor of the *Pennsylvania Magazine* and began promoting the idea of independence. In January 1776, he published a pamphlet called *Common Sense*. It called for the colonies to declare their independence and sold 120,000 copies in three months. Paine then joined the Continental Army and wrote a series of 16 pamphlets called *The American Crisis*. George Washington liked the ideas in the first pamphlet so much that he ordered it to be read to his troops just before battle. It starts: "These are the times that try men's souls. The summer soldier and the sunshine patriot will, in this crisis, shrink from the service of their country. . ."

After the war ended, Paine went to France and England. He published *The Rights of Man* in 1791–1792. This book defended the new French and American republics. Paine became a member of the French Convention, but he was put in prison when he refused to vote for the execution of the French king. While he was in prison, he wrote most of *The Age of Reason,* which contained his views on religion. Later he returned to the United States. Paine died in poverty on his farm in New Rochelle, New York in 1809.

▶▶▶▶ **FIND OUT MORE** ◀◀◀◀
American History; Revolutionary War

▲ Thomas Paine, a political writer who was active during the Revolutionary War.

PAINT

Paint is a colored liquid that is brushed, sprayed, or rolled onto a surface to protect or decorate it. When paint dries, it forms a thin, tough coating. Paint is made up of three parts—the *pigment*, the *body*, and the *vehicle*. The pigment gives the paint its color. It consists of a fine powder, often made of ground earth, stone, or minerals. The body of a paint forms the main protective covering when the paint dries. It is also made of a fine powder, usually white in color.

Until recently, white lead was the most commonly used paint body. Now titanium dioxide is used because lead is poisonous. Many children and animals have become very sick, and some have died, from licking or sucking lead paint.

The pigment and the body are mixed together in a liquid called the

▼ Oil, resins, and thinners are blended together thoroughly before the color pigment is added. The mixture is then ground in a ball mill until the paint is completely mixed.

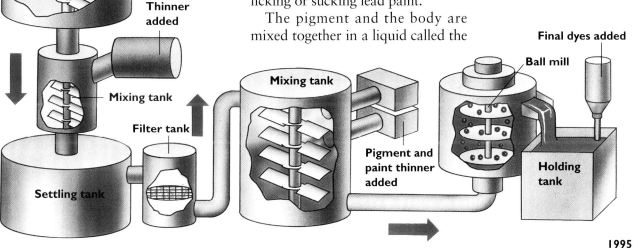

Oil and resin blended together

Thinner added

Mixing tank

Filter tank

Settling tank

Mixing tank

Pigment and paint thinner added

Final dyes added

Ball mill

Holding tank

vehicle. In *oil paints* the vehicle is an oil, such as linseed oil, combined with *a thinner,* such as turpentine. The thinner makes the paint flow on evenly. In *alkyd paints*, the vehicle contains a high percentage of man-made alkyd resins. *Latex paints* use water as the vehicle; these are very popular paints because of their low cost, quick-drying capability, and the ease with which the paintbrush can be cleaned.

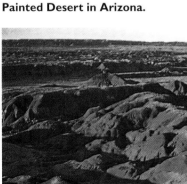

▲ **Emulsion paint is a mixture of two liquids whose particles are evenly mixed without being in a solution.**

▼ **The late afternoon sun casts a pattern of light and shadow over the hills of the Painted Desert in Arizona.**

People have been using paints for about 50,000 years. Primitive people learned to make pigment from natural materials, such as chalk, charcoal, and berries. Cave wall paintings discovered around the world contain natural pigments. The ancient Egyptians made blue paint from sand, soda, and copper and red paint from madder plants. They imported these red-rooted plants from India. As civilization spread, people began to use paints more and more. They learned to make longer-lasting and tougher paints from chemicals.

There are many types of paints available today. Paints are made especially for the *interior* (inside) or the *exterior* (outside) of homes and buildings. They may be made with a

gloss (very shiny), *semigloss* (less shiny), or *mat* (dull) finish. Gloss paints are often used by homeowners in their kitchens and bathrooms because they are washable. Mat paints are suitable for ceilings and some walls. Many other types of paints are used for specific purposes. There are *fluorescent paints* that glow at night when exposed to light. These paints are good for the sake of safety in and around the home. *Textured paints* have a thick body and are applied with special tools to give a textured effect on a ceiling or wall. They are especially useful at hiding cracks. Artists mix oil paints to obtain different tints and shades. And ship painters paint ship hulls with a special type of poisonous paint to keep barnacles away!

▶▶▶▶ **FIND OUT MORE** ◀◀◀◀
Painting

PAINTED DESERT

When early Spanish explorers in the American West saw a wasteland of buttes, mesas, and canyons glowing with pastel colors, they named the place *El Desierto Pintado*, meaning "The Painted Desert."

The Painted Desert is a dry region that extends across about 150 miles (250 km) of northeastern Arizona. Parts of it are in the Petrified Forest. The desert is unusual for the colors of its rocks and sand.

Iron oxides create the bright yellows and reds, and other chemical compounds make other colors in the desert. Shades of red, yellow, and purple mixed with white, gray, blue, and brown are seen. Colors seem to change with differences in heat and sunlight. Wind and rain have eroded the soft rocks into many strange shapes. Few plants grow there. An occasional scorpion or snake crawls across the hot ground. Sunset Crater, a volcano, stands in the Painted

Desert near Flagstaff, Arizona.

If you were to stand in the Painted Desert in late afternoon, you would see a kind of color movie show. As the sun sinks, the desert casts its reddish glow. Rocks change color before your eyes.

Look around in your own neighborhood and in fields and woods nearby. See if you can find any unusual color patterns that nature has provided. Make a list of them and try to discover what causes the different colors.

▶▶▶▶ **FIND OUT MORE** ◀◀◀◀
Arizona; Desert; Petrified Forest

PAINTING

Can you remember some of the paintings you have created? Perhaps you used fingerpaints, watercolors, or poster paints. You might have painted something real, such as a person you know or the street you live on. Maybe you painted an imaginary person or scene, or perhaps you just made a colorful design.

Painting means creating an *image,* or picture, by putting colors (called *pigments)* on a surface. There are two basic ways of doing this—*mural painting* and *easel painting.*

In mural painting, the artist applies pigments to a whole wall. The most lasting type of mural painting is the *fresco.* The artist uses a brush to paint with pigments on wet plaster. The plaster absorbs the colors. When dry, the fresco actually is part of the wall. The fresco artist must work with great speed, doing only one small section of the painting at a time before the plaster dries. Once completed, a fresco will last as long as the wall. The *Delphic Sibyl* (shown above right) is one of the great frescoes created by Michelangelo for the Sistine Chapel. *Fresco secco* (dry fresco) is painted on dry plaster. The pigments do not get absorbed by the

◀ *The Delphic Sibyl* **by Michelangelo, from the ceiling in the Sistine Chapel.**

plaster, and the colors can chip off easily if not carefully protected.

Easel painting is done on canvas, paper, wood, or any other movable surface—unlike a mural painting that cannot be moved because it is part of a building. An easel is a stand that holds a painting while the artist works on it. Easel paintings are usually framed and can be hung anywhere, whereas mural paintings must be created to fit the room in which they are painted. There are several techniques of easel painting.

FINGER PAINTING. The pigments used in finger painting are pasty substances that are mixed with water and smeared on slick paper with the fingers. Many designs can

▼ **These children are working on one large painting. Many great artists worked in studios aided by assistants, who mixed paints and helped on larger works.**

▼ **A palette holds the selection of colors being used by an artist. It eliminates the need to open a tube each time a particular color is used.**

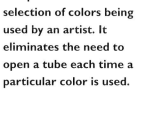

▲ *Fiord* by **Emil Nolde (1867–1956), a German printmaker and important Expressionist painter.**

be made by using different parts of your hands to smear the paint.

WATERCOLOR. Watercolor pigments are mixed with water and applied to paper with a brush. The colors are *transparent*, which means that if you paint over a color with another color, the color underneath will still show through. Mistakes are not easily correctable with watercolors. The painting by Joseph Turner (below) and Emile Nolde (left) are good examples of different effects you can get from watercolors. Turner used very pale colors. The white from the paper gives a glowing atmosphere to the scene. The city, water, and sky all blend together. Nolde used bright colors—blue, purple, orange, red, and yellow outlined in black. He has not blended the water and land together as Turner has.

Gouache, or poster paint, is a type of opaque watercolor. Colors can be painted over one another, and those

▲ **A detail from** *View of Venice from the Lagoon* **by J.M.W. Turner, a British painter of the early 1800s.**

underneath do not show through. *Casein* paint is similar to gouache, but when it dries it is very brittle. Casein should be used on a stiff surface, such as wood, rather than on paper or canvas.

TEMPERA. The word *tempera* usually means pigments that have

been mixed with egg and with water or oil. Egg tempera is painted on wooden boards that have been covered with a hard plaster called *gesso*. Tempera paints produce deep, rich colors and clear, sharp lines. Some Chinese tempera paintings were painted as early as the 1400s.

OIL PAINTING. Oil paints are made by mixing pigments with oil to form a thick substance, a little like toothpaste. Oil paints are usually applied to canvas material that has been stretched tight over a wooden frame or board and coated with a special white paint. Oil paints and the newly developed *plastic paints* (made from artificial materials, such as acrylics) are very popular with artists. Plastic paints are like oil paints to use, but they dry more quickly. They are also cheaper and do not discolor over the years, as oil paints do.

Oil paint can be thinned with turpentine so that it is transparent like watercolor. Or it can be applied in thick layers straight from the tube. The artist can apply the paints with a brush or, in the case of thick paint, with a flexible instrument called a *palette knife*. He or she can get effects by using an *impasto* technique, building up layers of paint to make it thicker in some spots. The artist can use a very dry pigment or leave brushmarks in the paint to achieve other effects. Oil paint dries very slowly, especially if it is thick. But once it dries, colors can be painted over and corrections made.

Still Life: Apples and Pomegranate by Gustave Courbet (pg. 1999) is very realistic. Compare it with the painting beneath it by Paul Klee, who has used paint to bring out the colors and shapes of his imaginary scene.

PASTELS. Pastel paints are pigments molded into sticks similar to chalk. The paints are drawn on paper or canvas in the same way you would use crayons. Once applied, pastel paints smudge easily and must be protected by being sprayed with a *fixative*, a preparation that keeps the pigments in place.

ENCAUSTIC. This painting technique was widely used in ancient Greece, Egypt, and Rome. The pigments are mixed with melted beeswax and then painted on a warm wooden surface. When the painting is complete, the surface is heated a final time to fuse the colors to each other and to the wood. The process takes a long time, and the artist must work in constant heat. Encaustic was finally replaced by tempera paints.

ILLUMINATION. Illumination is the application of pigments, often gold leaf and tempera, to book pages, certificates, and other items to make illustrations and decorative lettering. It was most popular before the invention of printing, around A.D. 1450, but it is still sometimes done today.

Elements of a Painting

When an artist paints, he or she organizes lines, shapes, colors, and textures to form a pleasing picture. By comparing four pictures of a similar subject, you will be able to see how different artists have used these elements. Four paintings shown on the following pages are all portraits of people, by Giovanni Bellini, Pierre Auguste Renoir, Henri Matisse, and Rufino Tamayo.

Each artist used the element of line in a different way. Bellini used soft lines at the edges of the face and hands to show the feel of skin. But the lines about the jewelry are sharp, indicating something hard. Renoir, however, used very soft and fuzzy lines all over. Matisse used dark lines to outline the girl. He put thicker lines about the face and thinner ones on the blouse and hands. The lines in Tamayo's painting are very angular, more like a design than a portrait. The lines in each painting are different, but they all mark edges or give a pattern or feeling.

The shapes in a painting may be

areas bordered by lines, or they might be just patches of color. In the Matisse painting, the girl's blouse is really one large white shape. The red background forms another shape, and the blue skirt yet another. In the Renoir, the lady's head and upper body form a definite shape, but so does the golden colored balcony wall separating her from the audience in the stalls. Bellini emphasized three important shapes—the woman's face, neck, and her hands. Notice how they stand out in comparison to the rest of the painting. The shapes in Tamayo's painting are set off both by lines and by colors. How many

▲ *Still Life: Apples and Pomegranate* (top) by French painter, **Gustave Courbet.** *Around the Fish* (above) by **Paul Klee.**

▲ *The Singer* by **Rufino Tamayo**, one of Mexico's leading modern painters, who was influenced by his exposure to European painters, such as Picasso.

▲ *The Rumanian Blouse* by **Henri Matisse**, who was well known for his love of using flat areas of bright colors.

▶ *Mary Magdalene* by **Giovanni Bellini (1432–1516)**. He contributed to the art of his time by his use of color and shade to create atmosphere in oil painting.

different shapes can you find in Tamayo's picture?

An artist can arrange colors to emphasize areas of a painting, to give a feeling of roundness to objects, or to give a special mood to a painting. Bellini used colors not only to record accurately the woman he painted, but also to set a mood. Notice that two or three areas of the portrait are quite light, but the rest is dark. What sort of feeling does this give you? Notice, too, that Bellini used shadings of color to show the shapes of objects. The tip of the woman's nose is a bright color, but the side of her nose is darker. Down at the bottom of the picture, Bellini even shaded dark areas to show the wrinkles of the woman's sleeve. This kind of shading is called *chiaroscuro*.

Renoir did not use a lot of different colors in this painting. Most of the painting is taken up with the blue shades of the dresses of the young woman and her chaperone. White is added for the neck and bonnet trimmings. The colors of the rest of the

audience are blurred. This gives a feeling of distance and depth to the picture. Notice how the shading on the chaperone's face contrasts with the pale lit face of the young woman.

Matisse used what is called *flat color*. There is very little shading at all, and the colors do not vary. Matisse has depended almost entirely on lines to *portray* (show) the girl's shape. Both Matisse and Tamayo have used colors that are very similar together. Notice the orange and red in the Matisse, and the red and violet in the Tamayo. Notice the patchlike use of color in the background of Tamayo's painting.

The *texture* in a painting is either the feel of the paint itself or the way the artist has represented objects in the painting. Bellini tried to paint so exactly that you almost seem to feel the texture of the woman's hair, skin, and jewelry. Renoir did not paint the girl *exactly* as she would be in real life. He blended and fused colors and lines so that the whole painting seems to have a soft, filmy feeling. Matisse did not use texture at all in his painting. The surface is very flat, and the colors and shapes do not suggest any special texture. Neither was Tamayo so concerned about texture. There seems to be no difference in feeling between the guitar, the hand, and the shirt.

All of these paintings have as their subject the same thing: a beautiful young woman. Yet each painting is very different. Why do you think this is? Every artist has a different way of *seeing* things. The greatest artists are those whose pictures make other people see things the way the artist saw them. Thus, Tamayo and Bellini are really trying to make you see the same sort of young woman, yet the visual images they produced are very different. If you go to an art gallery or museum, you will see paintings of young women by other painters. All will have the same subject, but all will be very different.

◄ **At The Theatre (La Premiere Sortie) by Pierre Auguste Renoir (1867–70).**

Perspective

Perspective is a way of creating the illusion of space and depth on a flat surface. You can do this by painting faraway objects much smaller. Lines that move off into the distance in your painting should be made to come closer together the farther away they get. Also, you cannot see a faraway object as clearly as you can one that is closer. By slightly blurring distant objects in your painting, they will seem farther away.

Notice the woman's left hand in the Bellini painting. The edges of the fingers are fuzzier than those on the right hand, which is closer to you. Also notice that the left-hand fingers are short little stumps. Because the hand is pointed away from you, the fingers are *foreshortened* (made to look shorter because they are headed into the distance). In the Tamayo painting, the lines marking the corners of the ceiling and walls are arranged in perspective so that the walls look as if they extend way back behind the guitar player.

Each of these paintings has a style, a mood, and a personality all its own because each of the artists was different. Therefore, each artist's work is unique.

The next time you decide to paint a picture, try experimenting with new ways of using lines, colors, textures, and shapes.

▶ ▶ ▶ ▶ **FIND OUT MORE** ◀ ◀ ◀ ◀

Art; Art History; Cartooning; Color; Design; Dimension; Drawing; Graphic Arts; Miniature; Paint
For individual artists see Index for artist's name.

SOME FAMOUS PAINTERS

Giotto di Bondone, Italian (c. 1266–1337)

Jan van Eyck, Flemish (c. 1387–1440)

Sandro Botticelli, Italian (c. 1444–1510)

Leonardo da Vinci, Italian (1452–1519)

Albrecht Durër, German (1471–1528)

Michelangelo, Italian (1475–1564)

Titian, Italian (1477–1576)

Raphael, Italian (1483–1520)

El Greco, Spanish (c. 1541–1614)

Rubens, Flemish (1577–1640)

Velasquez, Spanish (c. 1599–1666)

Rembrandt van Rijn, Dutch (1606–1669)

Goya, Spanish (1746–1828)

J. M. W. Turner, English (1775–1851)

Edouard Manet, French (1832–1883)

Paul Cezanne, French (1839–1906)

Mary Cassatt, American (1845–1926)

Vincent van Gogh, Dutch (1853–1890)

Vassily Kandinsky, Russian (1866–1944)

Henri Matisse, French (1869–1954)

Edward Hopper, U.S. (1882–1967)

Pablo Picasso, Spanish (1881–1973)

Georgia O'Keefe, American (1887–1986)

LEARN BY DOING

Mix flour or wallpaper paste with powder paint to make a thick colored mixture. Drop a spoonful of the paint mixture onto a sheet of paper. Spread it around with your fingers. You can use pieces of cardboard and sticks to make unusual patterns. Or smear wallpaper paste over the paper, then sprinkle on powder paint and spread with your hands. You can also use a drinking straw to blow drops of watery paint over the paper. Fold the paper in half and press the two sides together. What happens to the pattern?

PAKISTAN

Capital city
Islamabad
(204,000 people)

Area
307,374 square miles
(796,095 sq. km)

Population
122,666,000 people

Government
Islamic republic

Natural resources
Natural gas, coal,
copper, iron ore, oil

Export products
Cotton and cotton
goods, rice, wool
carpets, leather

Unit of money
Rupee

Official languages
Urdu, English

PAKISTAN

A country whose two sections were separated from each other by 1,000 miles (1,600 km) has now been made into two independent countries. Pakistan, formerly made up of West and East Pakistan, is now the name for the western part. Bangladesh has been the new name for East Pakistan since it became an independent country in 1971.

Pakistan covers an area about twice the size of California and has more than three-and-a-half times as many people as that state does. It is bordered by India on the east, Iran on the southwest, Afghanistan on the northwest, and the Arabian Sea on the south. Highlands and towering mountains cover most of western and northern Pakistan. Passes cut through the high mountains in several places. The famous Khyber Pass connects Pakistan with Afghanistan. Islamabad, the country's beautiful capital city, is located in the northern highlands.

Pakistan's chief river is the Indus,

which flows through the eastern half of the country. Wheat, rice, cotton, and other crops are grown on the fertile Punjab and Sind plains along the Indus. Most of Pakistan's people live in these areas. Karachi, the largest city, is on the Sind plain near the Indus River delta. Large deposits of natural gas have been discovered in central Pakistan. Copper and iron ore are in the highlands.

Pakistan, part of India until 1947, was invaded by many Asian peoples through the centuries. The Muslims came in several waves from the early 1000s to the 1500s. The British took control of the whole subcontinent of India in the 1700s.

In 1947, the mostly Muslim areas of India gained independence as Pakistan, which was divided into two widely separated sections. Muhammad Jinnah became Pakistan's first president. Fighting broke out between Muslims and Hindus. About 7 million Muslims fled from India to Pakistan, and about 6 million Hindus left Pakistan for India.

Later, the Bengali Muslims of East Pakistan wanted more self-government. West Pakistan refused their demands and sent troops to East Pakistan in 1971. The Indian army helped the Bengalis defeat the West Pakistan army. Bangladesh, meaning "Bengal nation," was born.

Pakistan is an Islamic republic. The civilian government was ousted in 1977, when a military group took control. The country's state and national assemblies were dissolved. Since 1988, however, there have been elections for civilian governments. Legislation is now moving toward the adoption of Islamic law. There are several million Afghan refugees living in Pakistan.

▶ ▶ ▶ ▶ **FIND OUT MORE** ◀ ◀ ◀ ◀
Bangladesh; India

⚙ PALEONTOLOGY

Living things have been on Earth for more than three billion years. The remains of some plants and animals that lived in the past have been preserved as *fossils*. Generally fossils are rocklike—the original animal or plant tissues have been replaced by substances that form stone. Fossils are also sometimes found in tar, in a mineral called amber, and in ice—these fossils are the preserved remains of the animal or plant.

Animal fossils most commonly include hard body parts, such as bones, teeth, and claws. Some animal fossils are just traces, such as footprints, claw marks, and burrows. Plant fossils are generally found in the form of leaf and stem imprints in rock and coal. But whole *petrified* (stonelike) plant stems and fruits have also been found.

Paleontology uses fossils to study the living things of the ancient past. It is usually thought of as a branch of *geology*—the study of the Earth, including its rocks—because most fossils are found in rocks. Paleontology is divided into two main parts: *paleobotany*, the study of plant fossils, and *paleozoology*, the study of animal fossils.

▶ **Sometimes a shell dissolves in a rock, leaving the "mold" shape. New minerals form a fossil cast.**

Millions of fossils have been found, but many, many more must still be buried in the rocks. The oldest fossils are usually buried the deepest. The very old rocks containing these fossils are exposed to view in only a few places. For this reason, there are gaps in our record of past life. *Paleontologists* (people who work in paleontology) spend much time and effort searching for fossils. They are always hoping that some of the fossils they find will fill in some of the gaps in our record of past life. By studying fossils, they can find out about *evolution*—the way living things change over millions of years.

Paleontology is useful to the oil industry. Paleontologists have found that certain kinds of very tiny fossils are found in and near rocks that contain oil, so finding the fossils helps find the oil.

▶ ▶ ▶ ▶ **FIND OUT MORE** ◀ ◀ ◀ ◀
Dinosaur; Earth History; Evolution; Fossil; Geology; Mammals of the Past; Plants of the Past

⚑ PALESTINE

Palestine is the "Holy Land" of the Bible. It is a region on the eastern coast of the Mediterranean Sea that is sacred to three religions—Christianity, Judaism, and Islam. Judaism and Christianity began here. Israel now covers most of this historic land.

The Phoenicians and Canaanites first lived in Palestine, then called Canaan. Between 1300 and 1100 B.C., tribes of Philistines and Israelites moved in. Palestine is the Hebrew word for *Philistine*. The Israelites slowly conquered the other tribes. Around 1030 B.C., the 12 tribes of the Israelites formed a kingdom.

The kingdom split in half around 933 B.C., becoming Judah (Judea) in the south and Israel in the north. Assyrians and Babylonians invaded. Next, Persians conquered the land. Then Alexander the Great added Palestine to his list of conquests. Egypt claimed it, and then Syria. In 63 B.C., Palestine became part of the Roman Empire and later the Byzantine Empire. And in A.D. 1516, Palestine became a Turkish province. During World War I, Great Britain took it over.

▲ **Baron George Cuvier (1769–1832), who *established* (began) the science of paleontology. He showed that rocks contained fossils of different ages.**

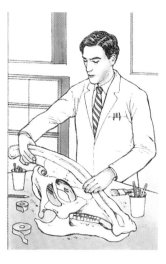

▲ **When paleontologists find fossils, they remove them carefully and take them to a laboratory where they are cleaned and identified.**

One million Arabs from Palestine left their homes and became refugees after the war with the Arab League in 1948. They were scared that Israel would act hostilely toward them.

Dates

Female coconut flower

Coconut

In 1917, the British government issued the Balfour Declaration, which favored the establishment of Palestine as the Jewish homeland. The League of Nations in 1922 appointed Great Britain to rule Palestine as a *mandate*. Part of Palestine had been made into the state of Trans-Jordan by the British in 1920. Jews came from many countries to settle in Palestine in the 1930s. The Arabs of Palestine wanted Palestine to be an Arab state and began fighting the Jews.

In 1947, the U.N. divided Palestine into two states: one Jewish, one Arab. Jerusalem was made an international city, and the British ended their mandate. Five Arab countries attacked the new state of Israel but were turned back. Israel won Jerusalem and other land in the Arab-Israeli War of 1967.

The Palestine Liberation Organization (PLO) was founded in 1964 to create a Palestinian state. The PLO continued bitter border fighting with Israel and withheld information about Israeli soldiers killed in action. In 1991, this information was released, helping to free many Western hostages, such as American Terry Anderson, held in the Middle East. The disputes between the PLO and Israel were one of the key issues of the 1991 Madrid Conference, which began the long process of seeking peace in the Middle East.

In 1993, Israelis and the PLO signed an agreement to settle their differences peacefully.

▶ ▶ ▶ ▶ **FIND OUT MORE** ◀ ◀ ◀ ◀
Dead Sea; Israel; Jerusalem; Jordan; Middle East

◀ Coconut palms are feather-leaved palms that can grow 60 to 100 feet (18 to 30 m) tall. They produce large clusters of coconuts. Thriving near water, they grow naturally on almost all the South Pacific islands. Dates come from the date palm.

PALM

Palms are among the most valuable of all plants. They grow in the warmer parts of the world. Palms provide people who live in tropical lands with a large number of things they need for daily living.

There are more than 2,600 kinds of palms. Most of them are trees, some of which grow more than 100 feet (30 m) tall. But some are shrubs that grow only 3 or 4 feet (90 to 120 cm) tall, and others have vinelike stems several hundred feet long. Most palms are evergreen. They produce leaves, flowers, and fruit all year long. Palms can be divided into two large groups according to the shape of their leaves—those with broad, flat leaves and those with feathery leaves. Most types of palm trees have no branches. The leaves usually form a tuft at the top of the trunk.

Palm leaves are often used to thatch the roofs of tropical houses. The tree trunks are used for timber. Strips of fresh leaves are woven into mats, baskets, and wall screens. Fibers from palm leaves are made into cloth for clothing and hats. Many kinds of palm fruits—including dates and coconuts—are nourishing foods.

Coconut palms are grown commercially for the many useful things they produce. Each coconut is a large one-seeded fruit with an outer tough fiber husk. Within this husk is the coconut you see in grocery stores— the "shell" is actually the hard inner layer of the fruit. Inside the shell is a thick layer of nourishing "meat," which surrounds a hollow filled with coconut "milk." The milk may be fermented to make a beverage. The meat is made into soap, wax, food, and oil. The coconut is an important ingredient in many of the tasty dishes in Indian cooking.

▶ ▶ ▶ ▶ **FIND OUT MORE** ◀ ◀ ◀ ◀
Plant; Plant Distribution; Plant Products; Tree

PANAMA

The Republic of Panama occupies the *isthmus* (narrow piece of land) that connects Central and South America. The Caribbean Sea (a part of the Atlantic Ocean) lies to the north and the Pacific Ocean lies to the south. Panama's eastern border with the South American nation of Colombia is in the jungles of the province of Darién. Its western border is high in the mountains touching the Central American nation of Costa Rica. At 29,208 square miles (75,643 sq. km) in area, Panama is slightly smaller than South Carolina and slightly larger than West Virginia.

Panama has a damp, tropical climate; the wettest region is on the northern side of the isthmus. The Panama Canal *bisects* (cuts into two parts) the country. From the western bank of the canal, the land rises from the low-lying canal area to the *llanos* (plains) of the central provinces, where much rice (Panama's chief crop) and sugarcane are grown. The land rises gradually to a level of more than 11,000 feet (3,350 m) at the extinct volcano Baru near the Costa Rican border. Here, coffee *fincas* (farms) lie on the mountainsides and orange groves in the valleys. Cattle ranches are in the lower land. The center of the cattle industry is the city of David, on the Pacific side of Panama, where modern meat-packing facilities are located. Near the Costa Rican border on both the Atlantic and Pacific coasts lie the banana plantations.

East of the Panama Canal lie the coastal ranges and swampy interior plain of Darién province. This land is chiefly inhabited by two groups of Indians, the Choco and the Cuna. Off Panama's Atlantic Darien coast is the San Blas archipelago, a string of a thousand little islands. The San Blas Indians have lived there since fleeing from the Spanish on the Darién mainland in the 1500s.

Panama's largest city and capital is Panama City, on the Pacific Ocean near the Pacific entrance to the Panama Canal. Tourism has become an important business. The location of the canal has brought shipping business to the city and has made it a small international finance center. Many ships are registered in Panama and fly its flag.

Most of the Panamanians are of mixed Spanish, Indian, and black ancestry. Spanish and English are the main languages spoken there.

Panama was ruled by Spain from about 1519 to 1821, when it became a province of Colombia. Panama later tried to break away from Colombian rule. In 1903, with U.S. help, it gained its independence. Panama then signed a treaty with the United States, giving permission for the construction, maintenance, and defense of an interoceanic canal within an area of Panama (the Panama Canal Zone).

Panama has usually had an unstable government. Since gaining its independence in 1903, the country has had more presidents than the United States has had in all its history. In 1978, two treaties were signed by the United States

PANAMA

Capital city
Panama City
(435,000 people)

Area
29,762 square miles
(77,082 sq. km)

Population
2,418,000 people

Government
Republic

Natural resources
Copper

Export products
Bananas, shrimp, coffee, sugar, clothing

Unit of money
Balboa

Official language
Spanish

In times past, mules were used to pull ships through canals. The powerful electric locomotives that pull ships through the locks of the Panama Canal are still called "mules."

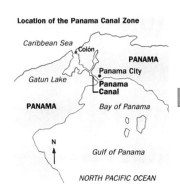

Location of the Panama Canal Zone

Caribbean Sea

Colón

PANAMA

Panama City

Panama Canal

Gatun Lake

PANAMA

Bay of Panama

N

Gulf of Panama

NORTH PACIFIC OCEAN

▼ The Panama Canal is the world's busiest ship canal. A series of locks raises ships 85 feet (26 m) above sea level. The canal gives ships a short route between the Pacific and the Atlantic oceans.

and Panama, providing for Panamanian control of the canal after December 31, 1999. In 1989, U.S. troops landed in Panama and arrested the ruler, General Manuel Noriega. He was later convicted of drug trafficking and money laundering. Guilerma Endara is now president.

▶ ▶ ▶ ▶ **FIND OUT MORE** ◀ ◀ ◀ ◀
Central America; Panama Canal;
South America

PANAMA CANAL

By cutting through the Isthmus of Panama, the Panama Canal connects the Atlantic and Pacific oceans. It also divides North and South America.

The ships of the world depend on this artificial waterway to save them traveling a distance of more than 13,000 miles (21,000 km) around the continent of South America. This was even more true when the Suez Canal in Egypt was closed to shipping from 1967 to 1975. Ships from Europe that once went east to Suez had to sail west to the Panama Canal to reach the Orient.

As a ship approaches the Panama Canal from the Atlantic Ocean at the town of Cristóbal, a Panama Canal pilot comes aboard and takes over the ship from the captain. Only a canal pilot with years of experience can

safely guide today's huge fast ships through the narrow channels, locks, and tricky currents of the canal that was built for small, slower ships of the early 1900s. The canal is 50 miles (80 km) long and at least 300 feet (91 m) wide. One or more pilots (four in the case of huge supertankers) guide the ship through the three sets of Gatun Locks, raising the ship about 28 feet (8.5 m) at a time to a height of 85 feet (26 m) above sea level—the height of Gatun Lake. The ship sails through Gatun Lake in a few hours. From Gatun Lake the ship proceeds into Gaillard Cut—the most hazardous part of the journey. The cut is wide enough here for ships to pass each other. The cut goes through the highest part of the isthmus.

At the end of the Gaillard Cut, the ship enters the Pedro Miguel Locks and goes down one 30-foot (9-m) step. Then it passes through the Miraflores Lake and into the Miraflores Locks. There, two sets of locks take the ship down to sea level in the Pacific Ocean, at the port of Balboa.

From 1881 to 1889, Ferdinand de Lesseps' French company (which had dug the Suez Canal) tried and failed to build a sea-level canal across the Isthmus of Panama. The United States later acquired the French rights and built the Panama Canal from 1904 to 1914. Colonel George Goethals of the U.S. Corps of Engineers headed the project. His ideas for simple, gravity-operated water systems have proved long-lasting in this tropical climate where heat and rust destroy complicated machinery. Colonel William Crawford Gorgas of the U.S. Army Medical Corps led the forces that controlled the yellow fever and malarial mosquitoes that had earlier caused the deaths of many French canal workers.

The Panama Canal is run by the Panama Canal Commission, a joint U.S. and Panamian authority. In 1903, the United States signed a

treaty with Panama and, for an annual payment to Panama, acquired *sovereignty* (full control) over the canal and the ten-mile-wide (16-km-wide) Panama Canal Zone. The zone was returned to Panamian control in 1979, though the U.S. retains access to vital areas of canal operation. Full control of the canal will be given to Panama after December 31, 1999.

▶▶▶▶ **FIND OUT MORE** ◀◀◀◀
Panama

PANDA

Two kinds of bearlike mammals that live in Asia are named panda. They are related to the raccoon family. The panda most often seen in pictures is the *giant panda*. It looks like a big black-and-white teddy bear, with white fur and black rings around its body and a black spot around each eye. It grows to be about 5 feet (1.5 m) tall and can weigh more than 200 pounds (90 kg). The giant panda is a rare animal. It lives in the bamboo forests in the mountains of China and eats chiefly bamboo shoots.

In 1972, the People's Republic of China gave the United States two giant pandas, which were housed in the National Zoo in Washington, D.C. Zoos around the world have begun breeding programs to raise pandas in captivity. In China, wild pandas and their bamboo forest habitats are protected by law. But in the past, many bamboo forests had been destroyed, endangering the giant panda.

The other kind of panda, called the *lesser panda*, resembles the raccoon. The lesser panda is about 2 or 3 feet (60 to 90 cm) long. It looks like a large, furry cat with a long, bushy tail. The tail has rings around it like a raccoon's tail. The lesser panda has white fur on its face and reddish fur on its body and it lives in the Himalaya Mountains. It climbs trees,

sleeps in a hollow tree trunk and eats bamboo shoots and leaves.

▶▶▶▶ **FIND OUT MORE** ◀◀◀◀
Bear; Mammal; Raccoon

PANDORA

To open a Pandora's box is an expression meaning to "let troubles out into the world." In Greek mythology, Pandora was the first *mortal* (human) woman. Her name means "all-gifted." Zeus, ruler of the gods, was angry with Prometheus, who had stolen fire from the gods. So he had the god of fire create Pandora. She was given a box and told never to open it. Zeus wanted her to bring misery to mankind. She was married to Prometheus' brother, Epimetheus, who allowed her to satisfy her curiosity and open the box. All the evils that afflict mankind flew out. Pandora slammed the box shut, saving one blessing—hope.

▶▶▶▶ **FIND OUT MORE** ◀◀◀◀
Mythology

▲ **It was once believed that the giant panda is strictly vegetarian, but some *carnivorous* (meat-eating) pandas have since been observed eating flesh—and also bones!**

Commedia dell'arte was a form of comedy that was popular in Italy. The same characters appeared in each play, and the actors *improvised* (made up) their lines as they went along.

 # PANTOMIME

Pantomime is a kind of entertainment in which actors perform without words. Ancient Roman audiences understood what was going on when the actors made broad gestures. The word *pantomime* comes from the Greek words *panto*, meaning "all," and *mime*, meaning "imitate."

In the 1500s, a form of pantomime called *commedia dell'arte* was developed in Italy. It featured delightful characters named Harlequin, a clown; Columbine, a young maid; and Pantaloon, a father. Pantomime came to England in the 1700s and became enormously popular. It included dancing and music and had clever machinery that made magic seem to happen right on stage. Lavish pantomimes of fairy tales are still performed at Christmastime in England today.

Some of the greatest actors began their careers in pantomime. Charlie Chaplin, Bert Lahr, and Buster Keaton were superb American pantomimists. The world's best known pantomimist is a Frenchman, Marcel Marceau. He and other mimes often play sad, gentle little people who are constantly victimized, or picked on, by others.

Many people enjoy playing a pantomime game called *charades*. A

player silently acts out a word while the others try to guess what it is. Can you act out "pantomime?"

▶ ▶ ▶ ▶ **FIND OUT MORE** ◀ ◀ ◀ ◀
Actors and Acting

PAPER

The world's first maker of paper was the wasp. The wasp chews tiny pieces of wood into a pulp. The pulp mixes with the saliva in the wasp's mouth. The wasp then spits out the wet pulp and smooths it into a thin sheet. When the pulp dries, it becomes paper and is used to build nests.

Today, we write on paper, but thousands of years ago, our ancestors communicated by drawing pictures on stones or animal horns. Later, people wrote on strips of bark from trees, on silk, or on skins of sheep or goats. Animal skins prepared for writing were called *parchment*.

Parchment and silk were costly. Tree bark was easily torn or cracked. People searched for something better to write on. They found it in the plant called *papyrus*, which grew along the Nile River banks in Egypt.

Papyrus is a reed, a kind of grass that grows in wet places. The Egyptians crisscrossed strips of papyrus to make small woven mats. Each mat was soaked in the river to soften the reeds. Then it was taken out, placed on a flat stone, and pounded with

▼ **During the Han dynasty the Chinese made paper by hand. Hemp was cut, mixed with water, and crushed into a paste. This paste was then mixed with ash, steamed, and pulped. Next, the pulped mixture was washed, squeezed, and pressed into frames to dry in the sun.**

another stone. This pounding broke up the fibers in the wet reeds and mashed them together so that they made a flat sheet. The sheet was dried in the sun. It could then be used instead of parchment as a writing surface.

But the first paper, as we know it, was produced in China about A.D. 105. It was made by a process similar to the one used by the wasp. The Chinese mashed tree bark into a wet pulp, squeezed out the water, and pressed the pulp into flat sheets, which dried into paper. The Arabs brought the secret of papermaking to Europe in the 1100s.

Today, paper is made by machines, but the basic process is the same as the one the Chinese used. Most paper is made on the Fourdrinier machine. This machine is named after the two Fourdrinier brothers who built the first one in 1803. It consists of a belt of wire mesh on which watery pulp is spread. The belt passes through a

paper an even smoother finish, called a machine finish. Finally, the paper is wound on spools into large rolls, slit into strips and cut into sheets.

The cheapest paper is made from wood pulp. Better quality paper is made from a pulp mixture of wood and cloth. The finest stationery is made entirely of cloth pulp, or rag fibers, usually cotton or linen. Paper containing rag fibers usually has a *watermark*. A watermark is a design pressed into the wet pulp by the dandy roll. When the pulp dries, the watermark becomes *translucent*— that is, the watermark can be seen clearly only when the paper is held to the light. The watermark may be a picture and may say "rag content."

Paper is used for many purposes besides writing. Money is made from paper. Groceries and other goods are carried in paper bags. Paper cups are used for drinking. Paper labels tell customers what cans of food contain. Books are made of paper. Paper is

The Chinese invented paper in about A.D. 105. In the eighth century, the Arabs captured some Chinese papermakers and took them off to Baghdad. There they started several state-owned paper mills. It was not until 1590 that the first paper mill was founded in England.

▼ Shown below is paper being made from wood pulp. The pulped wood is mixed with water and poured onto a wire mesh belt. The water is squeezed out, leaving a web of fibrous paper. This is then dried, rolled, and usually coated with substances to make it smooth and white.

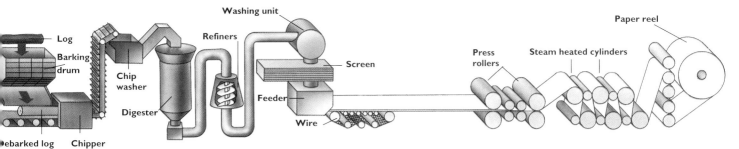

series of rollers, which presses the water out of the pulp. The belt then passes under a turning cylinder, called a *dandy roll*. The dandy roll gives the paper a woven or flat surface.

Near the end of the machine, the belt passes through two felt-covered couching rolls, which press out more water. It then goes through two sets of smooth metal press rolls. The press rolls give the paper a smooth finish. The last step before cutting is *calendering*, or pressing the paper between chilled rollers. Calendering gives the

used as a base for roofing and as a lining for wooden walls. Paper is used for wrapping industrial items. Tissue paper and wax paper are used in homes and offices every day. Nearly everyone reads newspapers and magazines. Artists draw and paint pictures on paper. Many goods come in cardboard boxes, which are paper products; in fact, almost half the paper we use is in the form of packaging.

▶ ▶ ▶ ▶ **FIND OUT MORE** ◀ ◀ ◀ ◀
Lumber and Lumbering

Americans use an average of more than 450 pounds (200 kg) of paper articles per person per year. Recycling newspapers cuts down on some waste.

LEARN BY DOING

You can make a Roman soldier's helmet out of paper. Blow up a balloon until it measures the same size as your head. Tear, or cut up, an old newspaper into very small pieces. Glue these onto the balloon carefully. Keep adding layer after layer until you have a thick, strong helmet shape. When the glue has dried, burst the balloon and trim the shape with scissors. Paint it with silver paint and add some cardboard trimmings. The "plume" can be made from strips of crepe paper.

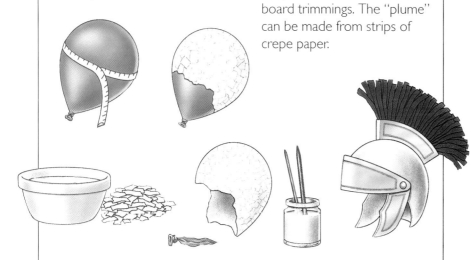

LEARN BY DOING

Here is how to make a paper penguin. 1. and 2. Fold and crease a square along the dotted lines so C meets D. 3. Fold point B up. 4. Fold point B down along the dotted line. 5. Fold and crease so that point F meets point E. 6. Fold point F along the dotted line to make the penguin's foot. 7. Turn the paper over and fold point E to make the other foot. 8. Fold point A down along the dotted line to make the head. 9. Unfold the paper so that the head points up again. Separate the folds of the head and push inward along the central crease. Cut to separate the tail. Fold the tail pieces back so that the penguin will stand. 10. Draw a pair of eyes.

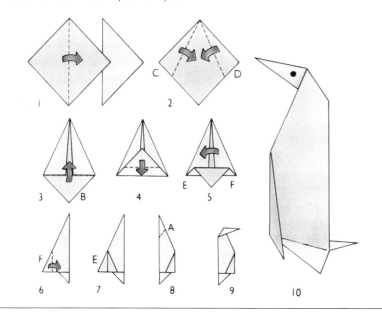

🎭 PAPER SCULPTURE

At Christmastime, many people make colorful paper chains to hang on Christmas trees. In hot weather, people often make fans of folded sheets of paper. Airplanes or gliders can be made from paper. All these are examples of paper sculpture. They are all made by changing flat paper into forms or shapes. The art of paper sculpture is hundreds of years old. Japanese children learn *origami*—the art of folding paper in special ways to make flowers and animals.

Experimenting with Paper Sculpture

You will need strong glue, tape, scissors, and paper for making sculptures. The paper may be construction or poster paper in all colors, typing paper, wallpaper, or brown paper from paper bags. Whichever paper you use, it must be stiff enough to keep the shapes you are folding.

Before making anything very complicated, you should experiment with paper to find out what you can do with it. Try bending and folding the paper in various ways. Try *pleating* it (making folds back and forth, like a fan). You can curl paper by pulling it along the edge of your scissors or wrapping it around a pencil. You can cut spirals from circles or squares by starting at the edge and cutting around and around in a circular or square pattern until you reach the center. Experiment with new ideas.

Papier-Mâché

Papier-mâché is a way of making solid sculpture out of wet paper and paste. Papier-mâché is a French term meaning "chewed paper." In France during the 1700s, old paper posters were ripped up and mixed with glue and paste to make boxes, trays, figurines, and other things.

 **FIND OUT MORE** ◄ ◄ ◄ ◄
Mask; Paper; Sculpture

PAPUA NEW GUINEA

Papua New Guinea occupies the eastern half of the island of New Guinea. It borders on the Indonesian province of Irian Jaya on the west. The country has lowlands along the coasts and dense forests and mountains inland. Until recently much of the country was unexplored by outsiders. Papua New Guinea is a little larger than California.

Papua New Guinea has high temperatures and heavy rainfall all year round. Many of the people live in isolated villages. They grow crops of sweet potatoes, bananas, rice, and fruits, and they also keep pigs. Beef cattle are now being raised on grassland areas.

Agricultural products include coconuts, cocoa, and coffee. Timber

means of communication.

Britain first claimed the southern half in 1884 and then gave it to Australia in 1905. Germany claimed the northern half in 1884, but Australia seized it in World War I. Much of Papua New Guinea was then administered by Australia, first under a League of Nations mandate and later through a U.N. trusteeship. The two parts of the country were given self-government in 1973 and complete independence in 1975.

Papua New Guinea is governed through a national parliament that meets in the capital, Port Moresby. The leader is a prime minister.

▶ ▶ ▶ ▶ **FIND OUT MORE** ◀ ◀ ◀ ◀
Melanesia; New Guinea; Pacific Islands

PAPUA NEW GUINEA

Capital city
Port Moresby
(152,000 people)

Area
178,260 square miles
(461,691 sq. km)

Population
3,671,000 people

Government
Parliamentary state

Natural resources
Copper, gold, silver, natural gas, potential for oil

Export products
Gold, copra, coffee, copper, palm oil, lobster, timber

Unit of money
Kina

Official language
English

and prawns (similar to shrimps) are also important. Copper is the principal mineral export, and some natural gas has been discovered.

The population of Papua New Guinea comes from many native Melanesian tribes, Australians, Europeans, and Chinese. Some 700 local languages are spoken, but *Pidgin* (simplified) *English* is the principal

PARACHUTE

The word *parachute* is a combination of an Italian word *parare*, "to protect", and a French word *chute*, "to fall." The use of the parachute was first suggested by Leonardo da Vinci, but the first practical parachute was not invented until the 1780s. A Frenchman, André Jacques

▲ **A drawing of Leonardo da Vinci's original design for a parachute.**

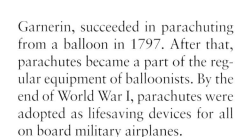

◄When parachutists free-fall, they descend to about 1,970 feet (just over 600 m) before pulling the ripcord to open the parachute pack. When two or more free-fall together, they can link hands and even do acrobatics in the air.

Garnerin, succeeded in parachuting from a balloon in 1797. After that, parachutes became a part of the regular equipment of balloonists. By the end of World War I, parachutes were adopted as lifesaving devices for all on board military airplanes.

During World War II, all the fighting nations transported troops behind enemy lines by plane, landing the soldiers from low altitudes by parachute. In the Korean War, the U.S. Air Force also used parachutes to drop heavy equipment, such as tanks, trucks, and field guns. Paratroopers dropped into the jungles of Southeast Asia during the Vietnam War.

The modern-day parachute is a canopy about 30 feet (9 m) across, made of panels of silk or nylon. A small hole in the center of the canopy lessens the jolt when the parachute opens. A series of shroud lines are sewn into the seams between the panels. The lines pass over the canopy and are connected at the ends by two metal rings. A harness, which fits around the shoulders and body and between the legs, attaches to the rings. The parachute is carefully folded in a canvas container worn on the jumper's back when not in use. The jumper pulls a small *ripcord* to release the folded parachute.

A parachute jumper dives from a plane and pulls the ripcord after about three seconds. The slight delay enables the jumper to fall far enough to be sure the opened parachute does not get entangled in the plane. Once the parachute opens, the jumper descends at a rate of about 17 feet (5 m) a second. The jumper hits the ground with about the same force as if he or she had jumped freely from a height of 10 feet (3 m). Paratroopers

usually jump with their parachutes attached to a static line that opens the parachute automatically.

Parachutes are often used to drop supplies and rescue crews at the sites of accidents, forest fires, and other disasters, where there is no available road or where land travel would take too much time. Spacecraft, manned or unmanned, have been lowered to the ground or into the sea by one parachute or by several parachutes. Supersonic fighter planes release braking parachutes to slow their speed when landing.

The exciting sports of parachute jumping and sky diving have been popular since the 1950s. Sports parachutists aim for pinpoint landings on targets. They often use parachutes with holes in them, so they can control the direction of their descent and landing point. The jumpers are in *free-fall* from the time they jump from the plane to the time they pull their ripcords. During free-fall, a sky diver sometimes delays opening the parachute and makes planned movements. Highly skilled sky divers can control their movements during more than 60 seconds of free-fall and can perform all kinds of acrobatics at more than 12,000 feet (3,500 m) above the ground.

▶▶▶▶ **FIND OUT MORE** ◄◄◄◄
Airplane; Airship; Balloon;
Hang Gliding

PARAGUAY

Paraguay is a South American country surrounded by other countries, so it has no seacoast. Brazil on the east, Bolivia on the north, and Argentina

In sports parachutes, like the one above, the canopy forms an aerofoil, which can be flown like a hang glider. Parachutes also are used to help some types of high-speed vehicles, such as dragsters, to slow down and stop more quickly.

on the south and west border Paraguay. The country, 157,047 square miles (406,720 sq. km) in area, is about the same size as California, but it has less than one-seventh of California's population.

Asunción, the country's capital city, is a busy port on the Paraguay River. The river flows into the Paraná River and into the Rió de la Plata (the large estuary that separates Argentina and Uruguay).

The Paraguay River divides the country into two regions. Eastern Paraguay is made up of a high, forested plateau and wooded hills and plains. Many crops are grown in the fertile eastern grasslands.

Few people live in western Paraguay, called the Chaco, a low plain covered with scrub forest and marshes. Oil and minerals have been found in the Chaco, but much of the land is unexplored. Rivers often overflow their banks in the eastern Chaco, but in the west, the land becomes drier, and water is scarce. Jaguars, *carpinchos* (large rodents), and tapirs live in the Chaco.

Most Paraguayans are *mestizos* (a people of mixed Spanish and Guaraní Indian ancestry) who are farmers. Cotton, soybeans, corn, sugarcane, tobacco, rice, and fruits are grown. Cattle raising is done on large plantations. Some people work in the forests, cutting down hardwood trees for export. Paraguay is one of Latin America's poorest and least industrialized countries. Televisions, radios, and telephones are not commonplace.

The Spanish explorer Juan de Salazar founded the city of Asunción in 1537. Paraguay was ruled by Spain until independence was won in 1811. A major political figure was Solano Lopez, Paraguay's most famous hero. Several dictators have ruled Paraguay. Alfredo Stroessner became president in 1954. He was reelected six times but was overthrown by General Andrés Rodriguez in 1989.

▶ ▶ ▶ ▶ **FIND OUT MORE** ◀ ◀ ◀ ◀
Conquistador; South America; Spanish History

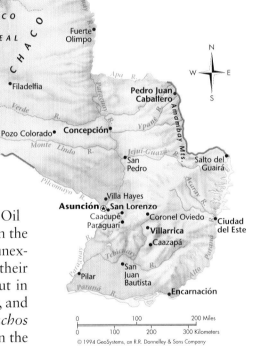

PARASITE

A parasite is an animal or plant that lives off another animal or plant, called a *host*. The parasite gets its nourishment either by taking some of the host's nourishment or by slowly eating the host. Most parasites are harmful to their hosts, but they do not usually kill them. If a parasite kills its host, then it must find another host. Many parasites cannot move on their own, so they die if the host dies.

PARAGUAY

Capital city
Asunción
(568,000 people)

Area
157,048 square miles
(406,752 sq. km)

Population
4,277,000 people

Government
Republic

Natural resources
Iron ore, manganese, limestone, hydroelectric potential

Export products
Cotton, soybeans, lumber, vegetable oils, coffee, tung oil, meat products, tobacco

Unit of money
Guarani

Official language
Spanish

The forests of Paraguay produce *quebracho,* one of the hardest woods in the world. (The name *quebracho* comes from the Spanish language and means "ax-breaker.") The wood is much used in building. The bark of the tree also produces *tannin,* a substance used in tanning leather.

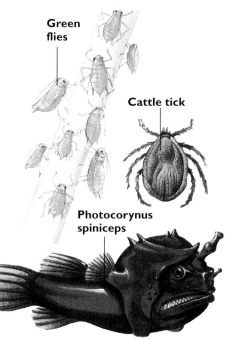

Green flies

Cattle tick

Photocorynus spiniceps

▲ Aphids suck plant sap. The tick lives on farm animals' blood. The male *Photocorynus spiniceps* attaches itself to the much larger female and lives by sucking her blood.

▼ The eggs of parastic flukes (1) hatch into larvae that live in water snails (2). These turn into a second type of larvae that live in water (3). These pass through the skin of human bathers (4) and change into adult flukes living in the gut (5). Their eggs pass out through feces into water (6).

Two kinds of parasites are *external* parasites and *internal* parasites. External means "outside." External parasites live on the outside of their host. Externally parasitic plants, such as mistletoe, send tubes through a host tree's bark to get nourishment. Fleas, mosquitoes, lice, ticks, and bedbugs are external animal parasites. They *pierce* (poke holes in) the host's skin and suck out nourishment. They are often not too different from their relatives that are not parasites.

Internal parasites live inside the host. They are very different from their nonparasitic relatives. Internal parasites have very complicated life cycles. A fairly typical internal parasite is the tapeworm. A tapeworm living in a person's *digestive tract* (stomach and intestines) lays eggs that pass out of the body with wastes.

If the eggs end up in water, they develop into a *larva* (young tapeworm) that can swim around. In order to develop further, the larva must be eaten by a certain kind of shrimp. Then the shrimp must be eaten by a fish. The larva moves from the shrimp to the muscles of the fish, where it *encysts* itself (covers itself with a hard coating). If a person eats the fish without cooking it well, the larva goes into the person's digestive tract, where it changes into an adult tapeworm. To avoid getting tape-

worms, or any of the many other parasitic worms, you should always cook foods well, especially meat and fish.

Although an internal parasite has a very complicated life cycle, it has a very simple body. An adult tapeworm has a *scolex*, or head, with hooks and suckers to hold onto the host. Behind the scolex grows a long chain of segments, which absorb food from the host's stomach. Each segment has male and female sex organs. Eggs are fertilized by sperm from the same tapeworm. When the segments are completely filled with fertilized eggs, they drop off and pass out of the host's body. The eggs grow into parasites.

The tapeworm has close relatives that have eyes, brains, and digestive *cavities* (stomachs). But the tapeworm has no eyes, brain, or stomach. It does not need them to live the kind of parasitic life it leads. Most internal parasites have lost almost everything but the ability to hook onto their host, absorb nourishment, and reproduce.

Some internal parasites are *microscopic*—too small to be seen except through a microscope. Malaria and sleeping sickness are caused by microscopic parasitic animals that are carried to their hosts by flies and mosquitoes. Nest parasites don't attach themselves to the host. They just take food from the host.

Many fungi, bacteria, and viruses are parasitic. Fungi can be internal or external parasites. Athlete's foot is a common disease caused by an external fungus.

Bacteria are microscopic plants that can cause disease and damage body tissue. Viruses are so small that they cannot be seen under an ordinary microscope and so *primitive* (simple) that biologists are not sure if they are living things at all. But viruses can cause a wide variety of diseases, including chicken pox.

Parasites are both very simple and very complicated. They have usually lost the ability to do certain things

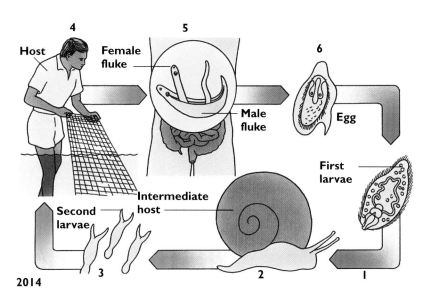

Host

Female fluke

Male fluke

Egg

First larvae

Second larvae

Intermediate host

4   5   6

3   2   1

for themselves, but to make up for this loss, they have developed very complicated ways of getting other animals to do things for them.

▶ ▶ ▶ ▶ **FIND OUT MORE** ◀ ◀ ◀ ◀
Animal; Animal Kingdom; Bacteria; Evolution; Virus

PARASITIC PLANT

Plants that live on and get their food from other live plants or animals are called *parasitic plants*. Almost all parasitic plants lack *chlorophyll*. Chlorophyll is the green coloring matter that makes it possible for most plants to make their own food. Because they cannot make their own food, parasitic plants get their nourishment by taking it from other plants and animals. These plants and animals are referred to as *hosts*.

Almost all bacteria are parasitic plants. So are some kinds of fungi. One parasitic fungus is wheat rust, which kills wheat plants. Dodder is a wiry, leafless plant parasite that destroys alfalfa, clover, and flax.

Mistletoe has some chlorophyll. It makes some of its own food but also grows as a parasite on many kinds of trees. Mistletoe has no true roots. It twines around the host tree. Thin tubes, called *haustoria,* grow from the mistletoe into the bark of the host. The haustoria anchor the mistletoe, and through them, the mistletoe draws sap from the host.

▶ ▶ ▶ ▶ **FIND OUT MORE** ◀ ◀ ◀ ◀
Parasite

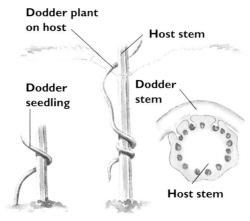

Dodder plant on host

Host stem

Dodder seedling

Dodder stem

Host stem

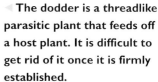

◀ The dodder is a threadlike parasitic plant that feeds off a host plant. It is difficult to get rid of it once it is firmly established.

△ The mistletoe grows on other plants, usually trees. It takes minerals and some water from its host. It also makes some of its own food in its leaves.

PARIS

Paris is the beautiful capital city of France. It is the artistic, commercial, scientific, and theatrical center of the country. Located on the Seine River, Paris is also a transportation center. A great network of rivers, canals, roads, and railroads meets in the city. More than two million people live in the central city of Paris, but about nine million people live in the entire metropolitan area.

Paris is often called the "City of Light," because so many great ideas and cultural achievements began there. The headquarters of UNESCO—the United Nations Educational, Scientific, and Cultural Organization—is in the city. Paris is also an international center of fashion design.

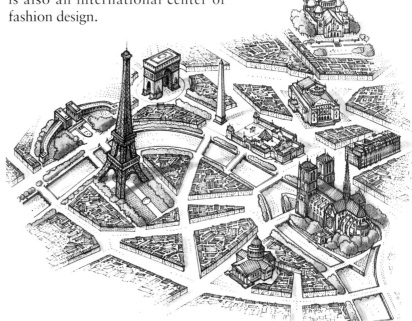

▶ On an island in the middle of the River Seine in Paris stands the Cathedral of Notre Dame. Although Paris has vastly expanded, the cathedral still stands at the heart of France's capital.

▲ **The Pompidou Center, Paris, contains an art museum, an industrial design center, an institute for music and research, and a library. It has brought life to a neglected area and attracts more visitors than the Louvre and Eiffel Tower combined.**

▼ **Central park stands in the center of Manhattan in New York City. With 840 acres (340 hectares) of grass, trees, and hills, it provides a place of escape from the crowded skyscrapers and bustling traffic.**

The Seine River divides the city of Paris in two. Thirty-two bridges cross the river. The oldest, and perhaps the most famous, of these is the Pont Neuf. It was built in the 1500s, but its name means "New Bridge." The Left (south) Bank of the river is popular with artists and students. The Sorbonne, one of the world's oldest universities, is located there. The Right (north) Bank is the business center. The white-domed church of Sacré Coeur (Sacred Heart) is a landmark there. It stands atop Montmartre, the tallest hill in Paris and a beautiful part of the city.

Perhaps the most famous landmark in Paris is the Eiffel Tower. The massive Arc de Triomphe (Arch of Triumph) celebrates French military victories. The Louvre, once a palace for French kings, is now one of the greatest art museums in the world.

Paris is named after a small tribe of Gauls called the Parisii, who built a village on Ile de la Cité in the Seine about 2,000 years ago. The Romans conquered the area and called the village "Lutetia Parisiorum," or "the muddy place of the Parisians." By the 1200s, Paris had become a great medieval center of learning.

▶ ▶ ▶ ▶ **FIND OUT MORE** ◀ ◀ ◀ ◀
Cathedral; France; Gothic Architecture; Louvre

 PARK

Parks are places set aside for public recreation. They offer many things to see and do. Parks may have playgrounds, baseball or football fields, flower gardens, lakes, swimming pools, or even zoos. Most parks have green lawns and trees, paths, and open places where people can take walks, have picnics, or just relax in the sunshine, away from the bustle of everyday life.

The first parks were forests that belonged only to the king. The king hunted antelope, deer, and other animals in his park. Ordinary people could not go into the park at all. In the 1600s and 1700s, nobles and other rich people had laid out different kinds of parks next to their castles and palaces. These parks were landscaped with trees, lakes, and broad lawns and had large flower gardens surrounded by stone walls or fences.

The kings of Prussia had a very lovely park called Sans Souci, which means "without care." The kings of France had large, beautiful parks next to their palaces in Versailles and Paris. Some of the large public parks in London, England, were once the private parks of wealthy nobles. Today, most of these gardens and parks are open to the public. Anyone can visit them and enjoy their beauty.

Parks made especially as places of recreation for ordinary people were first built only about 150 years ago. The best-known public park in the United States is Central Park in New York City. Originally, this land was used for farming. But as the city grew larger, people began to see the need for a public park. The city bought the land in the 1850s and two men, Calvert Vaux and Frederick Law Olmsted, designed the park. They laid out walks and drives, lakes and gardens, great lawns and playing fields, and a band shell, where people could listen to music.

Today, parks are found in almost every city and town. Most of them are owned and operated by local governments. The federal government and state governments have also set aside parks. These are often located in unusually scenic spots or in places of historic significance.

▶ ▶ ▶ ▶ **FIND OUT MORE** ◀ ◀ ◀ ◀
National Park

PARLIAMENT

A parliament is the highest *legislative*, or lawmaking, body in a country. The word *parliament* comes from the French word *parler*, which means "to talk." Thus parliament means a place to talk or debate. The British Parliament dates from 1295 and is one of the oldest. Known as the "Mother of Parliaments," it has been a model for lawmaking bodies the world over. Other countries also use the term "parliament" for their legislatures.

The British parliament is housed in the area of London called Westminster. It consists of two chambers, the House of Lords and the House of Commons. The House of Lords is made up of British *peers*, people who hold titles of nobility. Some titles are passed down from generation to generation. Others are granted for life, as a special honor. Important clergy also sit in the House of Lords. So do senior judges, called law lords. They hear cases appealed to the House of Lords, the highest court.

Members of the House of Commons are elected by the people of Great Britain. Each member represents a different *constituency*, or district. General elections are held at least every five years. Voters are usually offered a choice of representatives from several political parties.

The leader of the party with the most *seats*, or representatives, in parliament usually becomes *prime minister*. The prime minister is the most powerful government leader in the nation, but he or she is bound by law to follow the advice of parliament. (In this way the parliamentary system differs from the United States' *separation of powers*. In the U.S. each of three bodies—the President and executive staff, the Congress, and the Supreme Court—has well-defined limits of power, according to the U.S. Constitution.)

New laws and matters of national policy are discussed by both Houses. A vote is taken, and the legislation is passed if a majority of members favors it. The Lords seldom disagree with decisions made by the Commons. If they do disagree, they can only delay legislation for a period of six months. The Commons is by far the more powerful House. The king or queen of Great Britain must approve all laws before they can be put into practice. In modern times, however, this procedure has become only a formality.

▶ ▶ ▶ ▶ **FIND OUT MORE** ◀ ◀ ◀ ◀
Congress, United States;
Government; Legislature

> A single tree has been named a state park in Wye Mills, Maryland. The Wye Oak is the oldest oak in Maryland—more than 400 years old. It was made a state park in 1940.

▼ **The House of Commons, the legislative assembly of the British parliament, and the famous clocktower of Big Ben, seen behind Westminster Bridge.**

▲ **In the wild, budgerigars are green with yellow and black markings. The fancy colors of pet parakeets are obtained by selective breeding.**

▼ **The brightly colored macaws are becoming endangered, because much of their forest home is being destroyed. They are also caught and sold as pets.**

PARROTS AND PARAKEETS

Parrots are brightly colored birds that live in the warmer parts of the world. There are more than 310 kinds of parrots. They range in size from the pygmy parrot, only 3 inches (7.5 cm) long, to the macaws, which are more than 3 feet (90 cm) long.

Parrots have large beaks. Both the upper and lower parts of their beaks are hinged and can be moved up and down. Parrots use their beaks for cracking nuts and seeds, for smoothing their feathers, and for climbing. Some parrots hang by their beaks. Parrots have four-toed feet. The two front toes and the two rear toes can be closed like fingers of a hand. Parrots often use their feet like hands to hold their food when eating. Parrots also use their feet when climbing. They are among the world's best climbing birds. Most parrots are good fliers, and they walk easily on the ground.

Parrots have loud, harsh voices. The gray parrot of Africa and the green Amazon parrot can easily be taught to "talk." Parrots cannot understand what they say; they simply *mimic*, or imitate, the sounds of words.

Parakeets are middle-sized parrots that live in Australia, Asia, Africa, and the Polynesian islands of the Pacific Ocean. There were once large numbers of parakeets in the southern and eastern United States. But they were killed for their bright feathers, and because they ate fruit crops. The last of these parakeets was seen in 1910. The shell parakeet, or budgerigar ("budgie"), of Australia is a popular cage bird and also a good "talker." Lorikeets are similar to parakeets but are smaller.

Cockatoos are large, crested parrots of Australia and nearby islands. Cockatiels are similar but smaller. The pink cockatoo and the white cockatoo (which has yellow and red

▲ **Many breeds of parrots and parakeets are dying out, because they are killed for their beautiful, bright feathers.**

markings) are kept as pets. Macaws, which live in Central and South America, are the largest and most brightly colored parrots. Macaws can be scarlet and blue; red, yellow, and blue; or yellow and blue. Lovebirds are small, plump African parrots. They choose a mate for life and stay together in pairs.

▶▶▶▶ **FIND OUT MORE** ◀◀◀◀
Birds; Pets

PARTHENON

SEE ACROPOLIS

PARTICLE ACCELERATOR

All matter is made up of atoms. Scientists used to think that the atom was the smallest particle of all, but now they know that the atom itself is made up of even smaller particles. These are called *subatomic particles*.

Atoms are so small that they cannot be seen, even under a microscope. Subatomic particles are very much smaller! The only way that scientists can study them is to break up atoms. They do this using a machine called a

▶ **The two main types of particle accelerators are *linear,* which speed up particles moving in a straight line, and *circular,* such as a cyclotron. In the cyclotron the particles get faster and faster before being turned onto a target.**

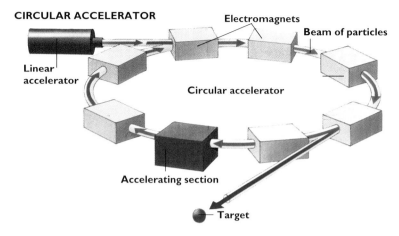

CIRCULAR ACCELERATOR

Electromagnets

Beam of particles

Linear accelerator

Circular accelerator

Accelerating section

Target

LINEAR ACCELERATOR   Beam of particles   Target

particle accelerator. This speeds up subatomic particles until they are traveling close to the velocity of light. When an atom is hit by a particle traveling at this speed, it disintegrates. The subatomic particles fly off in different directions. From the way in which they do this, physicists can tell a great deal about those particles. Today, for example, scientists believe that all matter is made up of subatomic particles called *quarks.* Quarks are believed to come together to form subatomic particles such as *protons, neutrons, and electrons.*

Particle accelerators were first made in the 1920s and 1930s. Modern ones are very big and expensive to build. The simplest type is the *linear accelerator,* or *linac.* The linac belonging to Stanford University in California is 2 miles (3.2 km) long.

Linacs accelerate particles in a straight line. Most big particle accelerators, however, are ring-shaped. In them, particles are accelerated to very high speeds as they travel around the ring. Accelerators of this type are called *synchrotrons.* One of the most important is at work near Geneva, in Switzerland.

▶▶▶▶ **FIND OUT MORE** ◀◀◀◀
Antimatter; Atom; Matter

⚙ **PARTICLE PHYSICS**

Particle physics is a branch of physics that studies the smallest building blocks that form all matter. These tiny building blocks are called *elementary particles.*

People have been trying to discover the smallest bits of matter for nearly 2,500 years. Most ancient Greeks thought that all matter was made up of four elements: earth, air, fire, and water. Others believed that tiny particles called *atoms* lay at the heart of all matter.

From about 1800, most scientists came to accept the theory of atoms. By the early 1900s, it became obvious that there were even smaller particles than atoms. In 1911, the British physicist Ernest Rutherford proved that tiny particles called *electrons* orbited around atoms. Scientists later showed that the core of these atoms consisted of other particles, called *protons* and *neutrons.*

In 1969, the U.S. physicist Murray Gell-Mann won the Nobel prize for his theory proposing that there were even smaller particles. Using a device called a *particle accelerator,* he and a team of physicists got protons and electrons to travel at almost the speed of light. These particles collided and gave off unusual, smaller particles that Gell-Mann called *quarks.*

Gell-Mann's explanation of quarks gave a new understanding of the basic structure of matter and gave birth to the study of particle physics. Quarks and other newly discovered particles, such as *leptons* and *bosons,* became known as elementary particles. They are 100 million times smaller than atoms and some exist

Ernest Walton

John Cockcroft

▲ **In 1932, a British physicist, John Cockcroft (above), and an Irish physicist, Ernest Walton (top), built a particle accelerator and split the atom. They were awarded the Nobel prize in physics (1951).**

▲ Richard Feynman (1918–1988), a U.S. physicist who discovered some of the rules that govern the interactions of subatomic particles. He worked out how particles can interact by exchanging *photons* (quanta of light). He shared the 1965 Nobel prize in physics.

▼ An example of a sentence broken down into adjectives, nouns, verbs, and adverbs.

for only about one-billionth of a second. Scientists now believe that they have succeeded in finding the smallest bits of matter.

Particle physicists now use computers, camera equipment, and accelerators to learn about elementary particles and their behavior. They hope to discover the forces that work on all things at the most basic level.

▶ ▶ ▶ **FIND OUT MORE** ◀ ◀ ◀
Atom; Nuclear Energy; Physics

PARTS OF SPEECH

In a play, actors take the parts of characters. Together, all the characters tell the story as the play is acted out. Each character or role is different from every other. In language, words are like actors. Each word takes a different part to help tell the story of the sentence. And just as in a play, each part is different.

There are eight main parts to our language—nouns, pronouns, verbs, adjectives, adverbs, prepositions, conjunctions, and interjections. These groups are called parts of speech. Every word belongs to one or more of these groups. Which part of speech a word belongs to depends on how the word is used in the sentence. A dictionary will tell you if a word is a noun, adjective, or some other part of speech.

A *noun* is a word that names. The name of everything in the world is a noun. It may be the name of a particular person (Frederick Douglass), a place (America), a thing (encyclope-dia), a quality (thoughtfulness), an idea (patriotism), or a unit of measure (inch). The subject of a sentence (what a sentence is *about*) is always a noun—or a pronoun.

A *pronoun* is a word that can be used in place of a noun to mean the same thing as the noun it replaces. The word *pronoun* means "for a noun." The most common pronouns are called *personal pronouns*. They show the person or persons speaking, or first person (I, we); the person spoken to, or second person (you); or the person or thing being talked about, or third person (he, she, it, they).

A *verb* is a word that expresses some action or a state of being.

LeRoy *threw* the ball.

He *was playing* in the yard.

A verb may be one word, as in the first sentence. A verb may also be more than one word, as in the second sentence. If it is more than one word, it is called a *verb phrase*. The verb is a word that tells you what happens in a sentence.

An *adjective* is a word that says something about a noun or pronoun. The adjective may describe or define the noun or pronoun in some way.

A *good* player needs a lot of energy.

His *dusty* car screeched to a stop.

There are many different types of adjectives. Among those used most often are words called *articles*. *A, an,* and *the* are the most common articles.

An *adverb modifies* (limits the meaning of) a verb, an adjective, or another adverb. An adverb indicates such things as *how, when, where,* or *why* something happened.

Frances arrived *late*. (modifies the verb *arrived*)

Chocolate pudding is an *extremely* sweet dessert. (modifies the adjective *sweet*)

Jim whistled *quite* softly. (modifies the adverb *softly*)

Put your books *down*. (modifies the verb *put*)

A *preposition* is a word or group of words whose purpose is to show

	Adjective		Noun	Verb

The sleek black cat meows sharply at the tiny mouse.

Adverb   Adjective   Noun

the relationship between a noun and another word in the sentence. Ideas about direction, position, source, and time are expressed by prepositions.

The plane flew *into* the sunset.

The lamp hangs low *over* the table.

The children can hardly wait *until* Christmas.

A *conjunction* is a word or group of words that join together other words or groups of words called *phrases* or *clauses*. The most familiar are the conjunctions *and, but, or,* and *nor.*

You *and* I can walk the dog.

I wanted to watch the late news, *but* I was too sleepy.

She doesn't know whether to stay *or* to go.

March seems like neither winter *nor* spring.

An *interjection* is a word or group of words used to express emotion.

Wow! What a game!

Oh, do you have to go already?

For goodness sake! I thought you'd never get here!

Prepositions, conjunctions, and interjections never change in their form (spelling). All other parts of speech change to show such things as how many are or who is (or was, or will be) talking and about whom or what. These changes in the form of words are called *inflections.* The inflection of nouns and pronouns is called *declension.* (For example, *boy* is singular, and *boys* is plural.) The change or inflection of a verb is known as *conjugation* (For example, I *sing,* but he *sings.*) And *comparison* is the word used to describe the inflection of adjectives and adverbs. (Tom is *tall.* His brother is *taller.* But his father is the *tallest* of the three.) These terms are used for inflections in foreign languages, as well as in the English language.

▶ ▶ ▶ ▶ **FIND OUT MORE** ◀ ◀ ◀ ◀
Grammar; Languages

⚙ PASCAL, BLAISE (1623–1662)

Blaise Pascal's father wanted him to be a student of ancient languages. However, the boy, born in Clermont Ferrand, France, proved to be so brilliant at mathematics that his father abandoned his early hopes.

Pascal was a genius. He was only 16 when he published his first math book, on geometry. It was so good that the great French scientist René Descartes refused at first to believe it had been written by someone only 16 years old. Before he was 21, Pascal built a mechanical calculator, or adding machine.

Pascal asked his brother-in-law to help with various experiments on the Earth's atmosphere. These involved climbing high mountains to see if the weight of the atmosphere was less the higher they went. This proved to be the case. An Italian scientist Evangelista Torricelli had done this experiment using a mercury barometer. Pascal did the same, but he used red wine instead of mercury. The barometer he built was 46 feet (14 m) long!

Pascal also concluded that if a *fluid* (liquid or gas) is in a container, the pressure that it exerts on the walls of the container should be the same in all directions. Again, he was proved correct.

▶ ▶ ▶ ▶ **FIND OUT MORE** ◀ ◀ ◀ ◀
Barometer; Fluid

⛩ PASSOVER

The joyful Jewish holiday of Passover *(Pesach)* celebrates the *exodus* (leaving) of the Hebrews from Egypt and their safe flight across the Red Sea.

Passover gets its name from an incident described in the Bible. According to the Old Testament, the Israelites, or Jews, were slaves in Egypt. Moses, a Hebrew prophet, was sent by God to ask the Egyptian

QUIZ

1. What are the eight main parts of speech?

2. The word *gracefully* is which part of speech?

3. Verbs come in different *tenses* to describe actions taking place at different times. What is the past tense of "I see" and "I go"?

4. Name the different parts of speech in this sentence: The *greedy monkey ate* the *grapes quickly.*

(Answers on page 2048)

▲ **Blaise Pascal (1623–1662) was only 20 when he made the first mechanical calculator.**

▲ The Passover feast, or *seder,* is a custom that has been celebrated for many centuries. It is conducted by the head of the family on the first two nights of the eight days of Passover.

▲ Louis Pasteur, who developed vaccines, also discovered that tiny yeast cells turn sugar into alcohol.

pharaoh to free the Hebrews. When the pharaoh refused, God sent ten *plagues* (disasters) against Egypt. The tenth plague was the killing of the eldest son of each family. Through Moses, God instructed the Jews to mark their doorposts with lamb's blood so that the angel of death would "pass over" their houses.

Passover is celebrated for eight days, beginning at sundown on the 14th day of the Jewish month of Nisan. This is usually about the same time as the Christian Holy Week before Easter. In Israel, Passover is celebrated for seven days. Before the first day of Passover, the home must be cleaned thoroughly to remove every crumb of non-Passover food. All meals during the holiday must be prepared and served in pots and dishes that are used only at Passover.

On the first two nights of Passover, a *seder,* a special service and meal, is held in the home. Various special dishes are served, each one symbolizing some hardship undergone by the slaves in Egypt. For instance, a mixture of apples, nuts, and spices represents *mortar,* a building material used in labor for the

Egyptians. Squares of *matzo,* or unleavened bread, are eaten instead of leavened bread throughout the holiday. This is to recall that when the Jews fled from Egypt, they did not have time to put leaven (yeast) in their bread to make it rise. It also recalls the unleavened bread they ate for 40 years after leaving Egypt.

The head of the family leads the others in giving thanks to the Lord and in reading from the *Haggadah,* which tells the story of the Jews in Egypt and their journey to the "Promised Land." The youngest person at the seder asks "Four Questions" about the meaning of Passover. The questions are answered by the person conducting the seder— usually the head of the family. The seder ends with joyous songs, extolling the exodus from Egypt.

▶▶▶▶ **FIND OUT MORE** ◀◀◀◀
Easter; Jewish History

PASTEUR, LOUIS (1822–1895)

Not much more than a century ago, no one knew what caused diseases such as cholera, anthrax, and rabies. Louis Pasteur, a French chemist, discovered that these diseases and many others are caused by *bacteria*, or germs. Because his work launched the science of *bacteriology* (the study of bacteria), Pasteur is called the "Father of Bacteriology."

Pasteur was born in Dole in eastern France. He studied chemistry at a college called the Ecole Normale in Paris. Within a year after his graduation, Pasteur made some very important discoveries about the structure of crystals. Shortly afterward, some French wine makers asked him to find out why their wines were turning sour. Pasteur found that a certain kind of bacteria was the cause. He showed the winemakers how to heat wines gently to kill the bacteria. This process, called *pasteurization*, is also used to kill harmful bacteria in milk.

Pasteur then began to battle disease. He proved that bacteria are living things and that they cause disease. He believed that people could be protected from certain diseases by receiving small infections of the bacteria that cause the diseases. In 1885, Pasteur proved his theory by saving the life of a small boy who had been bitten by a rabid dog. Pasteur prevented the boy from getting rabies by injecting weakened rabies bacteria into him. This method is still used to treat rabies.

▶ ▶ ▶ ▶ **FIND OUT MORE** ◀ ◀ ◀ ◀
Bacteria; Immunity; Medicine

PATENTS AND COPYRIGHTS

Patents and copyrights are legal protection against theft. Just as you would not want anyone to steal your belongings, you would not want any one to claim credit for a song you wrote or a soft drink you invented. Patents and copyrights protect writers, artists, composers, and inventors from people who would use their work without paying for it.

A patent is a grant (like a contract) issued by the government of a country to protect someone's invention from being copied and used by others. Newly manufactured products, machines, designs, and processes can be patented. Even new kinds of plants can be patented! The government must make sure that everything being patented is both useful and brand new, so the granting of a patent may take several years. A patent that is awarded in the United States protects against misuse only in this country.

A U.S. patent is granted to an inventor for 17 years. During that time, all others in the country cannot make, use, or sell his or her inven-

tion. (Patents on designs run for no more than 14 years.) In the United States, only an act of Congress can extend the term of a patent. The term "patent pending" is used to inform the public that an application for a patent is on file in the Patent Office for a certain item. Anyone using these terms falsely to deceive other people can be fined.

Just as a patent is a form of protection for an inventor, a copyright protects an author of a literary, dramatic, musical, or other artistic work. The owner of a copyright is granted by law certain exclusive rights to the work. He or she is given the right to print, reprint, and copy the work; the right to transform and revise the work; and the right to perform and record the work.

Most countries have copyright laws protecting works published by their own citizens. Treaties between some countries provide for copyright protection in all of the countries involved. No one but the author, or those receiving the right from him or her, can legally claim copyright. (Publishers, rather than authors, often obtain copyrights.) To obtain a copyright for a published work, the

> Among some of the more interesting patents issued in the last few years are a quiet alarm clock that will vibrate a pillow, a square ball that bounces exactly like a round one, a garbage collector for removing debris in space, and an electronic "walking stick" for the blind that detects objects in the way and, by means of a voice synthesizer, warns the owner.

▼ **The first elevator with protective safety devices was built by Elisha Otis. He gave a demonstration at a trade fair in New York City in 1854.**

In 60 years, the great inventor Thomas Alva Edison patented no fewer than 1,000 inventions, yet he said that genius was "One percent inspiration and 99 percent perspiration." It took him two years and thousands of experiments to find an effective filament for the incandescent light bulb.

author must publish the work and fill out a copyright application. When registering a claim in the Copyright Office of the Library of Congress after publication, he or she must supply two printed copies of the work.

The term of copyright in the United States begins on the day the work is published with the notice of copyright and runs for the duration of the author's life, plus 50 years.

▶ ▶ ▶ ▶ **FIND OUT MORE** ◀ ◀ ◀ ◀
Book; Invention

PATRICK, SAINT (about A.D. 389–461)

▶ After six years of being a slave, St. Patrick escaped and trained to be a Christian priest. He returned to Ireland in A.D. 435 to convert the Irish to Christianity.

Saint Patrick was the man who brought Christianity to Ireland about 1,500 years ago. Today, Saint Patrick is the *patron,* or special guardian, saint of Ireland. March 17 is Saint Patrick's feast day. This day is a special holiday for Irish people all over the world, when they celebrate the memory of Saint Patrick.

Saint Patrick's family were Christians who lived in ancient Britain. When Patrick was about 16 years old, he was taken prisoner by bandits and sold as a slave in Ireland. He escaped after six years and had many adventures before he returned home. He then had a dream in which the poor people he had known in Ireland asked him to come back to them.

Saint Patrick decided to become a priest and return to Ireland. Most of the Irish were *pagans* at that time. They believed in magic, magicians, and spirits. Saint Patrick spent the rest of his life in Ireland. He taught people about Christianity and founded many churches and monasteries.

▲ Saint Paul, beheaded for his Christian beliefs, is seen here in a fresco in a Spanish church in Barcelona.

▶ ▶ ▶ ▶ **FIND OUT MORE** ◀ ◀ ◀ ◀
Ireland; Saint

PAUL, SAINT (about A.D. 3–67)

Saint Paul was born in Tarsus, Cilicia (now Turkey). His name was originally Saul. His family was Jewish, and Saul studied in Jerusalem to become a teacher of religion. As a young man, he persecuted the followers of Jesus Christ. One day, as told in the New Testament of the Bible, he was traveling to Damascus, Syria. As he came near the city, a light from the sky suddenly flashed around him. He fell to the ground and heard a voice say, "Saul, Saul! Why do you persecute me?" The voice was that of Jesus Christ. This vision made him decide to be a Christian.

He changed his name to Paul and became one of the greatest *apostles* or witnesses of Christ. Everywhere he went, new communities of Christians sprang up. Paul wrote letters called *epistles* to the new communities. Some of these epistles are in the New Testament of the Bible. The letters told the new churches how to carry on their work.

Paul's teachings angered some of the Jews, who did not agree with his ideas. The Roman governors were afraid that he would stir up a rebellion. Paul was put into prison for four years. He was set free, but then was arrested again. In his second trial, Paul was condemned to die. He was beheaded (not crucified) because he was a Roman citizen.

▶ ▶ ▶ ▶ **FIND OUT MORE** ◀ ◀ ◀ ◀
Apostles; Christianity; Missionary; Saint

PAVLOV, IVAN (1849–1936)

Ivan Petrovich Pavlov was a Russian scientist who won the Nobel Prize in 1903 for his study of the digestion of food. He is better known, however, for his discovery of the conditioned reflex.

Pavlov studied medicine at the Military Medical Academy in St. Petersburg. He became a professor at the Academy of Medicine and Surgery in St. Petersburg in 1895, where he did important research.

In his most famous experiments, Pavlov showed food to a hungry dog. The dog drooled saliva. The saliva flowed in the dog's mouth, because it was needed to moisten and digest the food the dog was about to eat. The flow of saliva in the dog's mouth was a kind of *reflex*. Every time Pavlov gave food to the dog, he rang a bell. After Pavlov had done this a number of times, saliva flowed in the dog's mouth whenever it heard the bell, even though no food was in sight. The dog's saliva-producing reflex had been *conditioned* by the sound of the bell. Pavlov's discovery of the conditioned reflex had much influence on the developing science of psychology and the study of behavior.

▶▶▶▶ **FIND OUT MORE** ◀◀◀◀
Circulatory System; Digestion; Nervous System; Nobel Prize; Psychology

PAVLOVA, ANNA (1882–1931)

Anna Pavlova was so weak as a child that her parents feared she might not live. But she grew up to become one of the world's greatest ballet dancers.

Pavlova was born in St. Petersburg, Russia, the child of poor parents. She was taken to see a ballet when she was 8 years old, and from then on she dreamed only of dancing. At age 10, she was accepted at the Imperial Ballet School of the Russian Court, where she spent seven years in training. After graduation she danced small parts at the Imperial Theater. Her dancing was so brilliant that she became a *prima ballerina* (leading dancer).

When Sergei Diaghilev, the great ballet producer, took the Russian Ballet to Paris, Pavlova danced leading parts with his company. Often she was paired with the great dancer, Vaslav Nijinsky. After a time, she formed her own ballet company. Her performances in the United States brought a knowledge of ballet to thousands of people who had never before seen that kind of dancing.

Pavlova was unable to return to Russia after the revolution of 1917. When not on tour with a dance company, she spent her vacations in England. She died of pneumonia while on tour in Holland. Her desire for perfection, her great skill and precise body control, as well as her graceful beauty made her dancing unforgettable. Perhaps the most famous of all her dances was "The Dying Swan," which was *choreographed* (arranged) for her by Michel Fokine. In that dance, she enacted the death of a swan.

▶▶▶▶ **FIND OUT MORE** ◀◀◀◀
Ballet; Dance; Nijinsky, Vaslav

PAWNEES

The Pawnees were a group of tribes originally from the area of what is now Texas. From there they moved about, living throughout the Great Plains, especially in what is now Kansas and the Platte River valley of Nebraska. The Pawnees were both hunters and farmers. They raised crops such as corn, tobacco, squash, and beans in the fertile fields along the rivers. They hunted deer and buffalo. The houses of the Pawnee tribes were made of wooden frames cov-

▲ **Ivan Pavlov (1849–1936) was a Russian biologist who was the first to make a scientific study of learning by association. He discovered a reaction, which he named the *conditioned reflex*.**

▲ **A painting of Anna Pavlova, the great Russian ballerina, exiled from Russia after the 1917 revolution.**

▲ The Pawnee tribe once lived in villages made of a few large earth-covered houses and raised crops. Twice a year they would leave to hunt buffalo on the plains. During this period, they lived in tepees made of animal skins.

▼ A Peace Corps worker is helping prepare teaching materials in a Teacher's Resource Center, Kenya.

ered with earth and animal skins. They used *buckskin* (the skin of deer) to make clothes.

About 10,000 Pawnees lived on the plains during the 1700s. They were organized in small village groups. Children were named according to the mother's family, rather than the father's. The positions of chief and priest were passed on from father to son. Their main gods were the Sun, the Earth Mother, and the Morning Star.

Through a series of treaties, the U.S. Government took over the Pawnee land. Although the Pawnees fought with other tribes, they were friendly with white settlers. Many Pawnee men served as scouts for the U.S. Army during the numerous Native American wars of the 1800s. They also served as guards on the Union Pacific Railroad.

The Pawnee population got smaller as the result of tribal wars, mostly battling against the Sioux. Many Pawnees died from epidemics of cholera and smallpox—diseases of the white people. In 1876, the federal government moved the remaining Pawnee tribe to a reservation in Oklahoma.

▶ ▶ ▶ ▶ **FIND OUT MORE** ◀ ◀ ◀ ◀
Native Americans

PEACE CORPS

The Peace Corps is a United States government agency founded for the purpose of promoting world peace and friendship. The Peace Corps furnishes personnel to aid developing countries. The volunteers are given the opportunity to find out about life in less affluent countries, and the program also helps people in those poorer countries get to know and understand Americans.

Peace Corps members must be at least 18 years old and U.S. citizens. The Peace Corps matches the talents and skills of its volunteers with requests for aid from foreign countries. For example, if an African nation needs a medical technician to give vaccinations, the Peace Corps will send one. Peace Corps volunteers work in over 60 countries, mainly in agriculture, rural development, health, and education.

A person joining the Peace Corps starts a three-month training program. The volunteers learn to adapt their skills to the particular jobs they will have to do. They also learn about the countries where they will work and the language they will speak. The training period prepares them to live and work in other countries for at least two years.

The Peace Corps was founded by President John F. Kennedy in 1961. It proved so popular with Americans that in 1964, the federal government set up a similar program to help poor people in the United States. This program is called VISTA, for Volunteers in Service to America. The Peace Corps, VISTA, and other government volunteer programs became part of an independent Federal Government agency called ACTION in 1971. The Peace Corps was formerly part of the Department of State.

▶ ▶ ▶ ▶ **FIND OUT MORE** ◀ ◀ ◀ ◀
Kennedy, John Fitzgerald

PEANUT

SEE NUT

PEARL

Pearls form inside the shells of certain oysters and other kinds of mollusks. The pearl begins to form when a tiny particle, such as a grain of sand or a living parasite, gets inside the shell. The oyster coats the particle with a layer of smooth material called *nacre*, or *mother-of-pearl*. The nacre protects the body of the oyster from being irritated by the parasite or grain of sand. As time goes by, more layers of nacre are added, and gradually a pearl is formed.

Many mollusks besides oysters form pearls. The conch produces pink pearls. Pearls from some mollusks are a silvery black color. River pearls are produced by freshwater mussels. Cultured pearls are produced when a person places a tiny bead inside the oyster shell. The oyster covers the bead with nacre, and a large, round pearl results. Cultured pearls have been produced since the early 1900s, especially in Japan, where culturing pearls has become a major industry. There are still some pearl divers, people who dive underwater to gather natural oyster pearls.

▶ ▶ ▶ ▶ **FIND OUT MORE** ◀ ◀ ◀ ◀
Clams and Oysters; Gem;
Jewelry; Mollusk

PEARL HARBOR

It was Sunday on December 7, 1941. The blue-green waters of Pearl Harbor on the island of Oahu, Hawaii, were peaceful in the bright sunlight. The powerful battleships and cruisers of the U.S. Pacific Fleet floated at anchor. Headlines in the Sunday newspaper told about Japanese occupation of areas in Indochina, but no one expected trouble in Hawaii.

Suddenly, sirens wailed. Japanese torpedo planes screeched over the fleet. In a surprise attack that lasted less than two hours, about 360 Japanese aircraft pounded 5 battleships into useless hulks and destroyed 188 U.S. airplanes. Japanese submarines also attacked. The attacks severely damaged 13 other vessels.

The Japanese attack came as a complete surprise. People who lived in Honolulu thought at first that the smoke and noise came from make-believe war games. But when the smoke cleared, 2,280 Americans were dead, and nearly 1,200 were wounded.

December 7 marked Japan's entrance into World War II on the side of Germany and Italy. On December 8, the United States declared that a state of war had existed with Japan since the attack. President Franklin Roosevelt declared that December 7, 1941, was "a day that would live in infamy." Remember Pearl Harbor became a slogan during World War II.

▶ ▶ ▶ ▶ **FIND OUT MORE** ◀ ◀ ◀ ◀
Hawaii; Japan; World War II

The upper half of the oyster's crinkly shell is flat and sits on the saucer-shaped lower half like a lid.

The oysters we eat do not produce valuable pearls. The pearls of edible oysters are dull and do not gleam.

The attack by the Japanese naval air forces on Pearl Harbor brought the United States into World War II. Today, the U.S.S. *Arizona* Memorial, built over the wreck of the battleship that was destroyed in the attack, honors those who died at Pearl Harbor.

▲ Lester Pearson resigned as prime minister and as head of Canada's Liberal Party in 1968. He was succeeded by Pierre Trudeau.

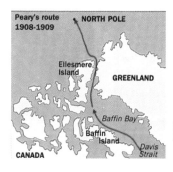

▲ Robert Peary and his team set off from Ellesmere Island in northern Canada, on March 1, 1909, for what was finally to be a successful trip to the North Pole.

PEARSON, LESTER (1897–1972)

The Canadian statesman Lester Bowles Pearson served as prime minister of Canada from 1963 to 1968. As an international diplomat, he worked for world peace.

Lester Pearson was born in Toronto, Canada. He joined the Canadian army at the outbreak of World War I, in 1914. After the war, he studied at the University of Toronto and won a scholarship to Oxford University, in England.

In 1928, Pearson joined the Canadian Department of External Affairs, which is similar to the U.S. Department of State. He served as ambassador to the United States from 1945 to 1946. Two years later, Pearson was elected a member of the Canadian parliament and appointed secretary of state for external affairs.

Pearson played a major part in the creation of the United Nations organization. He served as president of the United Nations General Assembly from 1952 to 1953. He also helped to found the North Atlantic Treaty Organization (NATO). Pearson was responsible for the United Nations settlement of the Suez Canal crisis in 1956, after Israel, Great Britain, and France had invaded Egypt. For this he was awarded the Nobel Peace Prize.

Pearson worked to build Canada's friendship with the United States, Great Britain, and other countries.

▶ ▶ ▶ ▶ **FIND OUT MORE** ◀ ◀ ◀ ◀
Canada; Trudeau, Pierre

PEARY, ROBERT (1856–1920)

Robert Edwin Peary was born in Cresson Springs, Pennsylvania. In 1881, he became a lieutenant in the U.S. Navy, working with the civil engineer corps. Between 1886 and 1897, Peary led several expeditions to Greenland. Among the valuable contributions he made to science were the proof that Greenland was an island and the discovery of large meteorites on Melville Bay. He tried unsuccessfully to reach the North Pole in 1902 and 1906.

On July 17, 1908, Peary sailed from New York City on his final expedition to the North Pole. The ship sailed northward for two months before the ice prevented it from going further. The crew lived on the ice-bound ship through the long Arctic winter. On March 1, 1909, Peary set out for the North Pole, about 450 miles (720 km) away. With him were 24 people on 19 *sledges* (sleds), pulled by 133 *huskies* (Eskimo dogs).

The entire route lay across floating ice, or ice floes. When they came to lanes of open water, they had to wait until the lanes closed up or froze over. If the ice cracked while they were on it, they might be stranded on the ice floe. One of Peary's men did fall into the icy water and died before the others could reach him. Most members of the expedition went only a part of the way, clearing a path, building igloos, and storing supplies to be used by the returning explorers.

On March 31, Peary and his fellow explorer, Matthew Henson, started the final march to the Pole. With them were four Eskimos and their dogs. On April 6, 1909, after taking readings from various instruments, Peary discovered that he had reached the North Pole. The next day, he planted the U.S. flag.

When he returned, Peary found that another explorer, Frederick Cook, claimed to have reached the Pole before him. The records of both men were studied. In 1910, the U.S. Congress decided by a special vote that Peary's claim was the real one. He was promoted to the rank of rear admiral in 1911.

▶ ▶ ▶ ▶ **FIND OUT MORE** ◀ ◀ ◀ ◀
Arctic; Exploration; Greenland; Henson, Matthew

PECOS BILL

When pioneers settled the American Southwest, they encountered many hardships. The land was rough and everyday life was hard and often lonely. In order to keep themselves amused, cowboys began telling tales about an imaginary "super cowboy" named Pecos Bill. Although there was never a real Pecos Bill, his fame grew as the tales about him were written down and published for everyone to read. Edward O'Reilly wrote some of the first Pecos Bill stories, which were published in *The Century Magazine* in the early 1900s.

According to stories, Pecos Bill fell out of his pioneer family's wagon when he was a baby. A pack of coyotes found him and raised him as one of their own. Pecos Bill grew up believing he was a coyote—until he noticed that he had no tail! Some of the amazing things Pecos Bill was said to have done were riding a cyclone, lassoing a railroad train, and digging the Rio Grande to get water for his cattle.

No one knows what became of Pecos Bill. One story tells how he put fish hooks and barbed wire into his whiskey to make it stronger—and died from indigestion.

▶▶▶▶ **FIND OUT MORE** ◀◀◀◀
Bunyan, Paul; Legend

PEKING

SEE BEIJING

PELICAN

A pelican is a large, web-footed, fish-eating bird. Pelicans range from 4 to 6 feet (1.2 to 1.8 m) long and have very powerful wings, with wing spreads of up to 10 feet (3 m). They have long beaks. The upper half of a pelican's beak is hooked at the end.

The lower half consists of an elastic pouch of skin that is attached to the neck. The pelican uses the pouch as a scoop to catch fish, which it swallows soon after it catches them. Young pelicans feed on half-digested fish brought up from the stomach into the pouch of the parent.

There are ten different kinds of pelicans distributed throughout the warm and temperate parts of the world. North American pelicans include the white pelican (the largest type of all) and the brown pelican.

White pelicans live in large colonies, usually on an island. Their nests are crude heaps of earth, gravel, and rubbish, in which they lay one to four white eggs. Brown pelicans nest in low trees. White pelicans catch fish by chasing them in the water. Brown pelicans dive upon fish to catch them.

▶▶▶▶ **FIND OUT MORE** ◀◀◀◀
Bird

▲ The tall stories surrounding the *fictional* (make-believe) character of Pecos Bill includes one that describes how he managed to ride a cyclone!

▼ The pelican drains the water out of its pouch, then gulps down any fish that it has managed to catch. Pelicans use their long beaks, to push shoals of fish into shallow waters where they can be more easily caught.

A pendulum is a *bob,* or weight, on the end of a string. When the weight swings out to one side, gravity pulls it back again. If left to swing, air resistance slows it to a halt.

The use of the pendulum to regulate clocks was first suggested by the great Italian scientist Galileo. While in Pisa cathedral during his first year at the university there, Galileo noticed that a lamp hanging from the ceiling was swinging to and fro with a very regular motion. He timed the swings by feeling the pulse on his wrist and discovered that as the distance of the swings grew less, the lamp slowed down. Each swing took exactly the same time whether the swing was big or small. Galileo was only 17 when he made this discovery.

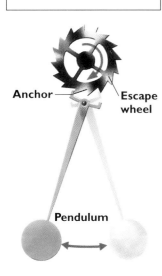

Anchor — Escape wheel

Pendulum

In a pendulum clock, the movement of the pendulum is transmitted to the hands of the clock through the *escapement,* made up of an escape wheel and anchor.

2030

☼ PENDULUM

Cuckoo clocks and grandfather clocks have pendulums. A clock pendulum is very simple. It is nothing more than a weight that swings on the end of a long metal rod. The pendulum makes the clock keep accurate time.

Watch a clock pendulum very closely. Notice that it does not slow down or speed up. It swings back and forth at a constant speed. A pendulum will slow down eventually, if it is left to swing by itself. But clocks have a special device, called an *escapement,* that gives the pendulum a tiny push at regular intervals. This tiny push keeps the pendulum swinging steadily. The escapement is driven by a spring or by a falling weight.

The weight on the end of the pendulum's rod is called the *bob.* A heavy bob will keep a pendulum swinging for a very long time. But it is the length of the rod that determines how fast the pendulum swings. If the pendulum has a long rod, the bob swings slowly. If the rod is short, the pendulum swings back and forth quickly. This is why the short pendulum on a cuckoo clock moves faster than the long pendulum on a grandfather clock.

The Foucault Pendulum

A French scientist, Jean Bernard Léon Foucault, invented a pendulum in 1851 that proved that the Earth turns. The Foucault pendulum is a very long wire with a heavy bob. It is usually hung from the ceiling so that it is free to swing to and fro in any direction. Sometimes the bottom of the bob is pointed, and it makes a mark in a circle of sand beneath the pendulum when it swings through its course. As long as nothing interferes with the swinging of the bob, the bob will con-

Bob

Movement

tinue to swing back and forth in the same direction through space. But the marks it makes in the sand will change, covering more and more of the circle. It looks as if the pendulum has been swinging in a circle.

Scientists know that, according to the laws of nature, the pendulum has kept on swinging in the same direction in space. It is the Earth that has turned around under the pendulum, changing the position of the circle of sand.

▶▶▶▶ **FIND OUT MORE** ◀◀◀◀
Clocks and Watches; Earth

❀ PENGUIN

Penguins are flightless swimming birds. They live in the Southern Hemisphere from the Antarctic regions to the Galápagos Islands, which are near the equator in the Pacific Ocean west of Ecuador. The 18 kinds of penguins range in height from 12 to 48 inches (30 to 120 cm).

Penguins look like small people in dress suits. They are white in the front, with black or blue-gray on the back and shoulders. In some species, the white feathers have patches of yellow or orange. The feathers of all species are tiny and thick.

Penguins' wings are rigid because they have no joints. The wings are useless for flight, but they make excellent flippers for swimming. When swimming, a penguin moves its wings together like oars—forward, then backward. Penguins stand erect on land because their short legs are placed so far back on their bodies. They walk slowly with a comically dignified waddle. However, penguins can move rapidly over ice and snow by sliding on their breasts and bellies.

Penguins feed on fish, crustaceans, and other sea animals, which they catch while in the water. A thick layer of body fat keeps them warm and enables them to go for long periods of time without eating.

At breeding time, penguins gather on land in large colonies. The female usually lays only one or two eggs. The male and female of most species take turns incubating the eggs. In some species, the eggs are kept warm in a pouch above the penguin's feet. The birds go without food during the 18 days it takes the eggs to hatch. Newly hatched penguin chicks are covered with grayish, downy feathers. The male of some species feeds the baby for a short time on a liquid food he brings up from his own stomach. Both parents usually share the responsibility of feeding the chicks' partly digested food.

The Antarctic emperor penguin, which is about 4 feet (120 cm) tall, is the largest species. The males incubate the eggs on their feet. The smallest penguin, about 12 inches (30 cm) tall, is the blue penguin of southern

▲ The male emperor penguin warms an egg between his legs for two months.

Australia and New Zealand. The jackass (or blackfoot) penguin of southern South America and South Africa is named for its braying, similar to that of a jackass.

▶ ▶ ▶ ▶ **FIND OUT MORE** ◀ ◀ ◀ ◀
Bird; Flightless Birds

PENICILLIN

SEE ANTIBIOTIC

PENN, WILLIAM (1644–1718)

William Penn, an English Quaker, founded the city of Philadelphia and the colony (now the state) of Pennsylvania. Penn, born in London, England, was converted to Quakerism while he was studying at Oxford University. Little religious freedom existed in England at that time, and the Society of Friends (the Quakers) was treated unfairly. Penn was imprisoned for writing religious and political essays based on Quaker beliefs.

In 1681, King Charles II gave Penn a grant of territory in North America in payment for a debt owed to Penn's father. Penn sent colonists to settle there, and then he sailed for America in 1682. He established friendly relations with the Native Americans, whom he generally treated fairly. Penn planned and named the city of Philadelphia. During his nearly 30 years as governor of Pennsylvania, he based the colony's government on Quaker ideals: peace, religious freedom, and democratic government. Because of this, many Quakers followed Penn to the new colony.

Penn had to return to England on business in 1701. He became very ill there and was never able to go back to the colony he had founded.

▶ ▶ ▶ ▶ **FIND OUT MORE** ◀ ◀ ◀ ◀
Pennsylvania; Society of Friends

Gentoo

Macaroni penguin

Chinstrap penguin

▲ **Chinstrap, macaroni, and gentoo penguins all breed on sub-Antarctic islands. All penguins live in the Southern Hemisphere and come ashore to raise their young.**

▲ **William Penn named Pennsylvania a "holy experiment" where people could worship freely.**

PENNSYLVANIA

Pennsylvania is called the "Keystone State" because it was in the center of the original 13 states. Six states were north and east of it, and 6 states were south of it.

Pennsylvania is one of the Middle Atlantic States. It is bordered on the north by Lake Erie and New York and on the east by the Delaware River, which separates the state from New York and New Jersey. Ohio and West Virginia are to the west, and West Virginia, Maryland, and Delaware border Pennsylvania on the south.

▲ The tranquil setting of an Amish farm in Lancaster County, Pennsylvania. The Amish are a people who live a simple life, in a community organized around strict rules.

The Land and Climate

Pennsylvania is mostly highland. It has two small lowlands. One is a narrow strip of plain beside Lake Erie. The other is part of the Atlantic Coastal Plain, along the Delaware River. All the rest of the state is in a highland, the Appalachian mountain system. Northern and western Pennsylvania are in the part called the Allegheny Plateau, formed by parallel mountain ranges curving through the center of the state. They begin at the Maryland border and run to the Delaware River. In the southeast is the rolling Piedmont, also running between Maryland and the Delaware River.

Two long rivers cut through the Appalachians in eastern Pennsylvania. One is the Susquehanna, and the other is the Delaware, which forms the state's eastern border.

Pennsylvania has a varied climate. The Allegheny Plateau is cold in winter. In summer, its ridges are pleasantly cool. The valleys between the ridges, however, are quite warm then. Summers in the Piedmont and on the strip of Atlantic Coastal Plain are long and hot, and the winters are mild. Mountains protect southeastern Pennsylvania from cold northwest winds. Rain and summer warmth help farming.

History

The most important Native Americans there were the Lenni-Lenape, who also lived in the valley of the Delaware River. They are usually called Delawares.

Swedish people were the first Europeans to settle in Pennsylvania. They had a colony in Delaware. Some of them moved a short distance north on the Delaware River. In 1643, they built a fort on an island. On the Pennsylvania side of the river, they built a village named Upland. In 1655, the Dutch made the Swedish settlements part of New Netherland. Nine years later, the English took over New Netherland, including the Swedish settlements.

Pennsylvania is also called the "Quaker State." The Quaker William Penn sent colonists from England to found the colony of Pennsylvania (meaning "Penn forest land") in 1681. Penn himself came a year later. Penn changed the name of the town of Upland to Chester. He signed treaties of friendship with the Delaware tribes and purchased land from them. He founded the city of Philadelphia.

The colony of Pennsylvania attracted settlers from many countries. Welsh Quakers, German Mennonites, Moravians, Italian and French religious groups, and people from other colonies came. Most of the early

STATE SYMBOLS

◄ The ruffed grouse is a wild game bird about the size of a chicken, but slightly plumper.

▼ The hemlock tree is a member of the pine family. Unlike the hemlock plant, it is not poisonous.

▲ In 1923, Governor Gifford Pinchot selected the mountain laurel as the state flower.

► The state seal depicts an eagle above a sailing ship, plow, sheaves of wheat, ears of corn, and an olive branch.

PENNSYLVANIA

Capital
Harrisburg
(52,376 people)

Area
45,308 square miles
(117,338 sq. km)
Rank: 33rd

Population
11,961,074 people
Rank: 5th

Statehood
December 12, 1787

Principal rivers
Allegheny River
Susquehanna River
Monongahela River
Delaware River

Highest point
Mt. Davis
3,213 feet (980 m)

Largest city
Philadelphia
(1,585,577 people)

Motto
"Virtue, Liberty and Independence"

Song
None

Famous people
James Buchanan, Stephen Foster, Martha Graham, Arnold Palmer, Betsy Ross, Benjamin West

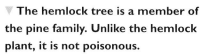

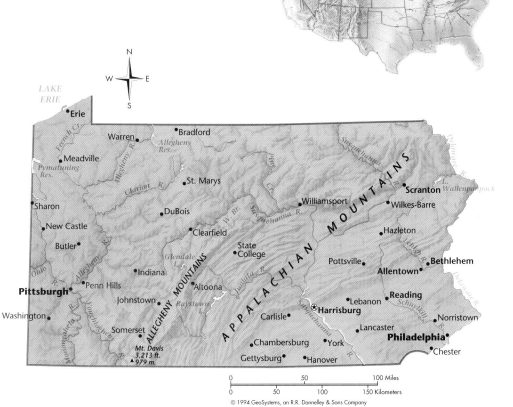

© 1994 GeoSystems, an R.R. Donnelley & Sons Company

Philadelphia, the largest city in Pennsylvania, is the fifth largest city in the United States. With its metropolitan area (including Trenton and Wilmington), Philadelphia has nearly 6 million inhabitants.

The triangular area between the Allegheny River (left) and the Monongahela River (right) is known as the Golden triangle. It is the major business center of Pittsburgh. On the tip is Point State Park.

colonists were Quakers from England, Wales, and Scotland. Germans who settled in Pennsylvania after the 1680s lived in their own groups on farms and spoke in a German dialect, which became known as "Pennsylvania Dutch."

The French built Fort Duquesne where Pittsburgh stands today. After the British won the French and Indian War of the 1700s, a British fort was built on the ruins of Fort Duquesne and was named Fort Pitt, after Britain's prime minister.

Pennsylvania played a big part in the Revolutionary War. The First Continental Congress met in Philadelphia in 1774. The Declaration of Independence was adopted in 1776 by the Second Continental Congress in Philadelphia's Independence Hall.

The Constitution of the United States was drawn up in Philadelphia. Delaware was the first state to *ratify* (approve) the Constitution and Pennsylvania was the second.

Coal mining boomed in Pennsylvania, as did the making of iron and, later, steel. Where rivers weren't deep enough for boats, canals were dug. Railroads were built. Pennsylvania grew into a state of miners and factory workers, as well as farmers.

During the Civil War, Pennsylvania was the only Northern state to be the site of a major battle. Confederates under General Robert E. Lee invaded it in 1863, but they were turned back at the Battle of Gettysburg, a turning point in the war.

Working in Pennsylvania

After the Civil War, the coal, steel, and oil industries expanded greatly in Pennsylvania. The Pittsburgh area in the west became a factory center. In the east, industry grew in the towns of Scranton, Reading, Easton, Allentown, and Bethlehem. Ships were built along the coast.

Pennsylvania is a good location for manufacturing. Millions of customers live in or near the state. Transportation by water, rail, and road is available. Iron ore from Minnesota can reach Pennsylvania easily by way of the Great Lakes. Ships from Philadelphia can reach the Atlantic Ocean by way of the Delaware River and Delaware Bay. Pittsburgh, a city with great iron and steel mills, is also an important river port. It is located where the Monongahela and Allegheny rivers join to make the Ohio River.

Nearly all the country's *anthracite* (hard) coal is mined in the state, which also has large deposits of *bituminous* (soft) coal. Petroleum, natural gas, and other minerals are found in the state. Pennsylvania leads in the making of iron and steel. The decline in heavy industry in the 1980s hit Pennsylvania hard. Many Pennsylvanians lost their jobs, and Pittsburgh's population dropped by more than 12 percent.

Other important industries include textiles, paper, lumber, and food products. On the farms, many fruits and vegetables are grown to supply city markets. Farms also yield livestock and dairy products.

The Pocono Mountains and many other woodland areas of Pennsylvania provide places to ski or to enjoy camping, boating, fishing, and hunting.

Historical areas also draw tourists to the state to view the restored Independence Hall at Philadelphia and walk on Revolutionary battlegrounds. Brandywine State Park near Delaware marks an old battlefield. British and German troops defeated the outnumbered Americans there in 1777. Washington's ragged little army camped at Valley Forge in Pennsylvania. The Valley Forge State Park has huts like those in which the soldiers lived. At the old ironworks in Hopewell Village National Historic Site, cannon were cast for General Washington.

▶▶▶▶ **FIND OUT MORE** ◀◀◀◀

Appalachian Mountains; Constitution, United States; Declaration of Independence; French and Indian War; Gettysburg Address; Independence Hall; Liberty Bell; Penn, William; Philadelphia; Society of Friends

PENS AND PENCILS

Pens and pencils are instruments used for writing. Pens are used for writing with ink. Pencils may contain one of several writing substances—graphite and clay, slate, or wax.

Probably the first writing instruments were sharp pieces of rock or bone. The ancient Egyptians and Greeks made pens from the reeds of the calamus plant. In the 100s B.C., the Romans began using *quills* (large, strong tail feathers of birds, such as geese and swans) as pens. The word *pen* comes from the Latin word *penna*, meaning "feather." Quills were widely used from the A.D. 700s to the 1800s, when metal pens were first made. These pens consisted of a *nib*, or metal pen point, attached to a wooden holder. As with the quill, the nib was dipped in ink for writing. Metal pens and holders are still used today, but mostly for special kinds of lettering.

These metal pens were replaced by more efficient pens. In 1884, Lewis E. Waterman, an American inventor, patented an improved *fountain pen*. It has an ink barrel in the holder and a metal point, permanently attached. The even flow of ink from the barrel to the point is controlled by an automatic "feeder," which releases ink to the tip as it is needed. Many fountain pens have disposable ink cartridges.

Ballpoint pens, first sold in 1946, also carry their own ink supply. But that ink is thicker and greasier than ordinary ink. Instead of a sharp point, a ballpoint pen has a tiny metal ball that turns, releasing ink evenly.

Two other types of pens in use today are *felt-tip marker pens*, first sold in 1951, and *fiber-tip marker pens*, introduced in the early 1960s. These pens can be used to write on paper, glass, plastic, and metal.

The lead pencil, another important tool for writing, has no lead in it at all! Lead was once used in pencils, so the modern pencil became known by the same name. The "lead" pencils most often used today consist of a mixture of *graphite* (a soft, black mineral) and clay encased in a painted wood covering.

Colored pencils are usually made of chalk, clay, or wax, mixed with coloring pigments. They may have wood casings, or they may have a strip of paper wound around them.

In modern graphite pencil factories, powdered graphite is mixed with water and clay to form the "leads." The more clay used, the harder the lead will be. (Soft

America's oil industry was born near Titusville in northwestern Pennsylvania. The first oil well was drilled there in August 1859 by a blacksmith, "Uncle Billy" Smith. He was working for Edwin Drake, a retired railroad conductor.

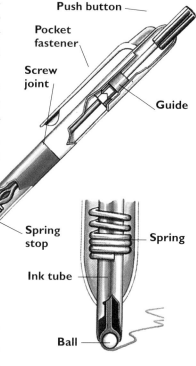

▲ Inside a ballpoint pen is a thin tube of ink. At the tip of the tube is an opening with a tiny ball in it. Many ballpoint pens have push-button actions that push the ink tube forward when it is needed for writing and retract it when it is not.

◀ The so-called "lead" in our pencils today is a mixture of clay and *graphite*. Graphite, once known as plumbago, is a form of pure carbon.

▲ Soft pencils make thick black lines. They are better for drawing a picture with shading, but care must be taken not to smudge the outline. Hard pencils make a fine, crisp line and are more useful for technical drawing.

pencils make a dark, thick line. Hard pencils make a light, thin line.) The pencil leads are inserted into the grooves in little slabs of wood. Other grooved slabs are glued over them. Machines then divide the slabs into pencils. Afterward, the pencils are polished and painted. Erasers are often attached on one end. The maker's name and a number indicating the pencil's softness are stamped on one side. The softest pencil is number 1 (mostly graphite), and the hardest is number 4 (mostly clay). The most widely used pencils are numbers 2 and 3.

▶▶▶▶ **FIND OUT MORE** ◀◀◀◀

Ink

⚙ PERCENTAGE

In mathematics you often have to work with parts of something. For example, you might want to know what part of all the voters cast votes for Mr. Pumpernickel. You can write this in fractions by saying that $\frac{3}{5}$ (three-fifths) of the voters voted for Mr. Pumpernickel.

Percentage is a way of writing a fraction. Percentage fractions always have a denominator of 100. ($20\% = \frac{20}{100}$ or $\frac{1}{5}$. $75\% = \frac{75}{100}$ or $\frac{3}{4}$.) The % sign means "percent." It comes from the Latin phrase *per centum*, meaning "per hundred." If $\frac{3}{5}$ of the people voted for Mr. Pumpernickel, this means that 60% (60 out of every 100) voted for him ($60\% = \frac{60}{100}$ or $\frac{3}{5}$). If 100% of the people voted for him, that would mean everyone ($\frac{100}{100}$) voted for him.

Stores often use percentages when having a sale. Let's say a bicycle that usually costs $220 is on sale for 20% off. This means the sale price is 20% lower than the regular price. $20\% = \frac{20}{100}$ or $\frac{1}{5}$. One-fifth of $220 is $44, which means that the bicycle is on sale for $44 less, or $176.

Percentage is easily written in dec-

imal numbers. To change from percentage to decimal, put the decimal point two places to the left in the percent number (60% = .60). If 60% of 17,640 people voted for Mr. Pumpernickel and you want to know the exact number of people who voted for him, just multiply 17,640 x .60 to get 10,584 Pumpernickel voters.

▶▶▶▶ **FIND OUT MORE** ◀◀◀◀
Decimal Number; Fraction;
Mathematics; Number

🎭 PERCUSSION INSTRUMENTS

If you have ever beaten a drum, shaken a rattle, or hit a tambourine, then you have played a percussion instrument. Percussion instruments are those that produce sound by being struck or shaken. In a band or orchestra, percussion instruments play the rhythm. Many percussion instruments have no definite pitch and so cannot play melodies. You cannot play a tune on a bass drum, for example. But pianos, xylophones, kettledrums, chimes, and sets of bells can sound various pitches and are able to play melodies.

The tone of a percussion instrument is made by striking metal (triangles, bells, chimes, gongs, cymbals), wood (rattles, woodblocks, castanets), or a stretched skin (drums, tambourines). The tone quality of each instrument depends on the material it is made of, as well as the way it is struck. In playing a drum, you can strike it with a wooden drumstick to produce a sharp, clear sound. Hitting it with a padded stick produces a duller, muffled sound. Hitting or rubbing the drum with a brushlike drumstick produces a swishy, crackling, or scratchy sound. Striking a drum with your hands produces a variety of different sounds.

Piano tone is produced by felt-covered *mallets* (hammers) striking

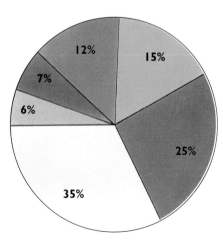

▲ The above pie chart shows pieces of a whole illustrated as percentages. You can see that the percentages all add up to 100 percent.

against tight metal strings each time a key is pressed. Kettledrums (timpani) can produce a variety of tones when the player tightens or loosens the skin of the drumhead. Chimes, xylophones, and marimbas are played by striking metal or wooden tubes or bars of varying lengths. Each tube or bar is tuned to a particular pitch. A celesta is a keyboard instrument that produces tones like a bell caused by hammers striking metal plates when the keys are pressed. The snare drum has a rattling sound along with the beat of the striking drumsticks. The rattle is caused by metal snares (wires stretched across the bottom, inside of the drum) that vibrate against the lower drumhead.

The musicians in the percussion section of a symphony orchestra or band must be skilled players of almost all the instruments mentioned in this article. In jazz and rock bands, the drummer often plays complicated rhythmic solos.

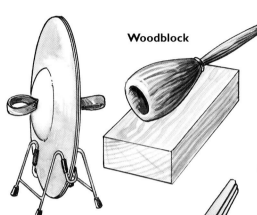

Woodblock

Gong

Tambourine

Cymbals

Castanets

Xylophone

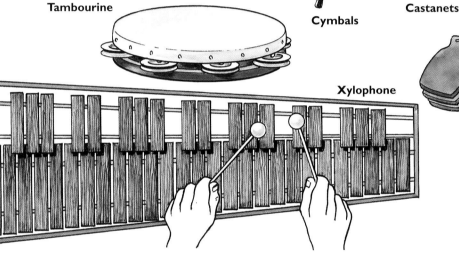

◁ There are many different types of percussion instruments with a wide range of sound between them. The triangle makes a light tinkling sound, but the gong makes a huge **BOOM!**

Vibrating skin

Steel drums make good musical instruments. During World War II, U.S. Navy oil drums were made into musical instruments on Caribbean islands. Empty oil drums of varying sizes produce a whole range of notes. The bottom surface is used as the drumhead and is struck with sticks or with the hands, producing soft, ringing tones.

The glockenspiel is a band instrument that looks like an upright xylophone. It is played by striking the metal bars. The glass harmonica consists of a set of glasses of various sizes that produce tones when the player draws a moistened finger around the rims of the glasses.

▷ ▷ ▷ ▷ **FIND OUT MORE** ◁ ◁ ◁ ◁
Bell; Music; Musical Instruments; Orchestras and Bands; Piano; Xylophone

PERFUME

Perfume is a substance that has a pleasant smell. Perfumes are used mainly in cosmetics. They may be in the form of a liquid that people put on their skin or clothes to make themselves smell pleasant. Or they may be mixed with a cream or soap. Face and body powders, lipsticks, and other cosmetics are often scented with perfume. Perfumes are also used

△ When a drum is struck, the instrument vibrates inside. As the vibrations lose energy, the sound of the drumbeat becomes quieter and quieter.

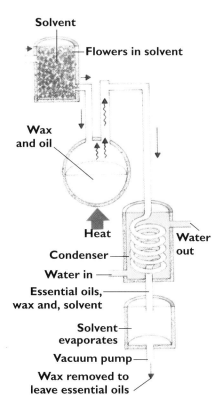

Solvent

Flowers in solvent

Wax and oil

Heat

Condenser

Water in

Essential oils, wax and, solvent

Solvent evaporates

Vacuum pump

Wax removed to leave essential oils

Water out

▲ The perfumer extracts the essential oils that contain the delicate fragrances. These are mixed with artificial substances, dissolved in solvents, and distilled in a vacuum.

to hide unpleasant odors in inks, paints, insecticides, and plastics.

Perfume is made of two types of ingredients. *Natural* perfume ingredients are those obtained from plants and animals. *Synthetic*, or artificial, perfume ingredients are made from chemicals. Synthetic ingredients give almost the same odors as natural ones. Most perfumes today are entirely synthetic or have many synthetic ingredients.

The most important part of a perfume is made up of one or more *essential oils*. These provide the distinctive odor of a natural perfume. The essential oil evaporates easily and quickly at ordinary temperatures. This evaporation carries the perfume into the air, so you can smell it. Essential oils come from various parts of plants. Rose scent comes from the essential oils pressed from rose petals. Violet and lavender scents come from both the flowers and the leaves of these plants. Bark and wood provide essential oils for cinnamon, rosewood, and cedar-scented perfumes. Fruits, such as oranges and lemons, and seeds, such as anise and nutmeg, also provide essential oils. *Aromatics* are synthetic products that give off strong odors.

Another part of a perfume is a *fixative*. It holds the perfume ingredients together and makes the odor last longer. The best fixatives are obtained from the scent glands of certain animals. Musk comes from the musk deer of Asia. Castor comes from beavers, and civet from civet cats. Another fixative is made from ambergris, which comes from the stomachs of sperm whales. Not everyone believes it is right to obtain fixatives from animals (especially rare ones). Synthetic and plant substances, however, can also be used as fixatives.

Solvents are the materials in which the essential oils, the aromatics, and the fixatives are dissolved. The most widely used solvent is a kind of alcohol. It has no odor and evaporates with the oils.

A perfume may be a mixture of as few as 10 ingredients or as many as 200. Most perfumes are made up of about one-tenth essential oils, aromatics, and fixative and nine-tenths solvent. Perfume may be mixed with *punk* (dried plant material) and pressed into cakes. This makes *incense,* which can be lighted and burned to give off a perfumed smoke.

Perfume making is an ancient art. The Egyptians used fragrant woods and flower petals to make perfumes. They often embalmed their dead with substances containing strong perfumes. The Greeks and the Romans learned to make perfumes from the Egyptians. But after the fall of the Roman Empire, Europeans stopped making perfumes until the 1500s. Today, France exports most of the world's expensive perfumes.

▶▶▶▶ **FIND OUT MORE** ◀◀◀◀
Cosmetics

LEARN BY DOING

You can make your own potpourri (mixture of dried flowers) to freshen and sweeten a room. The best time to pick the petals is when they are wide open. Rose petals are the most important ingredient. Some other plants you can use are lemon verbena, various mints, rosemary, and delphinium. Spread the petals on a sheet of paper and dry them in a dry, air-tight cupboard.

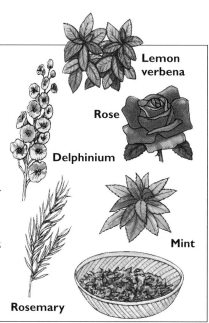

Lemon verbena

Rose

Delphinium

Mint

Rosemary

PERISCOPE

SEE LENS, SUBMARINE

PERON, JUAN (1895–1974) AND EVA (1919–1952)

Juan Domingo Perón was president of Argentina, first from 1946 to 1955 and again briefly from 1973 to 1974. He was born near Lobos, in Buenos Aires province, and became a soldier. In 1943, he helped overthrow the government of President Castillo. He sought the support of the country's workers, and on his election to the presidency in 1946 swore opposition to all who oppressed Argentina's poor.

Perón was greatly helped by his wife, Eva. They had married in 1945. Born Eva lbarguren in 1919, she had worked her way from poverty to success as a film actress. Alongside President Perón, she helped bring in reforms such as votes for women and better health services. "Evita," as she was known, became immensely popular. Her death in 1952 shocked Argentina. Because of her rise from poverty to be joint leader of her country, Eva Perón is still admired by many Argentinians.

Perón's policies did not bring economic success, and he was opposed by the Catholic Church. In 1955, the army overthrew his regime, and for years Perón lived in exile in Spain. But many Argentinians remembered "Perónism," and in 1973, he was elected as president once more. His government was short-lived, for Perón died in 1974. His second wife, Isabel, succeeded him, but her government was ended by military overthrow in 1976.

▶ ▶ ▶ ▶ **FIND OUT MORE** ◀ ◀ ◀ ◀
Argentina

PERPETUAL MOTION

Something that is perpetual will last forever. A perpetual motion machine would be a machine that could run forever without using any outside energy. It would have to supply all of its own energy. There are no perpetual motion machines.

There is one very good reason why no machine can supply all of its own energy. That reason is the *law of conservation of energy,* one of the basic laws of physics. This law says that energy can never be created or destroyed. Energy can only be changed from one form to another. For instance, when an automobile engine burns gasoline, it changes the chemical energy of the gasoline into heat energy. The heat energy in turn is changed into the mechanical energy that moves the automobile. You can make one kind of energy out of an other kind of energy, but you cannot end up with more energy than you started with. And this is just what a perpetual motion machine would have to do. It would have to make some energy out of no energy.

But what if we gave the machine a little push, just to get it started? Would this kind of perpetual motion machine be possible? The answer is still no, because of *friction.*

Whenever one thing rubs against another, friction resists the rubbing. Friction changes mechanical energy into heat energy. Even just moving through the air produces friction. A machine will always produce some friction. The friction will drain some of the machine's mechanical energy by changing it to heat energy.

The heat energy could not be used to run a perpetual motion machine because of the *second law of thermodynamics* (the study of heat energy). This law says that heat energy always flows from a warm body to a cold body. There is no way for a machine to keep all of the heat energy it

▲ Eva Perón rose from poverty to fame as the first lady of Argentina. Her death shocked the country.

▼ In this machine, the ball bearings were supposed to turn the wheel, which would drive the screw around and lift the balls back to the top. But energy is lost as friction, so the machine failed.

▲ The magnet attracts the ball up the slope. At the top, it should drop through the hole, and the process should repeat itself. But if the magnet is strong enough to pull the ball up, it will not let it fall down!

The nearest we can come to perpetual motion is an artificial satellite in orbit around the Earth. The initial push of the rocket that put it into orbit keeps it going for years. But eventually the satellite will fall to Earth, because even in space there are a few atoms of matter to cause friction and slow it down.

▶ An illustration from *Sleeping Beauty* in a modern children's storybook. Charles Perrault's collection of fairy tales are still popular today.

produces. Some of the heat energy is always going to escape. And if a machine loses any energy at all, it cannot be a perpetual motion machine. Pushing a perpetual motion machine to get it started gives it mechanical energy, but after a while, all of this mechanical energy will be eaten up by friction, and the machine will stop.

The first design for a perpetual motion machine was drawn up in the 1200s. Seven weights were attached to seven arms that swung from the rim of a wheel. The idea was that as the wheel turned, the weights coming over the top would swing out and down. At the same time the weights on the side moving up would be tucked in close to the wheel. The force of the moving weights would turn the wheel.

There were two things wrong with this idea. One was that the wheel lost energy through friction. The other was that there were always more weights tucked in on the "up" side than moving on the "down" side. The extra force each moving weight had was canceled out by the fact that there were more "dead" weights on the other side. Despite these problems, many people, including the great artist and inventor Leonardo da Vinci (1452–1519) have tried to invent a perpetual motion machine based on this idea.

Modern science has led to many new ideas for perpetual motion machines using atomic energy, electrical energy, or the heat energy held by lakes and oceans. However, the *law of conservation of energy* (now the law of conservation of mass-energy) and the second law of ther-

modynamics are still believed to be true. So there will never be a perpetual motion machine.

▶ ▶ ▶ **FIND OUT MORE** ◀ ◀ ◀
Energy; Friction; Physics; Relativity

PERRAULT, CHARLES (1628–1703)

Charles Perrault, a French poet, is best remembered for a collection of fairy tales. He was born in Paris. After studying in Orléans, he became a lawyer. Perrault later became secretary to the prime minister of King Louis XIV. In this position, he helped to promote the arts and sciences in France.

Perrault published *Contes de ma mére l'oye* (Tales of Mother Goose) in 1697. "Sleeping Beauty," "Little Red Riding Hood," "Hop-o'-My-Thumb," "Bluebeard," "Puss-in-Boots," and "Cinderella" are among the tales in the collection. Perrault's tales were translated into English in 1729. In 1765, John Newbery, an English publisher, brought out a book of children's poems called *Mother Goose's Melody*.

Perrault did not actually make up the stories in the first *Mother Goose* collection. They were already very old folktales passed down through the centuries from parent to child.

But Perrault was the first to write them down in simple language for children to enjoy.

▶ ▶ ▶ ▶ **FIND OUT MORE** ◀ ◀ ◀ ◀
Children's Literature; Fairy Tale

PERRY, OLIVER (1785–1819) AND MATTHEW (1794–1858)

The naval hero Oliver Hazard Perry was born in South Kingston, Rhode Island. His brother, Matthew Calbraith Perry, was born in Newport, Rhode Island. He too served in the U.S. Navy.

Oliver became a midshipman in the Navy and served in the Mediterranean Sea during the war with the Barbary pirates. At the outbreak of the War of 1812, Oliver Perry was given command of the U.S. naval force on Lake Erie. In 1813, at Erie, Pennsylvania, he ordered ten ships to be built, equipped, and manned. He met and defeated the British fleet on Lake Erie with these warships. During the battle, Perry sent the words, "We have met the enemy and they are ours." After the victory, he became a hero.

Oliver Perry was later sent to the Mediterranean Sea to fight the Barbary pirates. He caught yellow fever after completing a mission to Venezuela in 1819. He died in Trinidad. A monument in his honor stands in Newport, Rhode Island.

Matthew Perry followed in his brother's footsteps. He also joined the Navy and worked to change ships from sail to steam. He commanded the *Fulton*, one of the first steam-powered vessels and the first U.S. Navy steam warship.

In late 1852, Matthew Perry was sent on a mission by President Fillmore to negotiate a treaty with Japan for trade between the two countries. Until that time, Japan had refused to trade with the West. Perry anchored his fleet in Edo (now Tokyo) Bay when he arrived there on July 8, 1853. This display of armored sea power influenced the Japanese to agree to a treaty. The treaty was signed the following year, opening trade between Japan and America.

▶ ▶ ▶ ▶ **FIND OUT MORE** ◀ ◀ ◀ ◀
Japan, War of 1812

PERSEUS

According to Greek mythology, Perseus was a son of Zeus, the leader of the gods. His mother was a human woman named Dana. When Perseus was a grown man, a king named Polydectes fell in love with Dana and wanted to marry her. Knowing that Perseus was against the marriage, Polydectes sent him on a deadly errand. He ordered Perseus to kill the Medusa, a horrible female monster with snakes as hair. Polydectes thought that Perseus would never come back alive, because any man who looked at the Medusa would be turned into stone. Perseus

▲ During the battle of Lake Erie in the War of 1812, the *Lawrence,* Oliver Perry's ship, was put out of action. Perry and some of his crew rowed to the *Niagara,* another ship in his fleet. Aboard her, they defeated the British.

▲ To prevent himself from being turned into stone by Medusa's deadly stare, Perseus used his shield as a mirror. He used the Medusa's reflection to guide his weapon.

▼ The steps of the palace at Persepolis are overshadowed by huge carvings of King Darius' subjects paying him *homage* (respect) and bringing him gifts.

used a bright shield as a mirror with which to see the Medusa and cut off her head without looking straight at her. Perseus returned to Polydectes, holding the head of Medusa. In surprise, Polydectes looked at Medusa's head and was immediately turned into stone.

▶ ▶ ▶ ▶ **FIND OUT MORE** ◀ ◀ ◀ ◀
Gods and Goddesses; Legend; Mythology

PERSIA

The Persian Empire once stretched from India in the east to Greece in the west, north to the Danube River and southwest to Egypt on the African continent. Iran now occupies the area that once was the center of the empire.

Persian art and literature have lasted through the centuries. The religion called Zoroastrianism spread throughout the empire. A Persian teacher and prophet named Zoroaster (or Zarathustra) began the worship of Ahura Mazdah (or Ormazd), god of light, truth, and goodness, who waged cosmic war against the evil spirit Ahriman.

Persia was settled by *nomads* (wandering people) who moved down from the Caucasus Mountains in central Asia. People who settled in the mountains were known as Medes, and those who went to the valleys became known as Persians. Cyrus the Great united the tribes in the 500s B.C. and formed a nation. Cambyses II,

son of Cyrus, conquered Egypt.

Darius I extended the empire to its greatest area. The Persians governed their provinces by law—the Law of the Medes and the Persians. Roads were built. Coins were used in trade. Susa, the old capital, was a great city. Darius built a magnificent new capital, Persepolis. Its impressive buildings were decorated with carvings, many of them lifesize human figures.

The Greeks defeated Darius at the Battle of Marathon and later defeated his son, Xerxes. In the 300s B.C., Persia fell to Alexander the Great of Macedonia. The Arab conquest of Persia in the A.D. 600s introduced the Muslim faith, Islam, into Persia. Islam is still the main faith of Iran today. The word *Persian* is still used today to describe things that came from that part of the world, such as Persian cats and Persian rugs.

▶ ▶ ▶ ▶ **FIND OUT MORE** ◀ ◀ ◀ ◀
Alexander the Great; Ancient Civilizations; Iran; Iraq

PERSIAN GULF WAR

The largest military campaign since World War II ended in February 1991, when Iraq was forced to withdraw its forces from neighboring Kuwait.

Both Iraq and Kuwait have large oil reserves. In 1990, Iraq's president, Saddam Hussein, accused Kuwait of lowering the world price of oil by selling too much. He ordered an invasion on August 2. Iraqi troops took control of Kuwait within hours and pro-

claimed it to be a province of Iraq.

For several months the United Nations tried to persuade Iraq to pull out of Kuwait. It also agreed to an *embargo*, or halt, of trade with Iraq. The United States and other countries sent thousands of troops to Saudi Arabia to enforce the embargo.

On November 29, 1990, the U.N. agreed to the use of force if Iraq did not withdraw by January 15, 1991. On January 12, 1991, the U.S. Congress agreed to send in troops if Iraq ignored the deadline. Nearly 40 other Allies, such as Great Britain and France, also voted to send in troops.

The January 15 deadline passed. War began on January 17, with U.S. General H. Norman Schwarzkopf Jr. leading what became known as Operation Desert Storm. Allied planes flew more than 110,000 individual combat *sorties*, or missions, bombing military targets in Kuwait and Iraq.

"Smart" bombs, guided by lasers, scored many direct hits on targets. Iraq responded by firing Scud missiles at Israel and Saudi Arabia. Many of these poorly made missiles broke up in flight or were shot down by U.S. or Israeli defense forces using American-made Patriot missiles.

The ground war began on February 24, 1991. About 200,000 Allied troops attacked Iraqi forces in Kuwait and Iraq. Iraqi troops began leaving Kuwait two days later. As they retreated, the Iraqis set fire to hundreds of oil wells. On February 27, Iraq formally accepted the U.N. resolutions that required its forces to leave Kuwait. President Bush stopped military operations on that same day. It took almost a year to put out the fires and cap the wells.

Peace had been obtained, but the tensions have continued to create an unstable situation.

▶ ▶ ▶ ▶ **FIND OUT MORE** ◀ ◀ ◀ ◀
Iraq; Kuwait; United Nations; War

General H. Norman Schwarzkopf Jr., the commander of the Allied forces during the Persian Gulf War. He is seen here speaking to members of the *media* (the press and TV).

PERSPECTIVE

SEE DIMENSION, DRAWING, PAINTING

PERSPIRATION

SEE SKIN

PERU

Peru, the third largest South American country, was the center of the great Inca civilization. Later, it was the richest Spanish land in the Americas. Today, Peru is an interesting mixture of the Inca and Spanish past and the present.

The long coastline of western Peru extends along the Pacific Ocean.

Rising along the side of western South America are the Andes Mountains. The world's longest land range, they stretch from Cape Horn to Panama—a distance of 4,500 miles (7,200 km).

PERU

Capital city
Lima
(5,494,000 people)

Area
496,225 square miles
(1,285,216 sq. km)

Population
22,232,000 people

Government
Republic

Natural resources
Copper, iron ore, lead, oil, silver, zinc, gold, coal, phosphates, potash

Export products
Fish meal, cotton, sugar, petroleum, coffee, copper, iron ore, refined silver, lead, zinc

Unit of money
Sol

Official languages
Spanish, Quechua

▲ **Many Native South American villages dot the shores of Lake Titicaca. Boats, called *totoras,* made from the lake's reeds are used for fishing trips and provide transport for goods.**
2044

Ecuador and Colombia are Peru's northern neighbors. Brazil and Bolivia border Peru on the east, and Chile is south.

Peru is more than three times the size of California. It is divided lengthwise into three main regions. The costa, or coastal plain, has a dry climate. In the north, there are places where a whole year passes with no rainfall at all. Peru's capital, Lima, is located midway on the country's coast. It is a large city whose buildings reflect both Spanish colonial days and modern progress. Callao is the nearby seaport. The Sierra region is made up of the high plateaus and valleys of the Andes Mountains. The Andean region contains many valuable mineral resources. Peru has important copper and iron mines, and exports most of its metals.

An area known as the Montaña makes up the largest region. It consists of the steep eastern mountain slopes, foothills, and plains. Some of the densest forests in the world cover the Montaña, where primitive native tribes still live.

Native tribes make up nearly one-half of the Peruvian population. Most of them are poor and uneducated, and many speak only their tribal languages, although Spanish is the official language of the country.

Although the coastland is dry, farming is made possible by irrigation. Large farms raising cotton, rice, and sugarcane form green oases in the barren landscape. In the Andes Mountains, the Quechua and Aymara Indians farm

small plots of potatoes and grains suited to high elevations. Thousands of Indians work comfortably in the rich Sierra mines at higher altitudes than the lowland Indians and Europeans can stand. In the mountain regions, Indians tend flocks of sheep, llamas, and alpacas. The llama is used as a pack animal.

Peru is a world leader in the fishing industry. Fish meal and fish oil are leading products.

Spain ruled Peru for more than 250 years, until independence was won in 1821. The country is now ruled by a president and legislature. In 1992, President Fujimori dissolved the National Congress and brought in press censorship, which limits the knowledge of average people.

▶ ▶ ▶ ▶ **FIND OUT MORE** ◀ ◀ ◀ ◀
Conquistador; Inca; Pizarro, Francisco

PEST CONTROL

In 1980, the United States began fighting a war against an invader. The invader was a tiny insect, less than ⅛ inch long. It was the Medfly, or Mediterranean fruit fly, which threatened California fruit farms.

In Europe, these flies were not such a threat as they were in California. In America, they are a *pest*. A pest is an animal that eats or spoils our food, or any plant that grows on land we need for crops. Most animal pests are insects or other tiny creatures, but larger animals such as rats may also be pests.

People control pests in various ways. They kill rats by trapping them or putting down poison. Insects are generally attacked with *pesticides*, chemicals that kill the insects. One of the best-known pesticides is DDT, a chemical that is very efficient in killing insects. Unfortunately, DDT has harmful side effects. It remains in the ground for a long time. It is absorbed by plants and by the animals that eat the plants.

Animals at the top of the food chain, such as hawks, may be badly affected by the poison. So may humans. If we eat plants and animals sprayed with DDT, our bodies absorb the DDT. For these reasons, since 1972, the use of DDT has been banned in the United States.

Another way to control pests is *biologically*, by using the pests' natural predators to control them. For example, at one time, ladybugs were imported from Australia into California and Florida. Ladybugs feed upon the cottony-cushion scale insect, a major pest of citrus fruit.

In the 1920s, Australia had to import a moth to eat the prickly pear. This South American plant had been introduced as a garden ornament but became a pest when it spread over valuable grazing land.

▲ **Aerial crop spraying is one of the most effective ways of protecting large areas of potato plants from the devastating Colorado beetle.**

▶ ▶ ▶ ▶ **FIND OUT MORE** ◀ ◀ ◀ ◀
Caterpillar; Insect; Pollution;
Rats and Mice

PET

Having a pet can be fun, but with a pet come many responsibilities. You must feed most pets every day and take proper care of them so that they do not get sick. You must also housebreak some pets.

Talk with your parents and get their permission before selecting a pet. Decide with your parents where the pet will sleep or where its cage will be.

▽ **Pesticides can cause harm when they get into the food chain. Humans may eat crops, animals, or fish that have pesticides in them. The effects vary from a minor stomach upset to severe poisoning.**

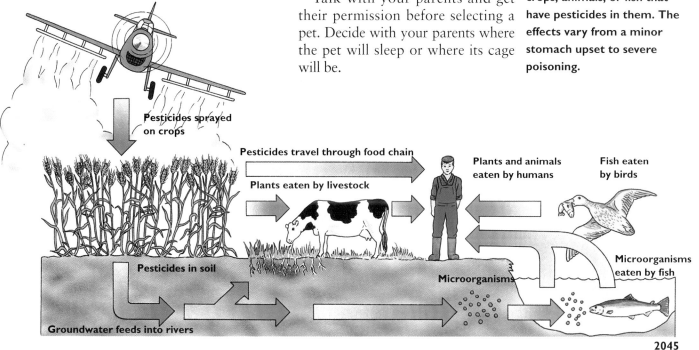

Pesticides sprayed on crops

Pesticides travel through food chain

Plants eaten by livestock

Plants and animals eaten by humans

Fish eaten by birds

Pesticides in soil

Microorganisms

Microorganisms eaten by fish

Groundwater feeds into rivers

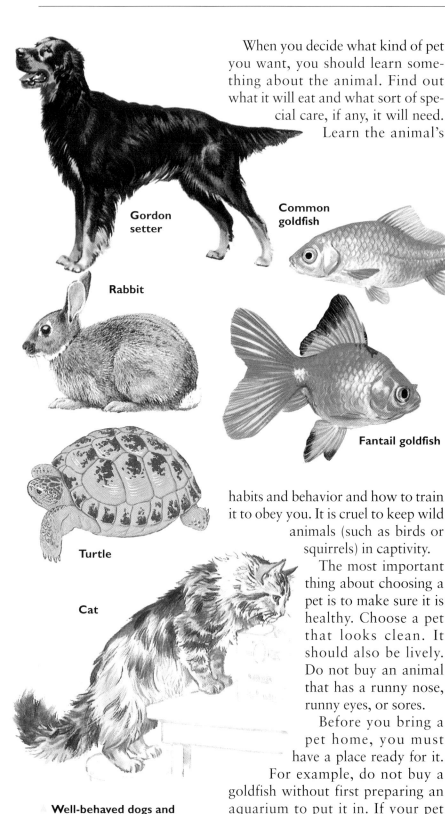

Gordon setter

Common goldfish

Rabbit

Fantail goldfish

Turtle

Cat

Well-behaved dogs and cats can roam quite freely in the home. Rabbits need a large hutch with separate sleeping quarters. Turtles must have a very large tank or pond and a place to hibernate if you live where the winters are cold.

When you decide what kind of pet you want, you should learn something about the animal. Find out what it will eat and what sort of special care, if any, it will need. Learn the animal's habits and behavior and how to train it to obey you. It is cruel to keep wild animals (such as birds or squirrels) in captivity.

The most important thing about choosing a pet is to make sure it is healthy. Choose a pet that looks clean. It should also be lively. Do not buy an animal that has a runny nose, runny eyes, or sores.

Before you bring a pet home, you must have a place ready for it. For example, do not buy a goldfish without first preparing an aquarium to put it in. If your pet needs a cage, the cage must be all ready when you bring the animal home. Have on hand the kind of food your pet eats. (Find out what foods are bad for your pet so that you can avoid them.) You must know how much food your pet eats so that you do not overfeed it.

Many new pets are nervous and frightened. You must give a new pet time to settle down and become used to its new home. Do not pick up your pet without first learning how to hold it properly. Some animals hate to be carried or handled very much.

Some Common Pets

CATS AND DOGS. These animals are the most popular pets in the world. They are also the friendliest and easiest animals to take care of.

Most dogs need room to run and plenty of exercise. Dogs also need to be trained. Cats also enjoy going outdoors, but they can live contentedly as "house cats." You may be able to get a free kitten or puppy by looking in the classified ads of a newspaper. People whose pets have litters are usually happy to give the babies to a good home as soon as they are old enough. If you want a purebred animal, however, you will probably have to pay a lot of money for it. Do not tease or try to frighten a cat or dog. They will scratch or bite you in self-defense.

FISH. Fish make very colorful and, of course, quiet pets. Even if you live in a small apartment, you probably have room for a fish tank. Before you buy any fish, you should have your aquarium and proper food ready. See the articles on AQUARIUM and TROPICAL FISH.

BIRDS. Certain birds have been bred as pets and are used to living in cages or in larger enclosures called aviaries. Canaries, which can be trained to sing, are very popular pets. Male canaries imitate the songs of other birds. Parakeets, parrots, and mynah birds also make interesting pets, because they can be taught to talk. Most birds will thrive on a diet of seeds, fruits, nuts, and green vegetables.

COMMON RODENT PETS. Hamsters, gerbils, and guinea pigs are the most popular rodent pets. See the article on GUINEA PIGS AND HAMSTERS .

Mice—from a pet store—also make good pets. Buy a mouse that has bright eyes and a smooth, shiny coat. You can keep a mouse in a wire cage or in an aquarium tank. Buy as large a cage or tank as you can because mice need room to run around and play. Mice also need a little closed room in their cage where they can sleep. The cage should always be kept clean.

You can feed a mouse either once or twice a day. Mice will eat oats and seeds and bread soaked in milk. Mice also eat green vegetables. Give your mouse only what it will eat at one meal. Make sure you clean the food dish every day. Always keep fresh water for the mouse to drink.

RABBITS. Rabbits make fairly inexpensive pets. Buy a bright-eyed, plump rabbit from a pet store. Pick it up gently and do not handle it very much until it gets used to you. *Never* pick up a rabbit by the ears.

A rabbit should live outside in a wire-mesh pen, or hutch. A rabbit likes privacy, so part of the pen should be closed off as its bedroom. Hay or straw make a nice bed. Change your rabbit's bedding at least twice a week, and clean the hutch once a week.

Rabbits eat greens, such as lettuce, spinach, clover, and beet greens, and grains, such as oats or bran. They also like turnips, carrots, and apples. They need a high nutrient diet, so they are usually fed a special food bought at a pet store. Keep fresh water and a piece of rock salt in your rabbit's hutch. It will also appreciate having some hay around for snacks. Rabbits need to chew on twigs to keep their teeth healthy. Wash your rabbit's dishes after each meal.

Whatever pet you choose, you must make sure that it stays clean, healthy, and well fed. Remember that your pet is unable to tell you how it feels. If your pet has runny eyes or a runny nose or seems sick or unusually inactive, you should take it to a *veterinarian,* or animal doctor.

▶ ▶ ▶ ▶ **FIND OUT MORE** ◀ ◀ ◀ ◀
Aquarium; Cat; Dog;
Domesticated Animals;
Guinea Pigs and Hamsters; Lizard;
Parrots and Parakeets; Rabbits and
Hares; Snake; Terrarium; Tropical Fish

**WHERE TO
DISCOVER MORE**

Caulkins, Janet. *Pets of the
Presidents.* New York:
Millbrook Press, 1992.

PETER THE GREAT (1672–1725)

Peter the Great was the name given to Peter I, the *czar* (ruler) of Russia. He was the first czar to make Russia into a great power in Europe.

Peter was crowned czar when he was 10 years old. He grew up to be tall and massively strong. He was fiercely independent. His great interest was in sailing and shipbuilding. When he was 17, Peter dismissed his sister Sophia, who had ruled during his childhood, and took control of the government. He traveled abroad to study, visiting England, Germany, and Holland.

Russia at that time was an inland country, with no seaports. Peter built a great fleet of ships and captured the Turkish port of Azov on the Black Sea. He then declared war on Sweden and seized several provinces along the Baltic Sea. In one of these provinces, he built a new capital, St. Petersburg.

Peter greatly admired the new inventions and modern governments of western Europe. Russia, in comparison, was a backward country. Peter began to reorganize the Russian government along Western lines. He made the Russian people adopt Western dress and habits. Anyone who continued to wear the traditional beard and long robes was heavily fined. Peter built new factories and encouraged trade with Western countries. The old Russian nobility, who rebelled against the

▲ **Parrots are often kept as pets. They sometimes show signs of distress by plucking out their feathers—a response something like human nail biting.**

▼ **Peter the Great, ruler of Russia, died after rescuing drowning sailors in freezing water.**

Peter the Great had such a passion for ships and shipbuilding that he worked in shipyards in Holland and England while he served as the czar of Russia.

changes, were put down with great cruelty. Before Peter died, he decreed that his wife, the empress Catherine, should succeed him. She was the first woman to rule Russia.

▶ ▶ ▶ ▶ **FIND OUT MORE** ◀ ◀ ◀ ◀
Catherine the Great; Russian History

PETRIFIED FOREST

▼ **These stone "tree trunks" are in the Petrified Forest National Park in Arizona.**

The Petrified Forest in northern Arizona is the world's largest and most colorful collection of petrified wood. About 200 million years ago, this area of the desert was a land of lakes and swamps. Trees grew in the highlands surrounding the swamps. When a tree died and fell, it was carried by streams into the swamps and became buried there. Water seeped through the mud into the dead tree. The minerals (mostly silica) in the mud and water seeped inside the tree cells and hardened, like plaster poured into a mold.

Gradually, the wood fibers were replaced by silica and *petrified* (hardened into stone). Every little detail of the log was preserved. Other minerals, such as iron oxide, jasper, agate, and quartz, added color and sparkle to the petrified wood.

Some of the stone logs in the Petrified Forest are more than 100 feet (30 m) long and 6 feet (2 m) in diameter. One arched log forms a natural bridge, called the Agate Bridge. Petrified wood is harder than steel and heavier than ordinary wood. One log of petrified wood weighs more than three logs of freshly cut wood of the same size.

The Petrified Forest officially became the Petrified Forest National Park in 1962. Visitors from all over the world come to see the magnificent petrified trees, as well as many relics of prehistoric Native Americans.

▶ ▶ ▶ ▶ **FIND OUT MORE** ◀ ◀ ◀ ◀
Fossil; Geology

QUIZ ANSWERS

Nutrition quiz, page 1946

1. Nutrients are the vitamins, minerals, proteins, and carbohydrates in foods that help us keep healthy.

2. Cholesterol is a type of fat. A little cholesterol will not harm you, but too much can help build up fat deposits in arteries. This increases the risk of clogged arteries and, as a result, of heart disease.

3. The most important minerals for health are calcium, phosphorus, iron, and iodine.

4. Foods that are particularly rich in vitamins include fresh fruits and vegetables.

5. Carbohydrates include cereals, bread, potatoes, rice, and pasta. These complex carbohydrates provide the body with energy.

Ocean quiz, page 1954

1. The total ocean area is about 140,000,000 square miles (362,000,000 sq. km), covering 71 percent of the Earth's surface.

2. No, the Great Lakes are not part of the world ocean.

3. A tsunami is a huge, dangerous wave caused by an earthquake or erupting volcano under the sea.

4. Since the Gulf Stream flows from the equator toward the North Pole, it is a warm current.

5. Cobalt, copper, gold, manganese, nickel, magnetite, tin, and titanium are some of the many useful minerals found in the ocean.

Olympic Games quiz, page 1966

1. The first modern Olympic Games were held in Athens, Greece, in 1896.

2. Paris (1900 and 1924), London (1908 and 1948), and Los Angeles (1932 and 1984) have all hosted the Summer Olympic Games more than once.

3. Five linked rings form the symbol of the Olympics.

4. Winter Olympic events include bobsledding, luge, biathlon, ice hockey, skating, and skiing. Summer events include archery, basketball, boxing, canoeing, cycling, equestrian, fencing, field hockey, gymnastics, judo, rowing, shooting, soccer, swimming, diving, table tennis, tennis, track-and-field events (such as running, high jump, long jump, hammer and discus throw, and the decathlon), volleyball, water polo, weight lifting, wrestling, and yachting.

5. No, they are usually held in two different cities, as this is more fair and less difficult to organize. Beginning in 1994, the Winter and Summer Games will no longer even be held in the same year, but two years apart. Therefore, in 1994, Norway hosted the Winter Games, while Atlanta, Georgia, will host the next Summer Games in 1996.

Parts of Speech quiz, page 2021

1. Adjectives, adverbs, nouns, pronouns, prepositions, verbs, conjunctions, and interjections are considered the eight main parts of speech.

2. *Gracefully* is an adverb, because it tells "how."

3. The past tense of "I see" is "I saw." The past tense of "I go" is "I went."

4. *Greedy* = adjective (modifying the noun *monkey*). *Monkey* = noun (singular). *Ate* = verb (past tense of "to eat"). *Grapes* = noun (plural). *Quickly* = adverb (modifying the verb *ate*).